New York
for less

"The
guidebook that
pays
for itself –
in one day"

TEXT BY

CHRISTINA PROSTANO
CHARLES W. WALDRON

Publisher Information

PUBLISHER

Metropolis International
222 Kensal Road
London W10 5BN
England

Telephone:
+44-(0)181-964-4242
(After May 2000, tel:
+44-(0)20-8964-4242)

Fax:
+44-(0)181-964-4141
(After May 2000, fax:
+44-(0)20-8964-4141)

E-mail:
admin@for-less.com

Web site:
http://www.for-less.com

FOR LESS TITLES

London for less
New York for less
Paris for less

FOR LESS TITLES COMPACT GUIDES

Amsterdam for less
Barcelona for less
Berlin for less
Brussels for less
Budapest for less
Florence for less
Florida for less
Lisbon for less
London for less
Madrid for less
New York for less
Paris for less
Prague for less
Rome for less
Venice for less
Vienna for less
plus forthcoming titles (see
page 5)

NEW YORK FOR LESS

First published in Great Britain in 1997 by Metropolis International (UK) Limited, a member of the New York Convention & Visitors Bureau.

Discounts by Metropolis International (UK) Limited. Text by Christina Prostano and Charles W. Waldron. Principal photography by Debra Sweeney.

ISBN 1-901811-31-X

COPYRIGHT

DISCLAIMER

Assessments of attractions, hotels, museums and so forth are based on the authors' impressions and therefore contain an element of subjective opinion which may not reflect the opinion of the publishers.

The contents of this publication are believed to be correct at the time of printing, however, details such as prices will change over time. We would advise you to call ahead to confirm important information.

Care has been taken in the preparation of this guidebook. However, the publisher cannot accept responsibility for errors or inaccuracies that may occur.

The publisher will not be held responsible for any loss, damage, injury, expense or inconvenience sustained by any person, howsoever caused, as a result of information or advice contained in this guide except insofar as the law prevents the exclusion of such liability.

Contents

for less guidebooks . . .

Unlike "budget guides", the series of stylish *for less* guidebooks enable every visitor, however much they anticipate spending, to save money at all the best places.

The *for less* guidebooks have 288 pages of information, plus a full range of discounts at top attractions, hotels, tours, restaurants, shops and entertainment venues.

Easy-to-use, informative, vividly written, packed with photos and maps, these comprehensive guidebooks are available for New York, London and Paris.

Maps

Fold-out street and underground maps come with each guidebook, with all the main attractions clearly located. They link to hundreds of mini-maps inside the book.

Discount Cards

The *for less* discount card that comes with each guidebook gives up to 4 people great savings at hundreds of places in each city.

Plus: Discount telephone card with £5 / $8 worth of free calls.

. . . *for less* Compact Guides

Slim enough to fit in your pocket, the *for less* Compact Guides combine quality text with discounts at top attractions, making them ideal for a shorter trip.

The area-by-area format and extensive information enable even first-time visitors to get the most out of their visit.

The series covers a number of destinations in Europe and the United States, and the list is constantly growing. Compact Guides can be purchased from all good bookstores. Many of the titles are available in French, Spanish, German and Dutch, as well as English.

Maps

Each guide comes with a detailed fold-out street and underground/Metro (subway) map. All the main tourist attractions are clearly located, making it easy for visitors to find their way around. Linked to the main map are hundreds of mini-maps in the guidebook.

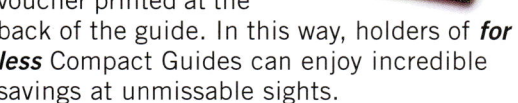

Discount Coupons

Visitors can obtain "2-for-1" discounts at an impressive range of top attractions and museums, simply by handing in the relevant voucher printed at the back of the guide. In this way, holders of *for less* Compact Guides can enjoy incredible savings at unmissable sights.

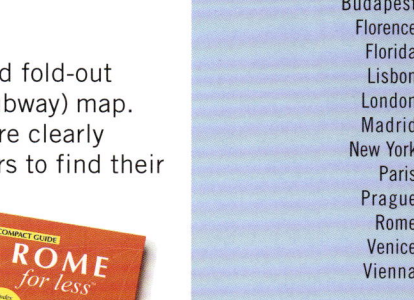

Plus: Discount telephone card with $5 / £3 worth of free calls.

AVAILABLE TITLES

Amsterdam
Barcelona
Berlin
Brussels
Budapest
Florence
Florida
Lisbon
London
Madrid
New York
Paris
Prague
Rome
Venice
Vienna

FORTHCOMING TITLES (from October 1999)

Athens
Bruges
California
Copenhagen
Dublin
Hawaii
Istanbul
Los Angeles
Las Vegas
Orlando
San Francisco

How to Use *New York for less*

New York for less has been created to enable visitors to save money by obtaining discounts at the best places in New York City. All discounts are applicable for up to four people for up to eight consecutive days. Each page is color coded as follows:

Attractions and Museums

Tours

Shops

Restaurants

Nightlife and Performing Arts

Before you use the card, you must validate it by following the instructions printed underneath it on the inside front cover. The card should always be presented when you request the bill (check) and before payment is made.

Discounts apply whatever method of payment you choose. However, **New York for less** cannot be used in conjunction with other offers or discounts.

Throughout this book, you will find the *for less* logo (pictured at left). Every time it appears, it indicates that you are entitled to a discount.

Use of the card or vouchers must conform to the instructions on pages 7 and 8 and to the specific instructions set out in each entry.

All organizations offering discounts in this guidebook have a contract with the publisher to give genuine discounts to holders of valid **for less** cards and/or vouchers.

Care has been taken to ensure that discounts are only offered at reputable establishments, however, the publisher and/or its agents cannot accept responsibility for the quality of merchandise or service provided, nor for errors or inaccuracies in this guidebook.

The publisher and/or its agents will not be responsible if any establishment breaches its contract (although it will attempt to secure compliance) or if any establishment changes ownership and the new owners refuse to honor the contract.

For post-publication updates and amendments to the discounts offered or for any additional information, call Metropolis International at (212) 587-0287 or visit our website at www.for-less.com.

CREDIT CARD SYMBOLS USED

AM = AMEX
VS = VISA
MC = MASTERCARD
DC = DINERS CLUB
DS = DISCOVER

How to Obtain Discounts...

ATTRACTIONS AND MUSEUMS

To obtain discounts at attractions or museums you have to either show your card or hand in a voucher which you will find at the back of the book (follow the particular instructions in each entry). When you hand in the voucher you should circle the number of people in your party and also show your *for less* card.

At most attractions, discounts are available on the adult, child, senior and student prices. Children are usually defined as under 12, seniors as over 65. An index of attractions, museums and galleries that offer *for less* discounts is on page 259.

TOURS AND TRANSPORTATION

New York for less offers large savings on airport transfers (pages 18-19), car rental (page 237), bus tours (pages 212-213 and 220), helicopter tours (page 217), walking tours (pages 218-219) and cruises (pages 214-216).

To obtain the discounts, you must book as instructed in each tour's entry. You cannot book through a travel agent, hotel concierge or other intermediary.

RESTAURANTS

New York for less entitles you to a flat 25% off the total bill (check), including food and beverages at more than 60 restaurants in Manhattan, listed on pages 262-263.

The price indicated is not a fixed or minimum price. It is only a guide to the average cost of a meal. It is based on a typical two-course meal for one person without an alcoholic drink. You are entitled to the discount however much you spend. To obtain the discount, you should present your card when you request the bill (check) and before payment is made.

You may return to each restaurant as many times as you wish and receive a discount every time as long as the card is valid.

So that the service is not reduced by the discount, it is recommended that you tip on the total amount of the bill, before the discount is applied. A standard tip in New York City is 15-20% of the bill.

SHOPS

New York for less offers a 20% discount at more than 50 Manhattan shops, listed on page 260-261. To obtain the discount, simply show the card before you pay for the goods. Discounts on goods already reduced in price or on sale are at the discretion of the shop's management.

Empire State Building

Cruising on the Hudson

Dining on Union Square

Soho shopping

. . . How to Obtain Discounts

Lincoln Center

NIGHTLIFE AND PERFORMING ARTS

New York for less offers you discounts on tickets for Broadway theater productions (see page 209). Unfortunately, we cannot guarantee that you will be able to obtain discounts at particular performances, as certain shows are frequently sold out.

TELEPHONE CALLING CARD

Broadway theaters

Enjoy savings of up to 70% on your international telephone calls by using your ***for less*** card as a calling card. Best of all, when you activate your card you will receive $8 worth of free calls.

A. To activate your *for less* card as a discount calling card:

When in New York, dial toll-free (freephone) 1-800-642-7410 and wait about 20 seconds for an operator (ignore the instruction to enter your card number and PIN).

Give the operator the last 8 digits of your ***for less*** card and your credit card details. You will then be given a secret Personal Identification Number (PIN).

B. To make a telephone call using your *for less* card:

1. Dial toll-free (freephone) 1-800-642-7410
2. Enter your unique card number and PIN
3. Wait for the greeting and then dial the country code + area code + telephone number you require (do not dial the international prefix "011")
4. If you have any problems dial * 0 and an operator will assist you at no charge.

Some hotels bar toll-free calls or even charge you for making them. To avoid this, use your calling card at any public telephone.

When you return home you will be sent a permanent Calling Card which you can continue to use to make great savings from home or abroad. Ask the operator for details.

Any questions relating to telephone calls, should be referred to Interglobe Telecommunications PLC *(☎ 44-(0)171-972-0800)*. Your credit card statement will show a charge from Interglobe calls you make after using up your free $8.

DIALING IN THE U.S.

Unless otherwise noted, all phone numbers listed in this book are within the (212) Manhattan area code. When a phone number is listed with an area code, such as (800) it should be prefaced by the number 1. See page 256 for more dialing information.

Introduction

Introduction to New York . . .

"The skyline of New York is a monument of a splendor that no pyramids or palaces will ever equal or approach." – Ayn Rand

Clustered together on the tiny island of **Manhattan**, like tall trees in a dense forest, New York's skyscrapers symbolize the energy, the dynamism and the unlimited possibilities that this great city seems to hold.

But it is on the streets below, in the shadows of the giant buildings and inside the busy offices, bustling shops and glamorous restaurants, that the vitality of the city and its people can be felt.

Perhaps no other city embodies the spirit of the 20th century as completely as New York. From the **Statue of Liberty**, to the **Empire State Building**, to the yellow taxi cabs, its images have been captured on film so often that, for many people across the globe, they now represent America and the American way of life.

And yet, it is only in the last 200 years that New York has transformed itself from a small town on the edge of an empty continent into a major metropolis.

Aerial view of Manhattan

REFLECTIONS

"New York is a different country. Maybe it ought to have a separate government. Everybody thinks differently, acts differently. They just don't know what the hell the rest of the United States is."
– Henry Ford

Founded by the Dutch as a trading colony, it was the capital of the United States for the first year of the new republic's life. However, it was as a commercial center, a place where business comes first, that New York established its pre-eminence.

With it gleaming corporate offices and **Wall Street** banks, its position as one of the world's foremost financial and business centers is

Statue of Liberty

secure. But New York today is about much more than business. The city is a mecca for fashion, art, theater and music that has few, if any, equals. It is also home to some of the world's largest and most diverse ethnic

. . . Introduction to New York . . .

communities. A giant melting pot that sometimes seems as though it might burst at the seams, New York

is perhaps the most diverse city in the world. Here the rich rub shoulders with the poor, and the cultural elite ride the subway with beggars.

Criticized for their brusque manner, New Yorkers have a reputation for being rude. People here undoubtedly have a tendency to speak bluntly and rarely waste time getting to the point. But

Hot dog vendor

although you may well see New York cabbies yelling at each other through their taxi windows, you will also find open-minded, friendly New Yorkers who will be happy to help as you travel about their city.

The diversity of the population contrasts with the remarkable symmetry of the streets. Thanks to the **Randel Plan**, devised in 1811, everything north of 14th Street fits into a uniform and easily comprehensible grid, with the avenues running north-south and streets running east-west.

To the visitor, New York may seem overwhelming. Yet, to New Yorkers, the city is divided into distinctive and definable neighborhoods each with their own history and style.

The busy streets of **Midtown**, with their notorious traffic, contrast with the quiet residential areas of the **West Village**, while the status-conscious shops of the **Upper East Side** are a world apart from the

View of New York from the Empire State Building

bohemian chic of the **East Village** or the historic streets of **Lower Manhattan**.

New York is far from being a purely urban landscape. In addition to its many small parks, it has one park of unparalleled size and magnificence: **Central Park**, New York's green playground. On a Sunday afternoon in summer, a visitor could be forgiven for thinking that the whole city was rollerblading, cycling or jogging around it.

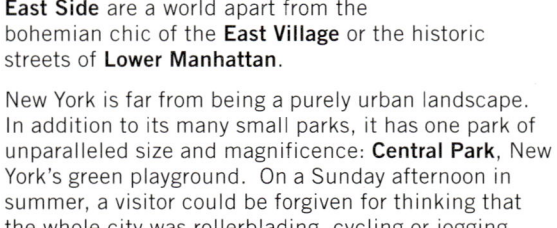

. . . Introduction to New York . . .

No matter how long you stay in New York, you will never exhaust the possibilities that await you. Indeed, more than 30 million visitors come here each year to experience its endless opportunities. You can view Manhattan's impressive skyline from the Empire State Building, tour the city in a double-decker bus, row a boat in

Winter in Central Park

Central Park, ice-skate at Rockefeller Center and still only scratch the surface of what this city has to offer.

In addition to world-class museums such as **The Met**, **Guggenheim**, **MoMA** and the **American Museum of Natural History**, New York has incredible restaurants, hotels, shopping and nightlife. Its **Broadway theaters**

New York Marathon

have been drawing crowds for nearly a century and its dance clubs prove that, when Frank Sinatra sang of "the city that never sleeps", he was telling the literal truth.

New York is in a constant state of flux. Barely a day goes by without a movie or theater premier, a new restaurant or shop being launched or an art exhibit opening. Whenever you come, there is likely to be something special happening. From the Macy's Thanksgiving Day Parade to the New York Marathon, the city's seasonal events will enrich your visit.

New Yorkers who have spent their whole lives here, still sometimes find themselves on a city block where they have never been before, or stumbling upon an unknown shop or restaurant that soon becomes a favorite. It is this marvelous variety, the sense that you can never get the measure of New York that makes it such a fascinating place to live or visit.

For most visitors, the 13-mile (22-km) island of Manhattan (taken from the Algonquin Indian name 'Mannahatta') *is* New York. However, of the 7.3 million residents, over 80% live in the outer boroughs of

. . . Introduction to New York

Brooklyn, the Bronx, Queens and Staten Island. While lacking the glamour of Manhattan, each of these is filled with a wealth of colorful neighborhoods and exciting attractions.

Brooklyn, which was originally a separate city, is connected to Manhattan by the spectacular Brooklyn Bridge. The Brooklyn Promenade, a short walk from the bridge, provides magnificent views of Lower Manhattan and New York Harbor. Brooklyn Heights, with its brownstone homes, tree-lined streets and excellent

Yankees' 1996 World Series victory parade

restaurants, bars and shops is fun to explore. Brooklyn is also home to a collection of ethnic enclaves including the Russian community at Brighton Beach.

For years, the South **Bronx** has been a byword for urban decay and inner-city blight. The North Bronx, in contrast, has a number of interesting attractions, including the New York Botanical Garden and the Bronx Wildlife Conservation Center, the largest zoo in America.

The Bronx even has its own Little Italy, arguably more authentic than its Manhattan counterpart. However, its outstanding attraction is probably the New York Yankees baseball team, whose die-hard fans could not have been more pleased by their victories in the 1996 and 1998 World Series.

Queens is brimming with dynamic and diverse ethnic communities. In the largely Greek area of Astoria, the American Museum of the Moving Image is worth a visit. Also stop by the Flushing Meadows-Corona Park which was the site of both the 1939 and 1964 World's Fairs.

Macy's parade

The other New York City island, **Staten Island**, is a short and pleasurable ferry ride from Lower Manhattan. The Staten Island Ferry offers breathtaking views of Lower Manhattan, the Statue of Liberty and New York Harbor. Best of all, it's free! For a visitor, places of interest include the Staten Island Zoo, Richmondtown Historic Restoration and the Alice Austen House.

REFLECTIONS

"That enfabled rock, that ship of life, that swarming, million-footed, tower-masted, sky-soaring citadel that bears the magic name of the Island of Manhattan."
– Thomas Wolfe

New York: Area by Area . . .

LOWER MANHATTAN

New York's old city mixes historic sights dating back to the early 17th century, with the modern financial institutions of Wall Street. Some of New York's top attractions are also located in the area, including the World Trade Center, South Street Seaport and Battery Park, where you can catch the ferry to the Statue of Liberty and Ellis Island. The combination of history and great sites make this one of the best places to begin sightseeing in New York.

SOHO, CHINATOWN AND THE LOWER EAST SIDE

Soho and Tribeca are filled with trendy shops, chic restaurants and art galleries. Unique to the area, cast-iron buildings house dramatic loft spaces which have become some of Manhattan's most expensive pieces of real estate. Further east, Chinatown, Little Italy and the Lower East Side are ethnic enclaves known for their authentic eateries and markets.

GREENWICH VILLAGE

Buzzing with activity, "the Village" is divided into the West and East Village, both filled with popular shops, bars and restaurants. In the West Village, Christopher Street is the center of New York's gay community. The East Village is the nucleus of the city's bohemian life. Its main street, St. Mark's Place, is crowded with funky boutiques and inexpensive restaurants.

CHELSEA, GRAMERCY AND THE FLATIRON DISTRICT

West Chelsea has recently become a center for art, as many new galleries have opened in its warehouse-sized buildings. There is also a thriving dining and nightlife scene. The heart of the Flatiron District revolves around the sophisticated bars and restaurants along Park Avenue South. Don't miss a trip to the top of one of the world's most famous skyscrapers – the Empire State Building.

. . . New York: Area by Area

MIDTOWN WEST

Midtown West is best known for its Broadway theaters. Centered around this hub of activity are many of the city's major hotels. You will also find the majority of Manhattan's theme restaurants and top attractions like Times Square and Rockefeller Center. For museum-goers, the Museum of Modern Art (MoMA) is a must-see. Fifth Avenue, the dividing line between Midtown West and East, is a shopper's paradise.

MIDTOWN EAST

Cleaner and quieter than its western counterpart, Midtown East is home to some of America's biggest corporations, housed in the enormous skyscrapers that comprise a large portion of Manhattan's famous skyline. On Fifth Avenue, there are designer shops and department stores like Saks Fifth Avenue and Tiffany & Co., as well as St. Patrick's Cathedral.

UPPER WEST SIDE
AND HARLEM

Lincoln Center, New York's foremost performing arts complex, and the American Museum of Natural History are the main attractions on the Upper West Side. Apartments along Central Park West are some of the grandest and most sought-after in the city. Further north, Harlem has a large African-American and Latin-American community. One of its star attractions is the illustrious Apollo Theater.

UPPER EAST SIDE

The Upper East Side is Manhattan's most exclusive residential area. Elegant townhouses and luxury apartment buildings fill the blocks near Central Park. On Fifth Avenue's Museum Mile, you can find some of the world's finest museums, including "The Met" and the Guggenheim. Nearby, The Whitney is located on chic Madison Avenue, home to many of Manhattan's most luxurious shops and designer boutiques.

Before You Go. . .

WHEN TO GO

New York's climate can vary dramatically, from extremely hot and humid summers, with temperatures reaching 95°F (35°C), to cold and snowy winters, with temperatures plummeting well below 32°F (0°C). Fall and spring are generally mild and perhaps the best time to visit. You will, however, find a multitude of activities and events throughout the year. See page 248 for a full calendar of seasonal events and activities.

Virgin Atlantic Airlines

VISAS AND ENTRY REQUIREMENTS

All visitors must have one, all or a combination of the following in order to enter the U.S.: a valid passport, a visitor's visa and a valid onward passage ticket (such as a return airplane ticket). Presently, passport holders from the UK, Canada, New Zealand, Japan and all western European countries (with the exception of Ireland, Portugal, Greece and Vatican City) are not required to have a visa if staying for less than 90 days. All other travelers must have visas. For more information, contact your local U.S. embassy or consulate.

Upon entering the country, customs allowances are limited to 200 cigarettes (or 50 cigars or 4.4 pounds (two kilograms) of tobacco), two pints (one liter) of alcohol and gifts worth no more than $100 (after that you must pay tax). In addition, no plants, fruit, produce or meat are allowed through customs at all.

Broadway Theaters

MONEY

The American currency is the dollar ($), divided into 100 cents (¢). Major credit cards, especially American Express, MasterCard and Visa, are accepted practically everywhere (including supermarkets and drug stores) and can also be used for cash advances at automated teller machines. Credit cards also offer the benefit of advanced bookings for everything from movie tickets to hotel accommodation. Traveler's checks are accepted in many stores and restaurants when accompanied by a photo identification.

. . . Before You Go

New York is a relatively expensive city and the average daily tourist budget, excluding accommodation but including entrance prices, meals, transportation and entertainment, is approximately $70 per person.

HEALTH AND INSURANCE

It is advisable to take out travel insurance before your departure. In addition to baggage loss and trip cancellation, you will want to be sure that your policy provides adequate medical coverage, since U.S. medical care is notoriously expensive.

Central Park in the fall

PACKING FOR NEW YORK

A warm coat, gloves and scarf are necessities during the winter. In the spring and fall, a light jacket or heavy sweater is appropriate. Summers can be very hot and short-sleeved shirts and shorts are sensible and acceptable attire at most attractions and restaurants. Electricity throughout the U.S. is 110 volts (at 60 hz) with two-pronged plugs. If you have electrical accessories with different voltages, you will need to purchase a travel plug adaptor and electric current converter.

BOOKING A HOTEL ROOM IN ADVANCE

New York hotels tend to be more expensive than in many other U.S. cities. When choosing a hotel, you might first think about a price category, then consider in which area you would like to stay. On pages 35-48, you will find a comprehensive listing of quality hotels. You will also find a wealth of information, including the names and phone numbers of several reputable hotel-booking agencies, to help you to choose something that will fit your needs and budget. It is strongly recommended that you book your hotel well in advance, particularly if you are traveling during the height of the tourist season when many hotels are completely sold out.

BOOKING THEATER TICKETS IN ADVANCE

If you are interested in seeing a particular show, it is best to book as far ahead as possible. It is also helpful if you book mid-week, rather than on a weekend. With your *for less* card, you can obtain substantial discounts on tickets for top Broadway productions and you can purchase your tickets in advance by phone, with a credit card (see page 209 for details).

Arriving in New York . . .

GETTING FROM THE AIRPORT

J.F.K. AIRPORT

for less From **J.F.K.** and **LaGuardia Airports**, the **Gray Line Airport Shuttle** is a frequent shuttle service that will take you from either of the airports to the front door of any Manhattan hotel that is located between 23rd and 63rd Streets. Upon arrival, you should proceed to the Ground Transportation Desk in your arriving terminal and present the voucher on page 285

LAGUARDIA AIRPORT

for a 20% discount. From J.F.K., shuttles depart every 15-30 minutes from 7am to 11pm daily. The ride takes 45-60 minutes and costs $19 each way. From LaGuardia, buses depart every 15-30 minutes from 7am until 11pm daily. Tickets are $16 each way and the trip takes 30-45 minutes.

J.F.K. Airport

Reservations are not required for the arrival transfer, but they *are* necessary for the departure transfer from your hotel back to the airport. Call (212) 315-3006 to make a reservation, one day before your flight. (To receive your 20% *for less* discount on the transfer back to the airport, you must present the voucher on page 285 at either Gray Line's Times Square Visitors Center *(Broadway between 46th and 47th Streets)* or the Gray Line Sightseeing Terminal *(Port Authority Bus Terminal, Broadway between 46th and 47th Streets)* any time during your stay in New York.)

LaGuardia Airport

Alternatively, from J.F.K., you can take the free airport shuttle to the Howard Beach subway station where you can catch the **A or C subway line** to Manhattan. Shuttles and trains depart approximately every 15 minutes. The ride takes about 50 minutes and costs $1.50.

A **taxi** from J.F.K. to midtown Manhattan takes 35-60 minutes depending on traffic and is fixed at cost of $30 plus tolls and tip. From LaGuardia airport, a **taxi** costs $15-25 plus tolls and tip and will take 20-40 minutes.

NEWARK AIRPORT

for less From **Newark Airport**, the **Gray Line Airport Shuttle** departs every 15-30 minutes, taking passengers to midtown hotels in Manhattan. The ride takes 30-45 minutes and costs $19. Shuttles run from 7am until 11pm, departing every 20-30 minutes. To

. . . Arriving in New York

obtain your 20% *for less* discount, go to your
terminal's Ground Transportation Desk and present the
voucher on page 285. For the return transfer going to
the airport, you must go to Gray Line's Times Square
Visitors Center *(Broadway between 46th and 47th Streets)*
or the Gray Line Sightseeing Terminal *(Port Authority Bus
Terminal, 42nd Street and 8th Avenue)* to purchase the
return transfer, and you must call (212) 315-3006
one day before your departure to reserve. A **taxi** from
Newark Airport takes 20-45 minutes and
cost $30-45 plus tolls and tip.

GETTING AROUND NEW YORK

New York is a relatively compact city which
makes sightseeing fairly easy. Careful trip
planning will allow you to do the majority of
your sightseeing on foot, once you have
reached a particular destination. This book
is organized by neighborhood so that you
can make the best use of your time.

Inside the subway

Bus Tours - Taking a guided tour is the best way
to orient yourself while visiting New York's major
sights. **New York Apple Tours** (pages 212-213) offers
double-decker sightseeing tours and a discount to *for
less* cardholders. Your discount at **Gray Line New York**
(page 220) applies to a fully-escorted tour on a luxury
coach.

Subway - Operating 24 hours a day, seven days a week,
the subway is the fastest and easiest way to get around
New York City. Trains run frequently (every 3-5
minutes during the day) and less frequently late at
night. The one-way fare is $1.50 (no matter how many
times you change trains without exiting the stations)
and can be paid with a Metrocard or a token bought at
any subway station. New Metrocards allow you to
purchase unlimited trips within a specified period of
time. Currently, a seven-day unlimited
Metrocard costs $17.

Bus - Most buses run 24 hours a day, seven
days a week. Traffic can make bus travel
slow and inconvenient during the day, but can
be a good alternative to a taxi in the
evenings. The fare is $1.50 and can be paid
with a MetroCard or a token.

New York City bus

Taxi - The ubiquitous yellow cabs are easily
recognizable. They are available when the center light
is on, but not when the "Off Duty" side lights are on as
well. Daytime traffic make cab rides a fairly expensive
method of transportation, even for short distances.

Planning Your Itinerary . . .

New York has so many sights and attractions that it can be rather overwhelming for a first-time visitor. This section will help you plan your trip by highlighting some of the best things to do and see in the city.

IF YOU HAVE ONE DAY

Sightseeing – Start the day by taking the New York Apple Tours Statue of Liberty Express (page 212) double-decker sightseeing tour; see the Statue of Liberty and Ellis Island. Upon returning, stop off at the World Trade Center (page 56) and admire the view from the Observation

A carriage ride in Central Park

Deck on the 107th Floor. If you have time, walk to the South Street Seaport (page 58), Trinity Church (page 62) and New York's financial center, Wall Street, all within a short distance of each other.

Lower Manhattan view from the Circle Line

Lunch/Dinner – New York has more than 17,000 eating establishments, serving a vast array of international cuisine. Choose from the many restaurants listed in this book and receive a 25% discount off the total bill.

Museums – Continue the bus tour to the Upper East Side to the Museum Mile (page 176), one the most famous art districts in the world. The "Met" (page 178), the Whitney (page 183) and the Solomon R. Guggenheim Museum (page 180) are a few of the many prestigious institutions that are worth visiting on this stretch of Fifth Avenue.

Evening – After an early dinner, take in a Broadway show in the Theater District (page 128). Or, if you prefer, a Circle Line Cruise (page 214) makes for an unforgettable New York experience, especially at sunset when the skyline views are amazing.

Empire State Building – After the theater, head to the Observatory at the top of the Empire State Building (page 114) to witness the extraordinary view of the Manhattan skyline at night.

IF YOU HAVE TWO DAYS

In addition to slowing down the pace of the previous itinerary, a second day in New York will give museum-goers a chance to visit the exceptional collections at

. . . Planning Your Itinerary

the Museum of Modern Art (page 130). Later, take a
walk through Central Park (page 199). The park's
main attraction, Wollman Memorial Rink (page 202),
is a great place for ice-skating and rollerblading.

IF YOU HAVE THREE-FOUR DAYS

Soho and its surrounding areas (page 74)
are an excellent place to explore.
Wander through the galleries and
fashionable boutiques before heading to
nearby Chinatown, Little Italy or the
Lower East Side (page 77) where you can
indulge in the ethnic foods for which
these neighborhoods are best known.
Before the sun sets, take a walk across
the Brooklyn Bridge for a breathtaking
view of the Manhattan skyline.

IF YOU HAVE A WEEK

Brooklyn Bridge

Visitors fortunate enough to have a week
in New York will begin to discover the full range of
what New York has to offer. An excellent way to
experience the city and all its curiosities is by
investigating its distinctive neighborhoods in-depth.

1. The Municipal Art Society (page 218) sponsors a
series of walking tours which focus on the
architecture, history and sites of some of Manhattan's
more interesting neighborhoods.

2. Historic Greenwich Village
(page 96) is a picturesque,
yet dynamic area. Its
charming old-world streets
contain historic brownstone
houses, contemporary
shopping, dining and nightlife
opportunities.

3. For an excellent dinner
and a view of the island of
Manhattan you will never
forget, take a World Yacht
Dinner Cruise (page 215).

*Greenwich Village
townhouses*

4. New York City's outer boroughs, often overlooked by
visitors, contain an array of historic and cultural sites
and attractions. Stroll along the Brooklyn Promenade
(page 222), directly across the river from Manhattan,
catch a baseball game at Yankee Stadium (page 228)
or take a ride on the Staten Island Ferry (page 65) for
great views of Lower Manhattan, the Statue of Liberty
and New York Harbor – for free!

If You Do One Thing . . .

These ten ideas may not be the most famous or popular destinations, but they are an honest selection of personal favorites.

If you visit one attraction:

Empire State Building Observatory (page 114)

If you go to one museum:

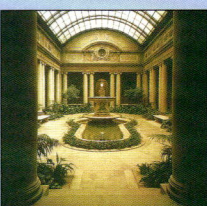

The Frick Collection (page 182)

If you take one walk:

Path along the Hudson River (page 67)

If you go to one nightclub:

Webster Hall (page 210)

If you take one tour:

New York Apple Tours' Statue of Liberty Express (page 213)

If you go to one restaurant:

Portfolio (page 122)

If you go to one store:

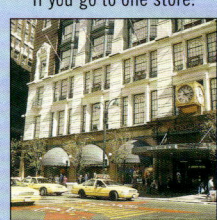

Macy's (page 142)

If you take one excursion:

Rent a car and drive to Philadelphia (page 240)

If you go to one brewery:

Heartland Brewery (page 122)

If you visit one church:

Cathedral of St. John the Divine (page 167)

History of
New York

History . . .

The history of New York began long before the arrival of European settlers. The **Algonquin** and **Iroquois**

Purchase of Manhattan from the Indians (1626)

Indians inhabited the region until the mid-1600s when they were forced out of the area by colonizing Europeans.

The first European settler to arrive in what is now New York Harbor was **Giovanni da Verrazano**. Traveling in the service of France, the Florentine Verrazzano arrived in 1524, not long after Columbus made his first voyage to America. Despite the fact that he wrote a detailed account of the new land to the king of France, it would be quite some time before any settlers arrived.

Eighty-five years later, in 1609, the Englishman **Henry Hudson**, working for the **Dutch East India Company**, was on a journey to find a westward route to the Indies. He failed, and inadvertently sailed his ship, the *Half-Moon*, up the river that today bears his name. His discovery of the fertile Hudson River Valley and the possibilities it had for trade sparked an interest with the company.

DeWit View (ca. 1672)

In 1624, the **Dutch West India Company** established a permanent colony on Manhattan Island as a trading outpost and named it **Nieuw Amsterdam (New Amsterdam)**. **Peter Minuit**, the colony's first governor, bought the island of Manhattan from the Indians for

. . . History . . .

$24 worth of beads, blankets and trinkets in 1626.

The industrious settlers set about taming the wild island formerly known by the Algonquin word "Manahatta". They groomed the land, built canals and created a self-sufficient town. In 1628 the **Reformed Dutch Church** was established, the first religious organization to be founded in New Amsterdam.

Before long, the colony was growing with incredible speed. Immigrants arrived from Britain and continental Europe; slaves were brought from the Caribbean; there is said to have been more than eighteen languages spoken in this small community.

Dance on the Battery in the Presence of Peter Stuyvesant (1838) by A. Durand

The relationship between the settlers and the natives was strained and often chaos ruled. During the 1640s, the Dutch, who had already started enforcing harsh laws towards the natives, launched a two and a half year war against them.

In 1647, **Peter Stuyvesant** became governor and implemented a strict plan to restore order and civility in what had become an unruly and lawless town. To keep warring Indians away he ordered a ditch to be dug and a wall to be installed at the present location of **Wall Street**, then the city's northern border. He remained governor for 17 years, during which time the settlement doubled in size and trading flourished.

New Amsterdam was seized by the English in 1664. The Dutch surrendered without a fight, and the town was renamed **New York**, in honor of the king's brother, the Duke of York.

Under the British flag, the colony prospered. Churches, a town hall and other public buildings were constructed. **King's College** was founded, later to become **Columbia University**.

. . . History . . .

In 1733, **John Peter Zenger** started a liberal paper called the *New York Weekly Journal*. His famous trial, on a libel charge, helped establish the American ideals of freedom of speech and freedom of the press which were later embodied in the **First Amendment to the Constitution**.

Pulling down the statue of George III at Bowling Green, July 1776

British control became increasingly stifling for the colonists. Divisions were drawn between the loyalists and patriots, and tensions were only mounting.

The patriots rallied behind **George Washington** who was on his way to Boston to head up the Continental Army.

In 1774, the colonists set up the **Continental Congress**. Soon after, **Thomas Jefferson's Declaration of Independence**, extolling the virtues of a democratic government, was adopted. Delegates from the Continental Congress, preparing for a revolution, asked colonists to band together and refuse to pay taxes.

In 1776, 200 British ships entered New

Portrait of George Washington (1796) by Gilbert Stuart

York Harbor and the **American Revolution** began. During this time, New York suffered from violence, over-crowding and starvation. After much bloodshed, British troops finally surrendered and began to withdraw from the colonies.

. . . History . . .

Initially, New York was named the first capital city of the newly formed **United States**. On April 23, 1789, General George Washington, hero of the American Revolution, was elected the nation's first president. He said farewell to his troops at the **Queen's Head Tavern** (now **Fraunces Tavern**) and was sworn in as president on the balcony of **Federal Hall** on Wall Street.

City Hall Park, early 1800s

In 1790, the capital of government was relocated to Philadelphia, but New York retained its import as a thriving commercial port. However, the population explosion brought along its own sets of problems, and in 1811, the street grid plan was devised for the future growth of the city.

New York City continued to flourish, and by 1850, the **Irish Potato Famine** had sparked a wave of **immigration** that brought the city's population to 300,000.

From 1855 to 1890, the number of immigrants who entered the U.S. via New York City totaled 8 million. To accommodate this influx, **Ellis Island Immigration Station** was built in 1892. After having seen nearly 16 million people pass through, it was finally closed in 1954.

The influx of cheap labor helped place turn-of-the-century New York City at the forefront of technological and industrial achievements, ushering in the "**Golden Age**". In the 1860s, the first **elevated trains** appeared, further expanding New York's geographical boundaries, while mansions were built on upper Fifth Avenue, overlooking the newly created **Central Park**. **Thomas Edison** first provided electricity to the general public in 1882 and soon thereafter New York watched in awe the completion and dedication of the **Brooklyn Bridge** and the **Statue of Liberty**. By 1900, the construction of the city's **subway** had begun.

Central Park Summer, Looking South (1865) John Bachmann

During this period, banker **J.P. Morgan** and industrial tycoons **Cornelius Vanderbilt**, **Andrew Carnegie** and

. . . History . . .

John D. Rockefeller monopolized the industry and wealth of the country and made names for themselves as the "**Robber Barons**". They went on to fund universities, libraries, museums and public institutions of all kinds, many of which still bear their names.

Immigrants on Battery Park, 1901

In 1917, America entered **World War I**. The eventual victory over Germany in 1918 introduced America as a world power while the country, and New York City in particular, profited immensely.

In 1920, the **women's suffrage movement** won the right to vote. At the same time, **Prohibition** gave rise to speakeasies – illegal drinking establishments run mainly by gangsters. **Jazz** flourished at nightclubs such as the **Cotton Club** in **Harlem** where **Duke Ellington** and **Cab Calloway** were regular performers.

The prosperity of the "**roaring 20s**" was followed by the **stock market crash** of October, 1929, and the **Great Depression**. Banks closed and people across the country lost their jobs and their homes.

Subway construction workers in a tunnel

President Franklin D. Roosevelt introduced the **New Deal** in an attempt to restore and revitalize public life by creating new jobs. At this time, great projects like the **Empire State Building** and **Rockefeller Center** were completed.

In 1933, **Fiorello LaGuardia** became mayor. Known for his stance against corruption and well-respected by the people, LaGuardia was re-elected twice. He led New York out of the Great Depression and through to the end of **World War II**.

The Second World War was as good to New York as the First had been. Government

New York skyline in 1932

. . . History

spending increased, jobs were created and New York Harbor filled with ships, soldiers and supplies bound for Europe.

During the 1950s, **Beat culture** became the latest in a long list of counter-cultural movements that have

The early days of the Flatiron Building

made New York a haven for progressive and radical thinkers. Nonetheless, the conservative influence of 1950s mainstream America was still dominant in New York.

In the 1960s, the struggle for racial equality led by African-American, Latin-American and other ethnic groups impacted the culture. **Equal rights** and **Anti-Vietnam demonstrations**, such as those at **Columbia University**, were in the nation's spotlight.

Tired of the chaos and crime, many middle-class families moved to the suburbs. The departure of workers and businesses took its toll on city coffers, which reached the point of near-collapse in the mid-1970s.

Federal and state loans were reluctantly granted and the **Municipal Assistance Corporation** was established to keep the city's expenditures in check. Mayor **Ed Koch**, elected in 1978, took control of city finances and remained in office for three terms.

In the 1980s, New York experienced another economic and building boom. The "yuppie" emerged as a symbol of wealth and excess typified by public figures like **Donald Trump**.

Hard-nosed lawyer and federal prosecutor **Rudolph Guiliani** became New York's mayor in 1994 on a platform of reducing crime and improving New York's quality of life. Although many people fear that he is attempting to suburbanize New York and strip it of its uniqueness, the crime rate, at least, has fallen to half its previous level.

Trump Tower: a tribute to the wealth and excess of the 1980s

Timeline . . .

1524 Giovanni da Verrazano becomes the first European to land on Manhattan.

1609 While on a voyage for the Dutch East India Company, Henry Hudson sails into the bay and river that now bear his name.

THE DUTCH ARRIVE

1624 The colony of New Amsterdam is founded by the Dutch.

1626 The first governor, Peter Minuit, purchases the island of Manhattan for the equivalent of $24 worth of trinkets.

1628 The Reformed Dutch Church is the first religious organization to be established in Manhattan.

1647 Peter Stuyvesant becomes governor. He establishes order in the chaotic, lawless city.

1653 New Amsterdam is declared a town and receives a charter. A protective wall is erected to control the fighting with neighboring Indians.

1654 Jewish settlers arrive in New Amsterdam for the first time.

1661 Poor civic management and wars with the Indians lead an unstable New Amsterdam to the brink of bankruptcy.

THE BRITISH ARRIVE

1664 The English invade and seize New Amsterdam, renaming it New York after the Duke of York, the King of England's brother.

1674 The Treaty of Westminster grants the colony of New Amsterdam permanently to the English.

1700 The population of the city reaches 20,000.

1725 William Bradford establishes New York's first newspaper - the *New York Gazette*.

1733-1734 John Peter Zenger founds the *New York Weekly Journal*.

1754 King's College, the city's first college is founded. It later becomes Columbia University.

1763 The 1763 Treaty of Paris ends the French and Indian War (also known as the 7 Years' War). The British are victorious and take control of the thirteen colonies.

THE AMERICAN REVOLUTION

1776 The Declaration of Independence is read in Bowling Green and the American Revolution begins. British ships are sent to New York Harbor.

. . . Timeline . . .

1783 On September 3, the 1783 Treaty of Paris is signed. The colonists are victorious and England recognizes the independence of the thirteen colonies.

1789-90 New York is capital of the United States.

1789 The Constitution of the United States is ratified and General George Washington is elected as the first president.

THE NEW REPUBLIC

1811 John Randel devises the street "grid plan" for the future growth of New York City.

1812-1814 The U.S. declares war on Britain. British ships are positioned in New York Harbor in order to block and isolate the city from trade. City Hall is built.

1825 The Eerie Canal is opened, leading the way for New York to become an important trading port.

1828 South Street Seaport becomes the center of New York's growing maritime trade.

INDUSTRIAL GROWTH

1858-1876 Central Park is constructed.

1860 Abraham Lincoln is elected President.

1861-1865 The Civil War. The Union (North) wins and slavery is abolished. President Abraham Lincoln is assassinated.

1868 The "El", New York's first elevated railway and the precursor to the subway, is erected.

1870 The Metropolitan Museum of Art is founded. Work on the Brooklyn Bridge begins.

1882 Thomas Edison's electrical plant, located in Lower Manhattan, offers electricity to the public for general use.

1883 The Brooklyn Bridge is completed and opened.

1886 The Statue of Liberty is unveiled and New York hosts its first "ticker tape parade" on lower Broadway.

MASS IMMIGRATION

1892 Ellis Island is opened as an immigration station and remains so until 1954.

1898 Brooklyn, the Bronx, Queens and Staten Island become part of New York City – making it the world's largest, with a population of more than 3 million.

1900 Construction of the subway begins.

1902 The Flatiron Building is erected and, at 21 stories, is the world's first skyscraper.

THE GREAT
DEPRESSION

POST-WAR
NEW YORK

. . . Timeline

1907 Metered taxis are introduced on the streets of New York.

1917 The United States enters World War I.

1920 The women's suffrage movement wins the right to vote. Prohibition laws are introduced.

1929 Wall Street crashes and ushers in the Great Depression. MoMA opens its first exhibition.

1931 The Empire State Building is completed and becomes the world's tallest structure.

1939 The World's Fair, held at Flushing Meadow Park in Queens, attracts over 44 million visitors.

1941 America enters World War II.

1946 The United Nations charter is signed in New York.

1947 Jackie Robinson of the Brooklyn Dodgers is the first black player in major league baseball.

1959 The Solomon R. Guggenheim Museum opens.

1962 Lincoln Center for the Performing Arts opens.

1964 Race riots occur in Brooklyn and Harlem. The Beatles play Shea Stadium in Queens.

1964-65 The World's Fair is held on the same site in Queens as it was in 1939-40.

1973 The World Trade Center is completed.

1977 A blackout lasts for 25 hours throughout the entire city.

1978 Ed Koch is elected mayor and begins economic turnaround.

1983 Trump Tower is completed by real estate developer and consummate yuppie Donald Trump.

1986 The stock market crashes again.

1990 New York's first black mayor, David Dinkens, is elected. Ellis Island reopens as a museum.

1993 Terrorists attempt to blow up the World Trade Center. Rudolph Guiliani is elected as New York City's first Republican mayor in 28 years.

1996 New York Yankees win the World Series. President Bill Clinton is re-elected for a second term.

1998 New York Yankees again win the World Series.

1999 Impeachment hearings of President Clinton.

Hotels

Booking a Hotel Room

New York hotels are notoriously expensive by international standards. In very recent years, demand often exceeds supply, pushing rates even higher and limiting availability, sometimes drastically. For these reasons, it is recommended that you book well in advance.

Lobby in the Tudor Hotel (page 43)

To make a booking, telephone the hotel directly and be prepared to confirm your booking by fax or letter. Alternatively, there are a number of hotel booking services, some of which offer discount rooms, that may be a simple way of checking out a multitude of options. These include *Quickbook* (☎ *(212) 686-7666)*, *Take Time to Travel* (☎ *(800) 522-9991 or (212) 840-8686)*, *Hotel Reservations Network* (☎ *(800) 964-6835)*, *Central Reservation Service* (☎ *(800) 950-0232 or (305) 274-6832)* and *The Room Exchange* (☎ *(800) 846-7000 or (212) 760-1000)*.

The hotels on the following pages are a general selection of those in the central areas of Manhattan, representing a variety of price categories. They are not necessarily recommended by *New York for less* and you cannot obtain a discount at them. They are grouped according to area in descending price order.

The $ symbols by each hotel's entry indicate the standard double room rates. $= under $149, $$= $150-199, $$$= $200-249, $$$$= $250-299, $$$$$= over $300.

The first thing to do after you decide how much you would like to spend is to decide in which area you would like to stay. Most hotels in Manhattan are located either in Midtown East or Midtown West. For a summary of New York's areas, see pages 14-15.

The number of stars under each hotel's name indicates its quality:

★★ : Basic amenities such as *en suite* bathrooms, air-conditioning, TVs and radios.

★★★ : Full reception services, more formal restaurant and bar arrangements, additional amenities.

★★★★ : More spacious accommodation offering high standards of comfort and food. The range of services includes porterage, room service, formal reception and often a selection of restaurants.

★★★★★ : The majority of rooms are of the highest international standard.

HOTEL FACILITIES

In addition to the amenities represented by the symbols below, all of the hotels listed on the following pages have *en suite* showers and baths, air conditioned bedrooms, satellite or cable TV, wake-up calls, laundry facilities and non-smoking rooms (available upon request).

 Minibar

 Tea/coffee facilities

Room service

24-hour room Service

 Radio

 Direct dial telephone

 Hairdryer

 Room safe

 Babysitting service

 Disabled facilities

Business Center

 Fitness Center

 Swimming Pool

Soho Grand Hotel

★ ★ ★ ★

310 West Broadway
Soho
☎ 965-3000

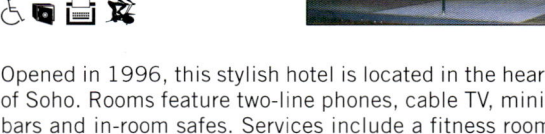

Opened in 1996, this stylish hotel is located in the heart of Soho. Rooms feature two-line phones, cable TV, mini-bars and in-room safes. Services include a fitness room and transportation to the Financial District. *(367 rooms)*

Southgate Towers

★ ★ ★

371 Seventh Avenue
Chelsea
☎ 563-1800

Located across from Madison Square Garden, every room in this all-suite hotel features a kitchen with a microwave and refrigerator. Services include business and fitness centers. *(522 suites)*

Rihga Royal

★ ★ ★ ★

151 West 54th Street
Midtown West
☎ 307-5000

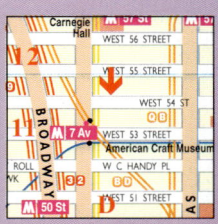

This 54-story luxury hotel has nearly 500 deluxe suites. Each has superb amenities including VCRs, electronic safes, televisions, phones and mini-bars. A full service restaurant is located on the ground floor. *(496 suites)*

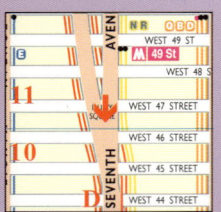

PRICE CATEGORY

$$$$

PRICE CATEGORY

$$$$

PRICE CATEGORY

$$$$

New York Renaissance

★ ★ ★ ★

714 Seventh Avenue
Midtown West
☎ 765-7676

Located in the heart of Times Square, this high-rise hotel provides quality accommodation and service. The rooms are modern and comfortable, and each of its 21 floors has a 24-hour butler. *(305 rooms)*

Doubletree Guest Suites

★ ★ ★ ★

1568 Broadway
Midtown West
☎ 719-1600

This all-suite hotel is located near Rockefeller Center and Radio City Music Hall. Each suite contains a living room, dining area with full kitchen, and bedroom as well as two TVs and three phones with voice mail. *(460 suites)*

Shoreham Hotel

★ ★ ★

33 West 55th Street
Midtown West
☎ 247-6700

The Shoreham is located one block from the Museum of Modern Art and is close to all the midtown attractions. Guest rooms are spacious and modern with cedar closets, refrigerators, cable TV and CD players. *(84 rooms)*

Royalton

★ ★ ★ ★

44 West 44th Street
Midtown West
☎ 869-4400

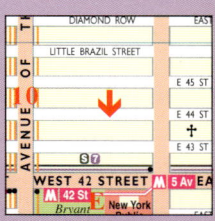

A favorite with many celebrities, the Royalton features luxurious rooms with fireplaces, roomy baths and large beds. Philippe Starck designed the hallway, lobby and the nautical-style rooms. *(167 rooms)*

Millennium Broadway

★ ★ ★ ★

145 West 44th Street
Midtown West
☎ 768-4400

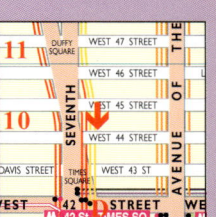

Floor-to-ceiling windows in each guest room look out onto the Theater District. Rockefeller Center and Fifth Avenue are all within walking distance. Amenities include multi-lingual voice mail and child services. *(638 rooms)*

Michelangelo

★ ★ ★ ★

152 West 51st Street
Midtown West
☎ 765-1900

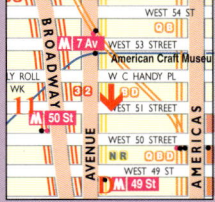

The Michelangelo is a first-class luxury hotel. The spacious rooms come with a complimentary breakfast and each features a marble foyer and Empire, Art Deco or Country French décor. *(178 rooms)*

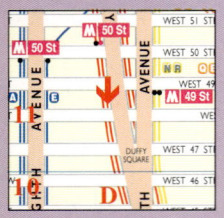

$$$$

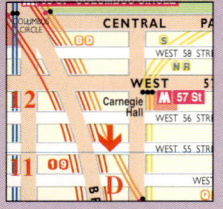

PRICE CATEGORY

$$$$

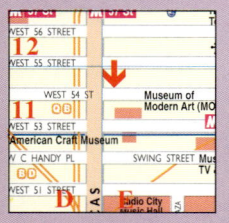

PRICE CATEGORY

$$$

Crowne Plaza

★ ★ ★

1605 Broadway
Midtown West
☎ 977-4000

Described by *Newsweek* as the "most gorgeous building in Manhattan", the Crowne Plaza has exceptional views, a full range of services and amenities, and Manhattan's largest indoor hotel pool. *(770 rooms)*

Hotel Gorham

★ ★ ★

136 West 55th Street
Midtown West
☎ 245-1800

This small luxury hotel has recently undergone a complete multi-million dollar renovation. Rooms and suites feature minibars, refrigerators, cable TVs, two-line phones, fax machines and in-room safes. *(122 rooms)*

The Warwick

★ ★ ★

65 West 54th Street
Midtown West
☎ 247-2700

Built by publisher William Randolph Hearst in 1927, the Warwick is located in the Theater District, and a short walk from Central Park. Rooms include cable TV, two-line phones and marble bathrooms. *(425 rooms)*

Novotel New York

★ ★ ★

226 West 52nd Street
Midtown West
☎ 315-0100

Located on Broadway in the heart of the Theater District, this hotel has a unique seven-floor lobby. Rooms feature either king-size beds and a pull-out sofa or two double beds, all with modern furnishings and baths. *(474 rooms)*

PRICE CATEGORY

$$$

Paramount

★ ★ ★

235 West 46th Street
Midtown West
☎ 764-5500

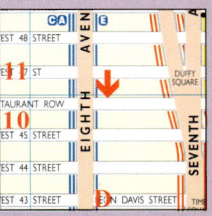

The Paramount is a chic, modern hotel often frequented by celebrities. A dramatic staircase is the centerpiece of Philippe Starck's stylish design. A coffee shop and trendy bar are located in the lobby. *(610 rooms)*

PRICE CATEGORY

$$$

New York Marriott Marquis

★ ★ ★ ★

1568 Broadway
Midtown West
☎ 398-1900

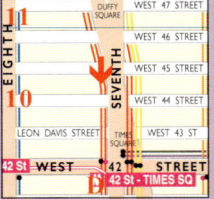

This 50-story hotel towers above Times Square. Rooms feature individual climate control, dual telephones and coffeemakers. Four eateries include The View – a revolving rooftop restaurant. *(1,911 rooms)*

PRICE CATEGORY

$$$

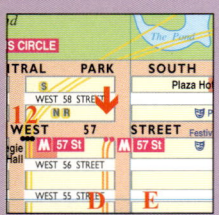

Salisbury

★★

123 West 57th Street
Midtown West
☎ 246-1300

PRICE CATEGORY

$$$

The Salisbury is situated across the street from Carnegie Hall and is a short walk from Fifth Avenue. Its central location and large rooms (many of which feature kitchenettes) make it perfect for families. *(320 rooms)*

Mansfield

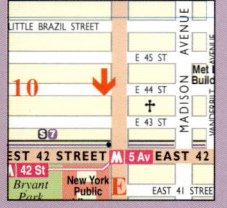

★★★

12 West 44th Street
Midtown West
☎ 944-6050

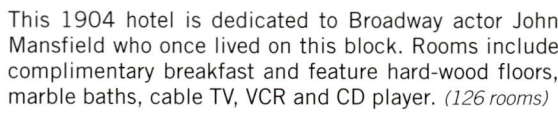

PRICE CATEGORY

$$

This 1904 hotel is dedicated to Broadway actor John Mansfield who once lived on this block. Rooms include complimentary breakfast and feature hard-wood floors, marble baths, cable TV, VCR and CD player. *(126 rooms)*

Best Western Woodward

★★

210 West 55th Street
Midtown West
☎ 247-2000

PRICE CATEGORY

$$

The Best Western Woodward is located in a Beaux Arts landmark building in the Theater District. Rooms feature modern conveniences and new bathrooms. Your stay also includes continental breakfast. *(200 rooms)*

Hotel Metro

★★

45 West 35th Street
Midtown West
☎ 947-2500

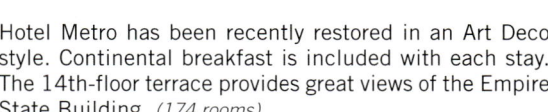

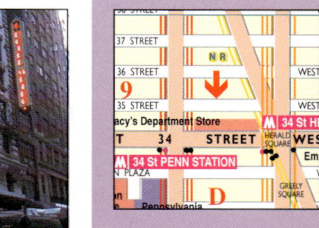

Hotel Metro has been recently restored in an Art Deco style. Continental breakfast is included with each stay. The 14th-floor terrace provides great views of the Empire State Building. *(174 rooms)*

Edison Hotel

★★

288 West 47th Street
Midtown West
☎ 840-5000

Built in 1931, the Edison Hotel is one of the best values in Manhattan hotels. Situated in the heart of the Theater District, each guest room has individual temperature controls and a modern bath. *(1,000 rooms)*

St. Moritz

★★

50 Central Park South
Midtown West
☎ 752-7760

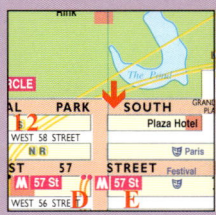

Ideally situated on Central Park South, the St. Moritz overlooks the park. This old-fashioned, affordable hotel has recently undergone a major renovation. It is located close to many of the midtown attractions. *(680 rooms)*

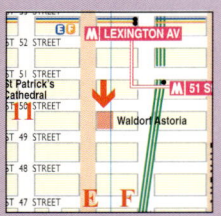

PRICE CATEGORY

$$$$$

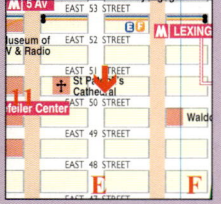

PRICE CATEGORY

$$$$

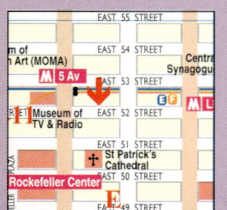

PRICE CATEGORY

$$$$

Waldorf-Astoria

★ ★ ★ ★ ★

301 Park Avenue
Midtown East
☎ 355-3000

Built in 1931, this world-famous hotel features a grand lobby decorated with painted murals, mahogany panelling and marble columns. The rooms contain beautiful French and English antiques. *(1,444 rooms)*

New York Palace

★ ★ ★ ★

445 Madison Avenue
Midtown East
☎ 888-7000

The New York Palace is annexed to the 1884 landmark Villard Houses. 55-stories high, this luxury hotel offers services which include business and fitness centers and several high quality restaurants. *(863 rooms)*

Omni Berkshire Place

★ ★ ★ ★

21 East 52nd Street
Midtown East
☎ 888-4705

Have a complimentary copy of the *New York Times* delivered to your door each morning at this luxurious hotel on fashionable Madison Avenue. The health club features a sun-deck and massage service. *(396 rooms)*

The Tudor

304 East 42nd Street
Midtown East
☎ 986-8800

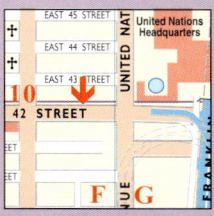

This hotel is located near the midtown sights. Small and modern, the Tudor is best known for its high levels of personal service. Rooms are contemporary and feature marble baths and in-room safes. *(300 rooms)*

PRICE CATEGORY

$$$$

Hotel Intercontinental

★ ★ ★ ★

111 East 48th Street
Midtown East
☎ 755-5900

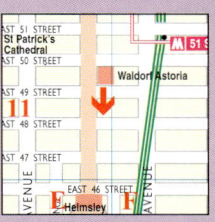

Built in 1926, the Hotel Intercontinental has been recently restored. Old-world in style, it has modern and comfortable guest rooms. Hotel services include a brand-new, state-of-the-art business center. *(861 rooms)*

PRICE CATEGORY

$$$$

Doral Park Avenue

★ ★ ★

70 Park Avenue
Midtown East
☎ 687-7050

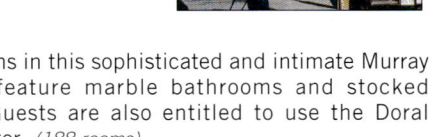

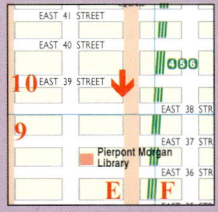

The bedrooms in this sophisticated and intimate Murray Hill hotel feature marble bathrooms and stocked minibars. Guests are also entitled to use the Doral Fitness Center. *(188 rooms)*

PRICE CATEGORY

$$$

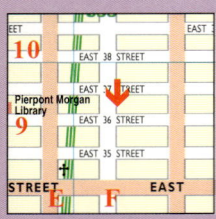

PRICE CATEGORY

$$$

PRICE CATEGORY

$$$

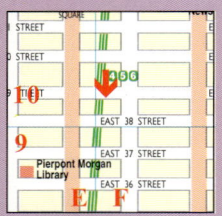

PRICE CATEGORY

$$$

Shelburne Murray Hotel

★ ★ ★

303 Lexington Avenue
Midtown East
☎ **689-5200**

The Shelburne Murray Hotel features spacious suites complete with full kitchen (including a microwave and refrigerator). Services include a multi-lingual staff, conference facilities and a fitness center. *(258 suites)*

Dumont Plaza

★ ★ ★

150 East 34th Street
Midtown East
☎ **481-7600**

Located in Murray Hill, the Dumont Plaza is a short walk from the Empire State Building and Macy's. The hotel features suite-style rooms with complete kitchen, cable TV and complimentary coffee and tea. *(247 suites)*

Doral Court

★ ★ ★

130 East 39th Street
Midtown East
☎ **685-1100**

The Doral Court is located in residential Murray Hill. This comfortable hotel has rooms that feature big-screen TVs, VCRs and walk-in closets. Guests are also welcome to use the Doral Fitness Center. *(199 rooms)*

Loews New York

★ ★ ★

569 Lexington Avenue
Midtown East
☎ 752-7000

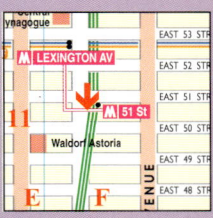

This moderately priced, high-quality hotel has recently received a multi-million dollar renovation. Guest rooms have modern furnishings including refrigerators, safes, TVs and two-line phones. *(688 rooms)*

PRICE CATEGORY

$$$

Morgans

★ ★ ★

237 Madison Avenue
Midtown East
☎ 686-0300

Morgans was built in 1929 to honor the early 19th-century banker J.P. Morgan. All rooms have modern amenities. Services include a baby-sitting service, fitness center and business facilities. *(113 rooms)*

PRICE CATEGORY

$$$

New York Helmsley

★ ★ ★

212 East 42nd Street
Midtown East
☎ 490-8900

The New York Helmsley is located near Grand Central Station. The hotel has 41 floors and services which include a multi-lingual staff and complimentary coffee and tea in the lobby. *(790 rooms)*

PRICE CATEGORY

$$$

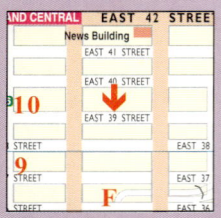

PRICE CATEGORY

$$

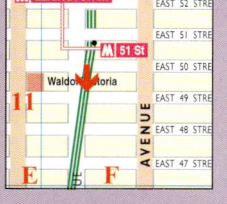

PRICE CATEGORY

$$

PRICE CATEGORY

$$

Eastgate Tower

★ ★ ★

222 East 39th Street
Midtown East
☎ 687-8000

Located close to the midtown attractions, Eastgate Tower offers comfortable all-suite accommodation. Each suite has a complete kitchen with microwave, coffeemaker and full stove. *(188 suites)*

Jolly Madison Towers

★ ★

22 East 38th Street
Midtown East
☎ 802-0600

Jolly Madison Tower is moderately priced and located near Madison Avenue. The lobby is decorated with white marble floors and a mirrored ceiling. The modern rooms feature rosewood furniture. *(246 rooms)*

Doral Inn

★ ★ ★

541 Lexington Avenue
Midtown East
☎ 755-1200

Located near Grand Central Station, the Doral Inn has rooms designed and furnished to a high standard, but is moderately priced. Guests can use the health club, sauna and squash courts. *(655 rooms)*

Radisson Empire

 ★ ★ ★

44 West 63rd Street
Upper West Side
☎ 265-7400

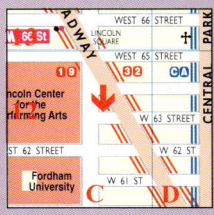

Across from Lincoln Center, every room at the Radisson Empire has a large bath, TV, VCR and stereo with CD player. The Tudor-style lobby is adorned with high ceilings, wood panelling and oil paintings. *(376 rooms)*

PRICE CATEGORY

$$

Regency

★ ★ ★ ★

540 Park Avenue
Upper East Side
☎ 759-4100

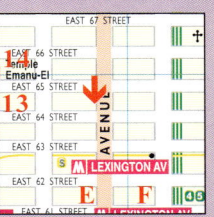

The exclusive Regency has nearly 400 elegant rooms. A full range of top-notch amenities includes 24-hour room service. Other hotel services include a fitness center and a business center. *(362 rooms)*

PRICE CATEGORY

$$$$

Hotel Delmonico

★ ★ ★ ★

502 Park Avenue
Upper East Side
☎ 355-2500

Located close to Central Park, Hotel Delmonico houses the famous Christie's auction house. It offers suites, each with modern amenities including a fully equipped kitchen, two color TVs and in-room safe. *(147 suites)*

PRICE CATEGORY

$$$$

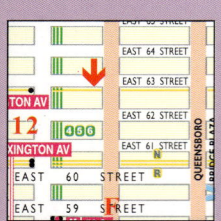

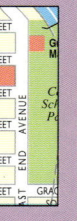

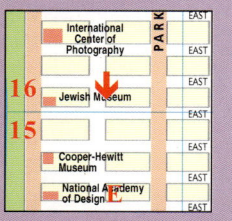

Barbizon

★ ★ ★

**140 East 63rd Street
Upper East Side
☎ 838-5700**

Once a safe haven for young ladies from wealthy families visiting the city, the Barbizon recently underwent a 40 million dollar renovation. Rooms are modern and are reasonably priced for this expensive area. *(344 rooms)*

Franklin

★ ★

**164 East 87th Street
Upper East Side
☎ 369-1000**

Located close to Museum Mile, the Franklin has an intimate, charming atmosphere. Each room has a canopied bed, spacious closets and a comfortable bath. Guests also receive complimentary breakfast. *(53 rooms)*

Hotel Wales

★ ★

**1295 Madison Avenue
Upper East Side
☎ 876-6000**

Located in the Carnegie Hill historic district, near Museum Mile, Hotel Wales has recently been restored to its original turn-of-the-century glory. Breakfast and tea are served in the Pied Piper Room. *(92 rooms)*

Lower Manhattan

Introduction . . .

In addition to being the home of one of the world's most important financial centers, Lower Manhattan contains many of New York's top attractions and historic sights, including **South Street Seaport** (page 58), the **World Trade Center** (page 56) and **Battery Park**, from where you can take the ferry to the **Statue of Liberty** and **Ellis Island** (pages 52-55). It is perhaps the best area to start a sightseeing tour of the city.

Statue of Liberty

Originally inhabited by the Iroquois and Algonquin Indians, Manhattan was named **New Amsterdam** by the Dutch who settled here in the 17th century. In 1653, a wall was built along the northern boundary of the settlement in order to keep its citizens safe from the wilderness and warring Indians beyond.

INSIDER'S TIP

Walking tours provide an in-depth look at the architecture, history and sights of a neighborhood. Heritage Trails New York (page 219) enables you to explore historic Lower Manhattan, either with a guide or on your own, by following the colored trail markers on sidewalks and streets.

Bowling Green

Today, **Wall Street**, as it came to be known, is the heart of the Financial District. The winding streets of the old Dutch town can still be traced among the looming skyscrapers of the modern metropolis.

Under British rule, the landscape of Lower Manhattan came to resemble the parks and squares of London. Many of these, such as **Bowling Green** (page 67) still remain - though the surrounding fence, which still stands, is no longer topped with English royal crowns.

As the nation's first capital, post-Revolutionary New York was the seat of government and Lower Manhattan held its courts and government offices. General **George Washington**, the nation's first president, took his oath of office in a building on Wall Street which is now

Brooklyn Bridge and the East River

Federal Hall National Memorial (page 61). Nearby, **Fraunces Tavern Museum** (page 60) is the site of the farewell speech he made to his officers.

. . . Introduction

North of the Financial District, Manhattan's **Civic Center** comprises the courthouses and offices of local, state and federal government. Its focal point, **City Hall** (page 63), was built in 1812 and since that time has been the site of many political protests and demonstrations.

Also in City Hall Park is the infamous **Old New York County Courthouse**. Begun in 1862 and not finished until a decade later, it is better known as "Tweed Courthouse". Legend has it that Boss Tweed, leader of the political faction Tammany Hall, corruptly pocketed $10 million of the $14 million dollars allotted to pay for its construction.

Overlooking City Hall, the much larger **Municipal Building** houses government offices of all kinds, including the marriage bureau. At the foot of this imposing building lies the entrance to the **Brooklyn Bridge** and its pedestrian walkway (page 63).

Municipal Building

South Street Seaport and Fulton Market

Further south, **Park Row**, which was once dubbed "Newspaper Row", was the hub of the early 19th-century daily newspaper business. It was also the home of **P.T. Barnum's American Museum** until it burned down in 1865.

In the 19th century, **South Street Seaport** (page 58-59) was the heart of the maritime trade. After a period of decline, it has now been delightfully restored as a seaport village, complete with 19th- and early 20th-century buildings and tall ships moored in the harbor.

Nearby, **Hanover Square** (page 66) was once the home of English pirate William Kidd, better known as Captain Kidd.

North of Battery Park, at the North Cove Marina on the Hudson River, you can see yachts from all around the world docked in front of the **World Financial Center** (page 71). This steel and glass structure rises to spectacular heights, allowing sunlight to illuminate the palm trees, marble piazza and grand staircase of its interior, a shopping arcade known as the **Wintergarden Atrium**.

Lower Manhattan

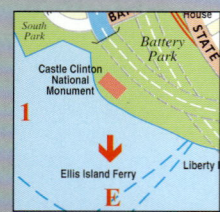

ADDRESS

Liberty Island is located
off the tip of Manhattan.
Ferries depart from
Battery Park.
For ferry times and prices,
☎ 269-5755.
For information about
the Statue of Liberty,
☎ 363-3200.

HOURS

Mon-Sun: 9.30am-5pm
(later in summer).
Ferries depart every
30-45 minutes.

PRICES

There is no admission
charge at the
Statue of Liberty.

GETTING THERE

Subway: 1/9 to South
Ferry, or 4/5 to Bowling
Green, then ferry from
Battery Park (see above).
New York Apple Tours stop:
Transfer stop #42,
Statue of Liberty Ferry-
Battery Park.

Statue of Liberty . . .

The Statue of Liberty was presented to the people of
the United States by the people of France in 1886, as
a symbol of friendship between the nations. Today, it
is recognized throughout the world as a symbol of
freedom.

Situated on **Liberty Island** in New York Harbor, the
Statue of Liberty rests on an 89-foot granite pedestal
and rises a total of 151 feet from base to torch. Lady
Liberty herself is more than 111 feet tall, and her
index finger alone is eight feet long. Her steel
framework and copper shell weigh a hefty 225 tons.

At the time of dedication, the statue was the tallest
structure in New York. Today, she is dwarfed by the
110-story World Trade Center which is clearly visible
from Liberty Island.

Although **the torch** is no
longer accessible to
visitors, you can go to
the crown by climbing
the 354 steps from the
bottom of the
monument.
Alternatively, there is an
elevator that takes you to
a panoramic observation
deck near the top of the
pedestal.

Statue of Liberty

Inside the statue's base,
there is an exhibit which
chronicles her
extraordinary creation
and history, including the unique fund-raising efforts
which make this monument a gift which is truly "from
the people".

The story of the Statue of Liberty began at a small
dinner party in 1865. The host was Edouard Rene
Lefebvre de Laboulaye, leader of the French "liberals"
– a political group established to promote a republican
government based on America's constitution.

Nearly a hundred years after the French had helped
America win its independence from Britain, French
and American dignitaries and guests reflected on the
relationship that had been forged between their
countries.

While discussing the approach of America's centennial
celebration, Laboulaye suggested that France should

. . . Statue of Liberty

give the U.S. a great monument as an everlasting symbol of their collective belief in human liberty and democracy.

Little could they anticipate what the Statue of Liberty would eventually mean to the millions of immigrants who were welcomed by the words of poet **Emma Lazarus**: "Give me your tired, your poor, your huddled masses, yearning to breathe free". Her poem, "The New Colossus", was written in 1883, but only gained fame after it was inscribed on a plaque and hung on a wall inside the pedestal, 20 years after it was written.

Under the direction of **Auguste Bartholdi**, a successful French sculptor, the copper sheets were shaped inside wooden molds, forming the "skin" of the statue. Famed engineer **Alexandre-Gustave Eiffel**, who later created the Eiffel Tower, joined the project by contributing the intricate "skeleton" support.

Since France's upper classes donated very little to the building of the statue, it became necessary to find a creative solution to spark public interest in the project. In the end, it was a lottery which proved successful in raising nearly all the necessary funds.

In the U.S., the appeal to the upper classes failed as miserably as it did in France. **Joseph Pulitzer**, a Hungarian immigrant, journalist and owner of the financial newspaper *The World*, saw a unique opportunity to use his paper as a way of raising funds while also boosting the circulation of his newspaper. He set a fund-raising goal of $100,000 and promised to publish in the newspaper the name of every individual contributor, no matter how small the amount. The goal was reached, then exceeded, and *The World*'s circulation dramatically increased.

The Unveiling of the Statue of Liberty Enlightening the World by Edward Moran

With the French paying for the statue and the Americans paying for the pedestal and foundation, the Statue of Liberty was unveiled to the world on October 28, 1886. Over a million spectators filled the streets to watch a parade of more than 20,000 people. Wall Street businessmen, working on this public holiday, threw streams of message tape from their windows, creating the first of the renowned New York "ticker-tape" parades.

INSIDER'S TIP

During peak seasons the wait may be incredibly long, and the view from the enclosed crown is limited. A better option might be the elevator, which takes you to a panoramic observation deck near the top of the pedestal.

You can also avoid the long lines for the ferry ticket and save money by taking the New York Apple Tours' Statue of Liberty Express (pages 212-213) which includes a double-decker sightseeing tour and a ferry ticket.

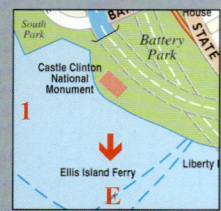

ADDRESS

Ellis Island is located off the tip of Manhattan. For ferry times and prices, ☎ 269-5755. For information about Ellis Island, ☎ 363-3200.

HOURS

Mon-Sun: 9.30am-5.30pm (later in summer). Ferries depart every 30-45 minutes.

The Great Hall

GETTING THERE

Subway: 1/9 to South Ferry, or 4/5 to Bowling Green, then ferry from Battery Park (see above). *New York Apple Tours stop:* Transfer stop #42, Statue of Liberty Ferry-Battery Park.

 # Ellis Island . . .

Between 1892 and 1954, the immigration station at Ellis Island processed more than 17 million immigrants – the ancestors of over 40% of Americans today. Some of the more famous immigrants who arrived at Ellis Island include author and scientist **Isaac Asimov**, composer **Irving Berlin** and actors **Rudolph Valentino** and **Bella Lugosi**.

Ellis Island Immigration Museum

The majority of immigrants were underprivileged Europeans seeking economic and political freedom in the "New World". Upon entering New York Harbor, they were overwhelmed with excitement at the sight of the Statue of Liberty - the embodiment of the American Dream. For many, however, this moment was soon replaced by the reality of strict screening processes, which often meant detention or even deportation. What was called by some the "Island of Hope", became known by others as the "Island of Tears".

As the 20th century advanced, the number of immigrants arriving at Ellis Island sharply declined. When the immigration station closed in 1954, the site was abandoned and left to decay. During the early 1980s, **President Ronald Reagan** initiated a major renovation project to restore both the Statue of Liberty and Ellis Island as major national landmarks.

The **Statue of Liberty-Ellis Island Foundation** was formed as a private sector fund-raising effort to reach a $230 million goal. The largest restoration project of its kind in American history, it enabled Ellis Island to be reopened to the public on September 10, 1990.

Today, the focal point of a visit here is the **Ellis Island Immigration Museum**. Housed in the 100,000 square-foot main building, the museum is dedicated to providing a thorough history of the island's processing station and the significant role that immigration has played in America's development.

... Ellis Island *for less*

On the second floor, by the Great Hall, the statue of a young girl commemorates fifteen-year-old Annie Moore, from Ireland, who was the first immigrant to be processed at Ellis Island. She was welcomed amidst great festivity and celebration before she and her brothers were reunited with their parents, who had arrived a few years earlier.

The many exhibits utilize a variety of different media to convey the immigration experience. The photographic exhibit "**Through America's Gates**" chronicles the rigorous step-by-step process faced by would-be Americans.

On the third floor, there are a number of permanent exhibits such as "**Treasures from Home**" which

includes artifacts, personal belongings and clothing brought from the immigrants' home countries.

A library features taped reminiscences of immigrants and former employees of the station, sharing their

Baggage Room at the museum

own personal views and experiences of Ellis Island. An evocative half-hour documentary, "**Island of Hope/ Island of Tears**", was created by Oscar-winning filmmaker **Charles Guggenheim**. The film is shown daily, at no charge, and is presented twice every hour on a rotating schedule in two separate theaters.

A good way to make the most out of your visit to the Ellis Island Immigration Museum is to use the **audio tour**. Narrated by news anchorman **Tom Brokaw**, it guides you through the museum's highlights (it is also available in foreign languages). With your *for less* voucher, two people can take an audio tour for the price of one. You can pick them up the tour at the booth located to the left of the main entrance on the first floor of the building.

View of Manhattan from Ellis Island

On the grounds outside of the main building, the **American Immigrant Wall of Honor** was created to commemorate the immigrants, and was funded by their descendants. From the monument there are great views of the Manhattan skyline and the Statue of Liberty.

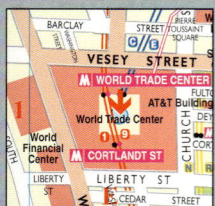

ADDRESS

Top of the World Trade Center is located in Tower Two of the World Trade Center, between Church Street and the West Side Highway, ☎ 323-2340.

HOURS

Observation deck:
Mon-Sun: 9.30am-9.30pm
(9.30am-11.30pm
in summer).

GETTING THERE

Subway: 1/9 or N/R to Cortlandt Street, or C/E to World Trade Center.
New York Apple Tours stop: Downtown/waterfront route to stop #41, World Trade Center.

Top of the World Trade Center . . .

The famed twin towers, which are known as Number One and Number Two, are certainly the best-known of the seven buildings which comprise the **World Trade Center**. In addition to the towers, there are three nine-story office buildings (numbers Four, Five and Six), a forty-seven-story office building (number Seven) and a 22-story hotel (number Three). The World Trade Center is the destination of approximately 50,000 people who work there each day.

Occupying a 16-acre site in Lower Manhattan, the complex is connected by an immense subterranean mall of shops and eateries (see page 72), as well as stations for the subway and PATH trains to New Jersey.

The **Austin J. Tobin Plaza**, a five-acre open space surrounding the buildings is a pleasant place for a picnic lunch, especially during summer when free entertainment is provided.

While excavation on the site began in 1966, it wasn't until 1970 that the first tenant moved into One World Trade Center, while 1972 saw the first occupants of Number Two.

In order to build the towers, it was necessary to excavate more than 1.2 million cubic yards of

The twin towers of the World Trade Center

earth and rock, which were used as landfill for the area now known as Battery Park City. Over 200,000 tons of steel were used in the construction, and, at peak times, more than 3,500 workers were on site.

When construction was completed, the Twin Towers were the tallest in the world. Today, they remain the tallest in New York, but lost the U.S. title to the Sears Tower in Chicago. To fully grasp the extreme height of the two buildings, stand in the plaza between them and look straight up at the sleek towers.

It is difficult to imagine some of the crazy stunts that have taken place here. In 1974, Philippe Petit tight-

. . . Top of the World Trade Center

roped his way between the rooftops of the twin towers, while, in 1977, George Willig scaled the northeast tower using suction cups. In addition, several mysterious parachuters have leapt from the building to a landing in the Hudson River.

The World Trade Center, dominating the Lower Manhattan skyline

Stunts aside, the best way to experience this New York landmark is to visit the **Observation Deck** at the **Top of the World Trade Center** in Tower Two. Since it opened in 1975, it has hosted nearly 30 million visitors.

For an incredible view of the city, ride one of the two main elevators at approximately 20 miles an hour to reach the Observatory on the 107th floor in less than one minute.

From the 232 viewing windows of the glass-enclosed Observatory, the city is spread out before you, and, with views of up to 55 miles, it is possible to see three states. Its location at the tip of Manhattan also makes it possible to take in a bird's eye view of the entire island of Manhattan, as well as the surrounding boroughs and waterways.

Located on the 110th floor, the **rooftop promenade** is the world's highest. Some of the best-known visible sights include the Brooklyn, Manhattan and Williamsburg Bridges, Empire State Building, South Street Seaport, the Statue of Liberty and Ellis Island.

In addition to providing great views, Top of the World Trade Center is also a virtual theme park in the sky. Fly on a **simulated helicopter ride** through the streets of New York or check out the **kinetic energy wall sculpture**.

Other points of interest are the **3-D map**, a **750-building model of Manhattan** and the **multi-lingual digital displays** providing an introduction to the view before you, highlighting the many famous and familiar buildings, bridges and monuments.

Important: to obtain the 20% *for less* discount you must go to ticket booth window 3 on the mezzanine (ground) level at the World Trade Center, Tower 2.

PRICES

Adult $12.50
Child (6-12) $6.25
(Under 6 free)
Senior $9.50
Student $10.75

DISCOUNT

20% off with your
for less card at ticket
booth window 3
on the mezzanine
(ground) level.

South Street Seaport

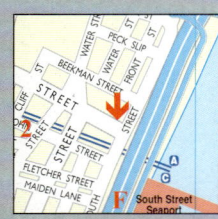

ADDRESS

The South Street Historic District is centered around Fulton and South Streets.

Visitors' Center & Museum Shop: 12-14 Fulton Street ☎ 748-8600

For sailing reservations on the *Pioneer*, ☎ 748-8786.

Although today the economic success of New York City is based on contributions from a wide range of industries, its initial fortune was largely the result of the success of its port. Ideally placed both for European trans-Atlantic trade and, via the Hudson River and the Erie Canal, for commerce with the rest of America, New York Harbor quickly became the most important port in North America.

During the 19th century, the South Street Seaport area was the center of New York's maritime trade.

Piers at the South Street Seaport

South Street itself was known as the "street of ships".

After a long period of decline in the 20th century, it has now been fully restored to a seaport village, complete with refurbished 19th-century buildings, cobble-stoned streets and tall ships moored in the harbor.

Schooner Pioneer against Lower Manhattan

This seaside village may seem somewhat out of place in such a busy city, but that is why New Yorkers flock here on their lunch breaks and after work to relax, shop or dine while enjoying great harbor views.

Jutting over the East River, **Pier 17** (page 68) is a modern, enclosed pedestrian mall with three floors of shops and restaurants. Exterior stairways and outdoor wooden terraces offer spectacular views of Brooklyn, the Brooklyn Bridge, the historic ships in the harbor and the colossal skyscrapers of Lower Manhattan. You can also glimpse the second-longest suspension bridge in the world, the **Verrazano-Narrows Bridge** (page 233), which links Brooklyn and Staten Island.

Nearby, Seaport Liberty Cruises (page 216) and the Schooner Pioneer (page 59) depart from Pier 16.

At the **Fulton Fish Market** (page 66), eight million pounds of fish are sold every year, making it the largest fish market in the United States.

GETTING THERE

Subway: 2/3, 4/5 or A/C to Fulton Street-Broadway Nassau.
New York Apple Tours stop: Transfer stop #44, South Street Seaport.

South Street Seaport Museum

Founded in 1967, the South Street Seaport Museum is comprised of exhibition galleries, historic art and archeological items and New York City's largest collection of restored early 19th-century buildings. Of these, the centerpiece redbrick Schermerhorn Row dates back to 1811-12. There are also historic ships, a maritime crafts center, museum stores, a library and a children's center – all contained within an 11-square-block landmark historic district.

Exhibitions and public programs focus on the economic, social and cultural importance of New York's maritime heritage. Many of the exhibits offer a hands-on experience. At the re-created printing shop Bowne & Co. Stationers, for example, you can learn to use a 19th-century printing press.

On Pier 16, you can explore the cabins and decks of one of the

South Street Seaport Museum

world's largest fleets of historic ships. Built in 1911, the *Peking* is a 347-foot, four-masted steel vessel once used to carry cargo from the U.S. to South America. On board there is a 15-minute film, *Peking at Sea*, which allows you to see the ship in its oceanic environment.

The 1893 wooden fishing schooner, *Lettie G. Howard*, sponsors marine education programs. The *Wavertree*, an 1885 iron full-rigged ship, the *Ambrose*, a 1908 steel lightship and the *W.O. Decker*, a 1930 tugboat, are also located on Pier 16.

Built in 1885, the Schooner *Pioneer* is an iron cargo schooner which provides memorable cruises through New York Harbor. Daily sails are available from May through mid-September, and a 20% discount is offered to *for less* cardholders.

Admission tickets to the museum include entry to all galleries, historic ships, films, district tours and ship tours. Tickets can be purchased at the Museum Visitors' Center and the Pier 16 Ticketbooth. Your *for less* voucher entitles you to two admissions for the price of one.

HOURS

Apr-Sep: Mon-Wed and
Fri-Sun: 10am-6pm
Thu: 10am-8pm
Oct-Mar: Mon and
Wed-Sun: 10am-5pm
Tue: closed

PRICES

Museum: Adult $6
Child (5-12) $3
(Under 5 free)
Senior $5
Student $4

Pioneer: Adult $20
Child $12
Senior $15
Student $15

DISCOUNT

2 admissions to the museum for the price of 1 with voucher on page 269.

20% discount on any ticket for the Schooner *Pioneer* with voucher on page 269.

10% discount in the museum shop with voucher on page 269.

The Peking

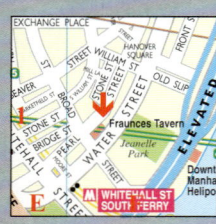

ADDRESS

54 Pearl Street
☎ 425-1778

HOURS

Mon-Fri: 10am-4.45pm
Sat-Sun: 12noon-4pm

PRICES

Adult $2.50
Child $1
Senior $1
Student $1

DISCOUNT

50% discount on
admission with
voucher on page 269.

10% discount in the
museum shop with
voucher on page 269.

 # Fraunces Tavern Museum

In old New York, taverns were more than just drinking
establishments – they were the center of social life.

During the Colonial
and Revolutionary
period, Samuel
Fraunces owned and
operated "The
Queen's Head
Tavern". In 1783,
George Washington,
who frequented the
Queen's Head,

Fraunces Tavern Museum

delivered his heartfelt farewell speech to his army
officers in its "Long Room". This room has been
preserved in the style of an 18th-century tavern dining
room and is open to visitors.

Located near Manhattan's financial district (on the
only National Historic Landmark block below Wall
Street), Fraunces Tavern Museum is housed in a
restored 18th-century building
and four adjacent 19th-century
buildings.

From 1785-1787, this building
housed the new nation's
departments of Foreign Affairs
(now called State), Treasury and
War (currently Defense). Since
then, it has been a mansion,
post office, transportation hub,
wax museum and even a dance
studio.

Fraunces Tavern Museum

Fraunces Tavern Museum,
founded in 1907, is committed
to the study and interpretation of early American
history and culture through a series of changing
exhibitions, period rooms, tours, public programs and
publications. There is also a constant schedule of
programs for children, including special activities such
as trying on costumes or learning to write with a quill
pen.

Past exhibitions and discussions have included "Myths
of American History", an investigative look at history
as portrayed in novels, films, on television and in
history books, and "Much Depends on Dinner", a look
at culinary customs in early New York.

The museum shop offers an interesting selection of
early American gift items and books and gives a
discount to *for less* cardholders.

Other Attractions . . .

The **New York Stock Exchange** started in the late 1700s with an agreement made by a small group of brokers who decided to trade only amongst themselves. Prior to this pact, trading occurred randomly on or near Wall Street. The NYSE has since grown into a formidable institution with a global effect on financial markets. Built in 1903, the present

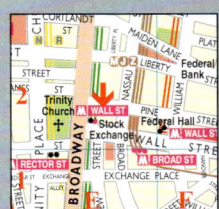

New York Stock Exchange

Wall Street, 1922

building's grand, neo-classical exterior is outstanding in the canyon of neighboring skyscrapers. Visitors can look out onto the action of the trading floor from a public viewing gallery. *(20 Broad Street, ☎ 656-5168. Mon-Fri: 9am-4.30pm. Sat-Sun: closed. Admission is free.)*

The statue of George Washington on the front steps of **Federal Hall National Memorial** heralds the site where he took his oath of office as the first president of the United States in 1789. On the corner of Broad and Wall

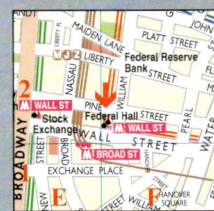

Federal Hall National Monument

Streets, where Federal Hall stands, many of the most important events of 18th-century American history took place. It was here that the government of the newly formed United States began to function: congress met for its first session in the original Federal Hall, the nation's first Capitol building. When the capital was moved to Philadelphia just a year later, the government of New York City moved into the building, using it as a City Hall. By the early 1800s, it became too small for the burgeoning bureaucracy of the largest city in the U.S., so the new City Hall (page 63) was built. The old Federal Hall was left to crumble and was eventually sold for scrap. The present building was built as

Federal Hall National Memorial

the U.S. Customs House in 1842, in the Greek Revival style. It now houses an historical exhibit on the Constitution and is the place to pick up the Heritage

. . . Other Attractions . . .

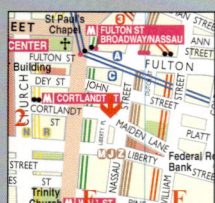
Federal Reserve Bank

Trails Walking Tours (page 225). *(26 Wall Street, ☎ 825-6870. Mon-Fri: 9am-5pm. Sat-Sun: closed. Admission is free.)*

Nearby, on Liberty Street, the imposing **Federal Reserve Bank** is the world's largest gold depository. It is also one of a dozen Federal Reserve banks nationwide. Currency printed here is identifiable by the letter B in the note's seal. Free guided tours are available four times a day, but reservations must be made 1-2 weeks in advance. Tours include a trip to the gold vault. *(33 Liberty Street, ☎ 720-6130. Tours: Mon-Fri: 10.30am, 11.30am, 1.30pm, 2.30pm. Sat-Sun: closed. Admission is free.)*

"The Bull" on lower Broadway

Trinity Church, which was the tallest structure in New York until the 1860s, is located at the western end of Wall Street. Its interior is an example of Gothic Revival architecture and its remarkable bronze doors, designed by Richard Morris Hunt, were modeled after Ghiberti's doors for the Florentine Baptistry in Italy. Captain Kidd is said to have loaned some equipment to help in the building of the church.

This Episcopalian parish is one of the oldest in America, dating back to 1697. Classical concerts are often given here and you can also attend services on Sundays at 11.15am (full mass), or at 9am (without a choir). *(Broadway at Wall Street, ☎ 602-0872. Mon-Fri: 7am-6pm. Sat: 8am-4pm. Sun: 7am-4pm.)*

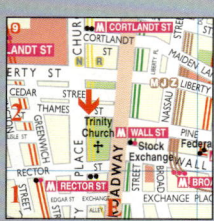
Trinity Church

Trinity Church

A few blocks north of Trinity Church on Broadway, **St. Paul's Chapel** is the oldest church building in Manhattan, surviving since 1766. Modeled after London's St. Martin-in-the-Fields, it is perhaps most famous for being the site of George Washington's inaugural prayer service. The pew where

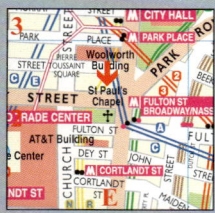
St. Paul's Chapel

. . . Other Attractions . . .

he prayed has been preserved in his name. *(Broadway at Fulton Street, ☎ 602-0874. Mon-Fri: 9am-3pm. Sun: 7am-3pm. Sat: Closed.)*

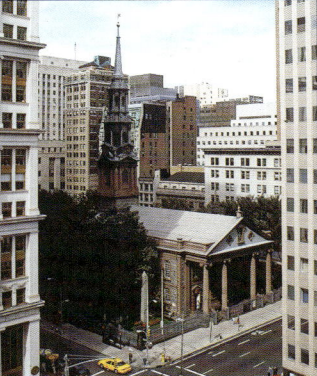
St. Paul's Church

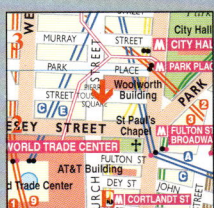
St. Peter's Church

St. Peter's Church is the oldest Catholic parish in New York State, originating in 1785. The current church with its classical facade and Greek Revival style was constructed in 1838. *(16 Barclay at Church Street, ☎ 233-8355. Mon-Fri: 6am-6pm and mass on Sat and Sun.)*

Walking across the **Brooklyn Bridge** is a pleasure often overlooked by visitors to New York. Completed in 1883, the Brooklyn Bridge was the first to be made of steel. Its construction, which took 16 years, claimed the lives of at least 20 men, including chief architect John A. Roebling. The view of Manhattan, Brooklyn and the bridge itself, with its massive network of overhead cables, was described by poet Walt Whitman as the best medicine his soul had ever experienced. The walkway begins by City Hall Park and continues for about a mile before arriving in Brooklyn Heights (see page 222). The bridge originally linked what were then the separate cities of Manhattan and Brooklyn. Twin Gothic arches tower some 277 feet above the East River, anchoring what was once the world's largest suspension bridge. *(Chambers Street at City Hall Park. Open 24 hours.)*

City Hall, built in 1812, is a charming example of early 19th-century American architecture. This Georgian-style structure was graced with marble on all sides except its north face because the architects underestimated the future growth of New

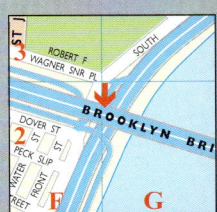
Brooklyn Bridge

Brooklyn Bridge, 1912

. . . Other Attractions . . .

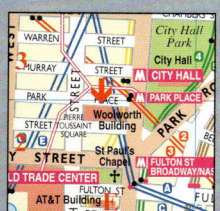
City Hall

York City and assumed that the city would never expand north of the building. To say the least, they were mistaken. You can visit City Hall during the hours listed below, but you must call two weeks ahead to book. *(City Hall Park, below Chambers Street, ☎ 788-6865 (group tours). Mon-Fri: 10am-4pm. Sat-Sun: closed. Admission is free.)*

Constructed as headquarters for the thriving Woolworth 5 & 10 department stores, the 1913

City Hall

Woolworth Building became New York's tallest structure, a position it held for 17 years. Nicknamed the Cathedral of Commerce, this $13.5 million dollar edifice, until the recent closing of the company, housed the headquarters of the Woolworth company. The lobby features caricatures of founder Frank W. Woolworth (who paid for the building in cash) and architect Cass Gilbert. The detail and design is spectacular and the lobby alone is worth a visit if you are nearby. *(233 Broadway. Open office hours.)*

The Shrine of Elizabeth Ann Seton is dedicated to the first American-born saint canonized by the Catholic Church. The house where she lived from 1801-1803

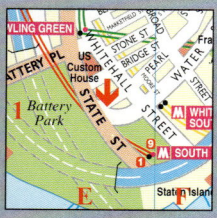
Woolworth Building

is a Federal-style building, curved to the shape of the road. Originally built in 1793, it is one of the few remaining examples of the early mansions of Lower Manhattan. *(7-8 State Street, ☎ 269-6865. Mon-Fri: 6:30am-5pm. Masses are held daily and on Saturdays and Sundays at the following times: Sat: 12noon and 4.30pm. Sun: 9am and 12noon.)*

Woolworth Building

Situated in Battery Park, **Castle Clinton National Monument** was built in the early 1800s as a defense against the recently expelled British. It never saw a battle, but over the years has instead been used as a theater, an aquarium

Shrine of Elizabeth Ann Seton

. . . Other Attractions . . .

and, before the opening of Ellis Island, as an

Castle Clinton National Monument

immigration center. In 1850, singer Jenny Lind, the "Swedish Nightingale", made her American debut here in front of an audience of over 6,000. Today, Castle Clinton features historical displays and acts as a visitors' center. It is also the place to buy tickets for the ferry to Liberty and Ellis Islands (pages 52-55). In warm weather, it is often rented out as a unique party space. *(Battery Park, ☎ 344-7220. Mon-Sun: 8.30am-5pm.)*

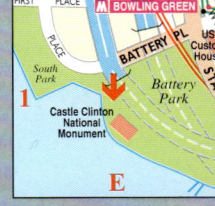

Castle Clinton National Monument

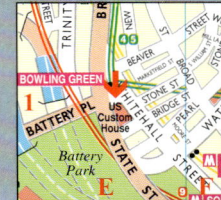

National Museum of the American Indian

Built in 1907, the **US Custom House** is a charming example of Beaux Arts architecture. Recently, the **Gustav Heye Center of the National Museum of the American Indian** has taken over three floors of the building. Part of the national Smithsonian Institute, the museum actively promotes the past and current cultures of the indigenous people of the Americas through fascinating exhibits and live performances. *(1 Bowling Green, ☎ 668-6624. Mon-Wed and Fri-Sun: 10am-5pm. Thu: 10am-8pm. Admission is free.)*

The **Staten Island Ferry** was started in 1810 by a young Staten Islander named Cornelius Vanderbilt. The ferry has carried commuters between the islands since and is a fun (and free!) way to get great views of New York Harbor and the Statue of Liberty. As for Vanderbilt, he went on to become one of the great 19th-century industrialists, making his immense fortune on the railroads. *(Whitehall Street, ☎ 806-6940. Mon-Sun: 24 hours a day. Ferries run every half hour. Free.)*

National Museum of the American Indian

The waterside **Vietnam Veterans' Plaza** pays tribute to veterans with a memorial wall of green glass. Designed by Maya Lin, famous for creating the Vietnam Veteran's Memorial in Washington, D.C. (page 238), it is etched with touching letters and writings from the veterans to their families. *(Water and South Streets.)*

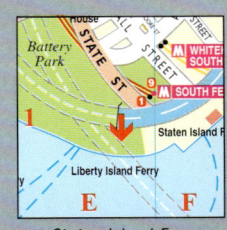

Staten Island Ferry

. . . Other Attractions

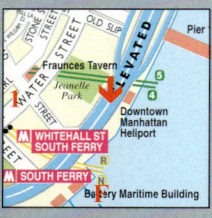

Hanover Square

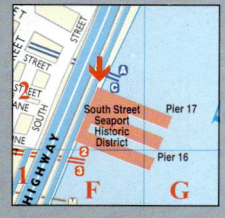

Vietnam Veterans' Plaza

In **Hanover Square**, a statue of Dutch mayor Abraham de Peyster stands near the house where he was born in 1657. At 1 Hanover Square, the brownstone **India House** was once the location of the New York Cotton Exchange, but is now home to Harry Cipriani's famous restaurant Harry's of Hanover Square (see page 69). *(Hanover Square at Pearl and Hanover Street.)*

Statue of Dutch mayor Abraham de Peyster

Next to the Staten Island Ferry, the **Battery Maritime Building** once served as a terminal for ferries to Brooklyn, but is now used by the U.S. Coast Guard for service to Governor's Island. *(11 South Street. Closed to the public.)*

Once the ticketing center for the Cunard passenger ship company, the magnificent **Cunard Building** is now a U.S. Post Office. The Great Hall has a colorful domed ceiling, with frescoes and detailed murals. *(25 Broadway, ☎ 363-9490. Mon-Fri: 8am-6pm. Sat-Sun: closed.)*

When **Fulton Fish Market** was established in the early 1800s, the fish arrived fresh every day from boats in the harbor. Today they arrive by land, but the market remains a source of quality seafood that is sold to many of the city's best restaurants. If you get up early enough (or stay up late enough), you can watch the traders in action any day of the week from midnight to about 8am. You can also take a guided tour of America's biggest and most famous fish market. *(South Street at Beekman Street, ☎ 748-8590 for tours.)*

City Hall Park

Heritage Trails New York offers walking tours which tell the interesting history of Lower Manhattan and its sights. It is an excellent way to familiarize yourself with the history and sights of Lower Manhattan, especially if you have a limited amount of time. On page 219 you will find more information about Heritage Trails New York and how to pick up the tours which originate at Federal Hall National Memorial.

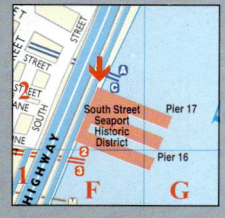

Fulton Fish Market

Open Spaces

Named after the battery of cannons which stood to protect the city, **Battery Park** is now the hub of downtown offshore activity. Ferries to the Statue of

Liberty and Ellis Island (pages 52-55) depart from here, and the Staten Island Ferry (page 65) is nearby.

Just north of Battery Park, the triangular **Bowling Green** was the city's first public park, established in

Battery Park

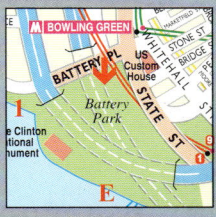

Battery Park

1733. It has been used as a cattle market, a place for public bowling and today is once again a small green park. In 1776, after the signing of the Declaration of Independence, a demonstration took place here and rioters did some renovating of their own, removing the statue of Britain's King George III and the royal crowns that once topped the surviving fence.

One of the best recent redevelopment projects has been the major overhaul of the area along the Hudson River, including a paved path which has become a favorite place for joggers, rollerbladers and office workers out for a lunchtime stroll. Originating at Battery Park, the riverside

Esplanade along the Hudson River

esplanade provides views of the Statue of Liberty and Ellis Island and is lined with benches, trees and neatly landscaped borders.

Hudson River Park

Continuing north, **Hudson River Park** is an open grassy expanse along the once seedy and run-down waterfront. Instead of decrepit piers and empty docks, there is now a large park which, on warm afternoons, is packed with New

Yorkers sunbathing or playing ball – a secret Central Park for the downtown set.

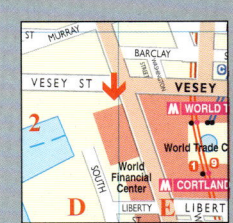

Hudson River Park

By the Brooklyn Bridge, the early 19th-century **City Hall Park** was the place where the Declaration of Independence was read to Washington and his troops. The park contains multiple subway stations, a working fountain flanked by colorful flower gardens, and chess tables on which fierce competitions rage at lunch hour.

Eating and Drinking . . .

Eating in the **Financial District** generally means take-out and fast food. Many of the restaurants here are casual places serving basic "pub grub" alongside a vast selection of beers. After 5pm, Wall Streeters flock to the pubs, where they socialize and take advantage of the multitude of "happy hours" where drink specials are often served with complimentary snacks and bar food. One of the best-known after-work haunts is **John Street Bar and Grill** (page 70) where early evening drink specials draw a full house almost every night of the week.

Recently, the invasion of "brew pubs" throughout New York has finally reached the Wall Street area. **Wall Street Kitchen and Bar** *(70 Broad Street, ☎ 797-7070)* is the latest addition. It marks a shift in the neighborhood's atmosphere, as late-night bars and restaurants are helping to change Lower Manhattan into an around-the-clock area – a sharp contrast to its past life as a ghost town after working hours.

Throughout the downtown area, there are also plenty of typical New York deli's which offer hot and cold buffets (selling food by the pound), sandwiches and just about anything else you might find in a grocery store. Pizzerias sell

Lower Manhattan Streets

pizza by the slice (see page 70), hot breads and other quick and inexpensive items that provide sustenance during a busy day of sightseeing.

The food court on the third floor of **Pier 17** allows you to eat your meal in the large cafeteria-style dining room, or to sit outside on the deck overlooking Brooklyn and the Brooklyn Bridge with the seaport down below.

One of the most historical restaurants in Manhattan is **Delmonico's** *(56 Beaver Street, ☎ 509-1144)* in Hanover Square. Throughout the 19th and 20th centuries, it attracted society figures such as Mark Twain, who celebrated his birthday here. Though it closed in the early 1990s after more than a hundred years, it has recently re-opened, freshly refurbished.

INSIDER'S TIP

To avoid overpriced food at the Statue of Liberty, Ellis Island and on the ferry, stop by one of the delicatessens or pizzerias near Battery Park before boarding (see pages 69-70 for discounts).

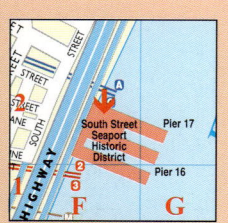

Pier 17 and the South Street Seaport

. . . Eating and Drinking

Legendary Harry Cipriani, famous for his New York and Venetian restaurants, founded **Harry's of Hanover Square** (1 Hanover Square, ☎ 425-3412) in the old India House. These institutions are known as "boys clubs", and more suits can be found here than on the racks at Macy's.

If a view is what you are after, visit **Windows on the World** (One World Trade Center, 107th Floor, ☎ 524-7000) where the view has always been more important than the food. Celebrity chef Michael Lomonaco just might change that, but if the prices seem as high as the 107th-floor location, you might be better off with a drink at the **Greatest Bar on Earth**, just next to the restaurant.

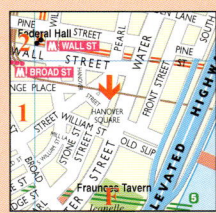

Harry's of Hanover Square

Mercantile Grill

American

126 Pearl Street
☎ 482-1221

Average meal: $10-15
for less discount: 25%
AM/VS/MC/DC

This charming pub-style grill features exposed brick walls and an oak bar. Wholesome Irish and American dishes are served. Around the corner from the World Trade Center, this is a great place to have lunch.

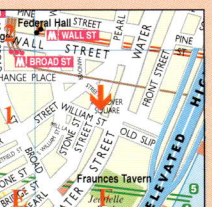

HOURS

Mon-Wed: 11am-10pm
Thu-Fri: 11am-12midnight
Sat-Sun: closed

The Beekman

International

15-17 Beekman Street
☎ 732-7333

Average meal: $10-15
for less discount: 25%
AM/MC/VS/DC/DS

The Beekman is close to the Brooklyn Bridge, City Hall and South Street Seaport. Classic cuisine is served in a friendly, old-world pub atmosphere. Try favorites like corned beef, *shrimp fra diablo* or *sole française*.

HOURS

Mon-Fri: 11am-2am
Sat-Sun: closed

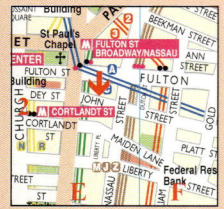

HOURS

Mon-Fri: 11am-9pm
Sat: 12noon-10pm
Sun: closed

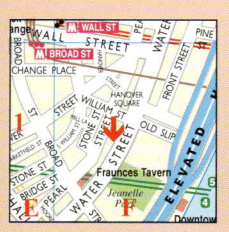

HOURS

Mon-Sun: 11.30am-11pm

HOURS

Mon-Fri: 8am-8pm
Sat: 11am-5pm
Sun: closed

Bennie's Thai Cafe

Thai

88 Fulton Street
☎ **587-8930**

Average meal: $10-15
for less discount: 25%
AM

Bennie's, located near the South Street Seaport, is a casual restaurant where you can find authentic Thai and vegetarian cuisine at excellent prices. Specialty dishes include the *pad-Thai* and *tom-yum*.

John Street Bar and Grill

American

17 John Street
☎ **349-3278**

Average meal: $10-15
for less discount: 25%
AM/MC/VS

This roomy restaurant and pub serves American fare in a casual setting. Enjoy hearty dishes and pub fare like buffalo wings, burgers and sandwiches. There is a wide variety of international beers, both bottled and on tap.

Pranzo Pizzeria

Pizzeria

34 Water Street
☎ **344-8068**

Average meal: $5-10
for less discount: 25%
AM/MC/VS

Situated near Battery Park, Pranzo is a good place for traditional NYC pizza. Visit this pizzeria before boarding the ferry for Liberty and Ellis Islands. Hot and cold sandwiches, pastas and salads are also available.

Shopping

To New Yorkers, downtown shopping conjures up the word "bargain". Two of the best discount stores in town are located here: **Syms** *(42 Trinity Place, ☎ 797-1199)*, a warehouse discounter, and **Century 21** *(22 Cortlandt Street, ☎ 227-9092)*, a department store which carries everything from watches to perfume and designer clothing – all at a discount. Popular with the Wall Street crowd, these stores can be extremely crowded at lunch time and after work.

World Financial Center

Pier 17 and the South Street Seaport

Also scattered below Chambers Street, west of Broadway, are a variety of discount stores carrying excess stock and buy-outs at big savings. These are not, however, the kind of places to shop if you are looking for something specific as they have limited selections.

For a more pleasant (and perhaps more expensive) shopping experience, visit the stores around the **South Street Seaport** and in **Pier 17**. Branches of familiar chains such as **J. Crew** *(203 Front Street, ☎ 385-3500)*, and **The Sharper Image** *(89 South Street, Pier 17, 1st level, ☎ 693-0477)* can be found here, as well as interesting specialty and gift shops. The **South Street Seaport Museum Shop** (page 59), which offers a discount to *for less* cardholders, has a selection of items that make good souvenirs or gifts.

Another place to shop downtown is at the **World Financial Center** in Battery

Pier 17 at the South Street Seaport

Park City. Here you will find major stores like **Barneys New York** *(☎ 945-1600)* and **Ann Taylor**, as well as specialty shops like **Godiva Chocolatier**, **Caswell-Massey** and **Gap Kids**.

Introduction . . .

During the 19th century, **Soho**, the area <u>SO</u>uth of <u>HO</u>uston Street (pronounced "HOWston"), was an industrial district, filled with warehouses and factories. Today, it is overrun with chic galleries, boutiques, trendy bistros and bars (see pages 84-88).

Ethiopian Art from the Museum for African Art

The birthplace of industrial and pop art during the 1960s, Soho is still famous for its world-renowned art scene. **West Broadway**, the area's main thoroughfare, is home to some of the most important commercial galleries in New York City. Recently, however, a slow migration of some major galleries to Chelsea is threatening to split New York's art world into two separate spheres.

Soho also contains some well-known museums, the majority of which exhibit modern art. On Broadway, the **Guggenheim Museum Soho** (page 78) exhibits works with a focus on technology. Within a few blocks, you can also find the **New Museum of Contemporary Art** (page 80), the **Alternative Museum** (page 81) and the **Museum for African Art** (page 78) which displays a wide variety of African and African-American art, including sculpture and costumes.

DON'T MISS

Take a break from shopping in Soho to check out the cast-iron architecture that lines the streets, especially along Greene and Prince Streets.

Besides its famed art scene, Soho is also notable for having the world's largest collection of **cast-iron buildings**. Erected between 1860 and 1890 in the American-Industrial style, these iron buildings were shaped and painted with exquisite detail, mimicking Italianate, neo-Grecian and

Soho cast-iron buildings

Victorian Gothic styles. At 84 Leonard Street, you can see a cast-iron building designed by **John Bogurdas**, inventor of this unique architecture.

In addition to spacious interiors and large windows, cast-iron architectural highlights include large iron

. . . Introduction . . .

loading bays and sidewalks covered with raised circular glass disks to let light into basement areas.

The original purpose of these structures was to house the factories and sweatshops which were abundant in this part of town. When these closed in the 1950s, the area became what the City Club called in 1962, "the wasteland of New York".

The abandoned cast-iron buildings provided well-lit loft spaces that became very desirable to artists. Many of the buildings were renovated, and a program of redevelopment was pioneered by residents and developers who officially made the neighborhood an historic area in 1973. Throughout the 1970s, gentrification continued to transform this former industrial slum into the high-priced, cosmopolitan hot spot it is today.

Of particular architectural interest, the **St. Nicholas Hotel** *(521-523 Broadway)* was built in the mid-1800s as a luxury hotel. Though it no longer exists, remains of its former glory can still be seen in its marble exterior.

Just south of Soho, **Tribeca**, the TRIangle BElow CAnal is essentially a residential area favored by the likes of

A realistic mural of a cast-iron building painted on the side of a plain brick one

John F. Kennedy, Jr. and Robert DeNiro. In addition to his **Tribeca Film Center** *(325 Greenwich Street)*, DeNiro is co-owner of a collection of restaurants throughout the neighborhood, many of which are frequented by people in the film industry.

Modern Tribeca offers a glimpse of what Soho was like prior to its current commercialization. When Soho's real-estate prices skyrocketed during the late 1970s, artists, photographers and other creative types migrated to this previously undeveloped area, making use of its large converted loft spaces to live and work.

Just west of Greenwich Street, numbers 37-41 Harrison Street comprise a surviving row of early 18th-century Federal-style townhouses, beautifully restored and slightly out-of-place amongst the industrial-style buildings that surround it.

Part of Tribeca's charm lies in its experimental

. . . Introduction . . .

galleries, small theaters and live music venues. To find out more about Tribeca's happenings and history, pick up the area's free monthly newspaper – the "**Tribeca Trib**".

Sidewalk dining in Little Italy

Despite Tribeca's recent revitalization, corporate America, with its coffeeshop, book and clothing store chains, has not yet invaded this territory. Instead, you will find an assortment of cozy coffee spots, "local" bars and some of the city's best restaurants (see page 84-85).

The areas east of Soho and Tribeca are ethnic enclaves that represent the lasting impact of immigration on New York. Population shifts have certainly changed the faces of these neighborhoods, but their original character remains.

Manhattan's **Chinatown** contains one of the largest Asian communities in the western world. The area centered around **Mott Street** is populated by more than 150,000 Chinese (mostly from Hong Kong), Taiwanese, Vietnamese, Thai and other Asian communities. All of these cultures are represented by a multitude of authentic restaurants (see page 84-85) offering some of the most delicious and inexpensive cuisine in town.

Confucius Plaza, *(Bowery and Division Street)*, is marked by a big stone statue of the ancient Chinese philosopher. Nearby, at Chatham Square, the **Kimlau War Memorial** is dedicated to the Chinese who were killed pursuing freedom and democracy in American wars.

Buddhist temples abound, including the **Eastern States Buddhist Temple of America** (page 82). Around the corner, on Bayard Street, the **Wall of Democracy** posts newspaper

Chinatown streets

clippings and political writings about the political and social situation in China.

Observe the signs on the buildings and listen to the conversations of the locals. You will realize that the

INSIDER'S TIP

For a bigger and more authentic Little Italy, visit the Belmont section of the Bronx (see page 227), a short walk from the Bronx Zoo and the Botanical Gardens (page 228).

. . . Introduction

area is completely self-sufficient, and that over half of its residents do not speak any English at all. The architecture also reflects the Chinese style – even the phone boxes are shaped to resemble Chinese pagodas.

Lower East Side, 1936.

In January and February, the streets swell with the festivities of **Chinese New Year**. Chinatown also becomes a focal point around the Fourth of July, when it supplies (illegal) fireworks to celebrants from all parts of the city and beyond.

Tenement buildings

Little Italy is slowly disappearing as Chinatown expands into it, but **Mulberry Street** remains intact. The multitude of restaurants (see page 84-85) that run its length are the main reason to visit.

During the **San Gennaro Festival**, held each September, Mulberry Street is brought to life with food stalls, games and entertainment in a carnival-like atmosphere. If you can tolerate the crowds, you can sample Italian specialties such as fried dough or pastries.

DON'T MISS

A chance to catch a New York neighborhood in the process of gentrification – the Lower East Side (especially along Ludlow Street, below Howston) is a great place to shop and explore the streets before it is colonized by corporate America's stores and restaurants.

The character of the **Lower East Side** has been shaped by the millions of Russian and Eastern European Jews who settled the area in the late 19th and early 20th centuries. The **Lower East Side Tenement Museum** (page 79) provides a fascinating history of these settlers and their subsequent impact on America, as well as a glimpse of what living conditions were like in the crowded tenement buildings, many of which still stand. Today, the area is only 10-15% Jewish, but many cultural institutions remain, including historic synagogues and distinct eating establishments (see page 85).

Artist Marco at work in his studio

In recent years, a progressive, young community has formed on the Lower East Side and a number of lively shops, restaurants and bars have sprung up (see page 90).

Attractions . . .

The Guggenheim Museum Soho is the downtown branch of the Solomon R. Guggenheim Museum. Opened to the public in 1992, it is located in a 19th-century landmark building in Soho's Cast-Iron Historic District. Designed by renowned architect Arata Isozaki, this unique gallery space features special exhibitions that complement those at the uptown Guggenheim.

Guggenheim Museum Soho

Expanded and renovated in June 1996, the Guggenheim Museum Soho has a new focus on technology and the arts. With the support of German telecommunications carrier Deutsche Telekom A.G., four galleries on the main floor have been reconstructed and dedicated primarily to the presentation of multimedia art.

Additional exhibitions continue to present contemporary art, along with the Guggenheim's permanent collection.

Private guided tours, available in English and other languages, focus on the museum's art, architecture and special exhibitions.

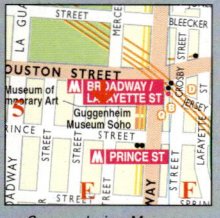

Guggenheim Museum Soho

Due to a possible renovation and expansion in 1999, it is best to phone ahead for details before visiting to the museum. *(575 Broadway, ☎ 423-3500. Wed-Fri and Sun: 11am-6pm. Sat: 11am-8pm. Mon-Tue: closed. Adult $8, child free, senior $5, student $5. 2 admissions for the price of 1 with voucher on page 271.)*

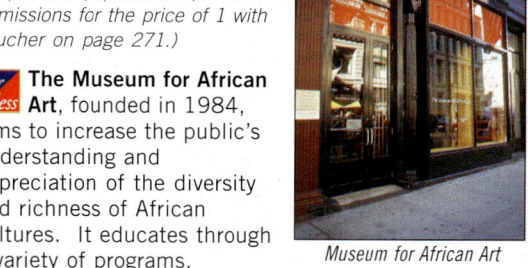

Museum for African Art

The Museum for African Art, founded in 1984, aims to increase the public's understanding and appreciation of the diversity and richness of African cultures. It educates through a variety of programs, including music and dance performances, storytelling series and film screenings.

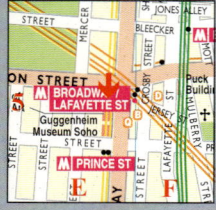

Museum for African Art

One of the world's foremost publishers on the subject of African Art, the museum publishes informative catalogues for its past and current exhibits.

The museum has one of the best displays of African art in the U.S. Exhibits change at least twice a year and

. . . Attractions . . .

feature decorative and ceremonial art, costumes, masks and other artistic representations of culture.

The museum's interior was designed by acclaimed artist Maya Lin, who is perhaps most famous for her creation of the Vietnam Veterans' Memorial in Washington, D.C.

The museum shop has an assortment of books, textiles and crafts, all of which can be purchased at a discount with the voucher on page 271. *(593 Broadway, ☎ 966-1313. Tue-Fri: 10.30am-5.30pm. Sat: 12pm-8pm. Sun: 12noon-6pm. Mon: closed. Adult $5, child $2.50, senior $2.50, student $2.50. 2 admissions for the price of 1 and 10% discount at the museum shop with vouchers on page 271.)*

Preserved room at the Lower East Side Tenement Museum

The Lower East Side Tenement Museum is located in an 1863 tenement building, which has been designated a National Historic Landmark and an affiliated site of the National Park Service and the National Trust for Historic Preservation.

It stands as a powerful reminder of the challenges and hardships faced by the millions of immigrants who came to America during the late 19th and early 20th centuries. After passing through Castle Clinton and, after 1892, Ellis Island (pages 54-55), many of the new arrivals settled on the Lower East Side.

Lower East Side Tenement Museum

Presently, apartments have been restored in an effort to chronicle the lives of their former tenants. The tour of a 19th-century tenement visits the apartments of the Gumpertzes, a German-Jewish family from the 1870s, the Rogarshevskys, an Orthodox-Jewish Lithuanian family from 1918, and the Baldizzis, an Italian-Catholic family from the 1930s.

The Confino Program is based on a Sephardic Jewish family from Turkey in 1916. In this "living history" apartment, visitors can see what it would have been like to be a member of an immigrant family. (This was exhibit was especially designed for families.)

Immigrant family apartment at the Lower East Side

Guided tours, exhibits, performances and media presentations recount and preserve the lives of the

. . . Attractions . . .

people who lived here between 1863 and 1935, numbering close to 7,000 and coming from over 20 nations. *(90 Orchard Street, ☎ 431-0233. Visitor's Center: Tue-Fri: 12noon-5pm. Sat-Sun: 11am-4.30pm. Mon: closed. Tours: Tue-Fri: 1pm, 2pm, 3pm and 4pm. Sat-Sun: 11am-4:15pm, every 45 minutes. Gallery: free. Tours: adult $8, child $6, senior $6, student $6. 50% discount on tours and 10% discount at the museum shop with vouchers on page 271.)*

Eldridge Street Synagogue

 When the **Eldridge Street Synagogue** first opened its doors in 1887 it was the pride of the neighborhood. Its interior was richly decorated and its stained glass windows were spectacular. A decreasing congregation cut the need for such a large synagogue and its doors were closed in the 1930s. A large-scale restoration project is now underway. Tours allow visitors to watch the work being undertaken to restore this elegant Moorish building to its former glory. The Victorian fixtures and fittings, the beautiful stenciled walls and much of the original furnishings can be seen. The synagogue also contains a small collection of artifacts and documents about life on the Lower East Side. *(12 Eldridge Street, ☎ 219-0888. Tours: Tue and Thu: 11.30am and 2.30pm. Sun: 11am-4pm, every hour. Mon, Wed and Fri-Sat: closed. Adult $4, child $2.50, senior $2.50, student $2.50. 50% discount on admission with voucher on page 271.)*

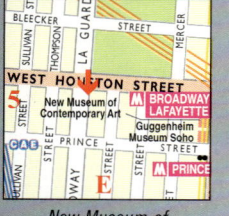

New Museum of Contemporary Art

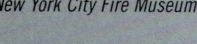 **The New Museum of Contemporary Art** is the younger version of the Museum of Modern Art, displaying the latest in the contemporary art scene. The museum houses no permanent collection, but instead showcases the works of innovative contemporary artists. *(583 Broadway, ☎ 219-1222. Thu-Sat: 12noon-*

New York City Fire Museum

New Museum of Contemporary Art

8pm. Wed and Sun: 12noon-6pm. Mon-Tue: closed. Adult $5, child free, senior $3, student $3, artist $3. 50% off with discount voucher on page 273.)

Other Attractions . . .

Across the street, the **Alternative Museum** specializes in avant garde works of art. It emphasizes socio-political consciousness and vision in art. *(594 Broadway, 4th floor, ☎ 966-4444. Tue-Sat: 11am-6pm. Sun-Mon: closed. Suggested admission $3.)*

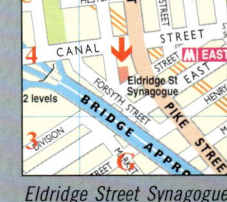

Eldridge Street Synagogue

The New York City Fire Museum displays a fine collection of 18th- and 19th-century fire fighting memorabilia and equipment. Tours of the 1904 firehouse and its collection are given by New York City firefighters. *(278 Spring Street, ☎ 691-1303. Tue-Sun: 10am-4pm. Mon: closed. Suggested admission $4.)*

A.I.R. Gallery has been dedicated to showcasing women artists for over 20 years. *(40 Wooster Street, ☎ 966-0799. Tue-Sat: 11am-6pm. Sun-Mon: closed. Admission is free.)*

The prestigious **Gagosian Gallery** is run by Larry Gagosian, who has another eponymous gallery uptown (page 190) on Madison Avenue. Both have featured many contemporary and well-known works by artists such as Jasper Johns and Roy Lichtenstein. *(136 Wooster Street, ☎ 228-2828. Tue-Sat: 10am-6pm. Sun-Mon: closed. Admission is free.)*

420 West Broadway contains six separate galleries including some of Soho's best known names. One of these, **Leo Castelli**, was the headquarters for pop art during the 1960s and is now a haven for new artists. *(420 West Broadway, ☎ 431-5160. Tue-Sat: 10am-6pm. Sun-Mon: closed. Admission is free.)*

Alternative Museum

NY Earth Room is Walter de Maria's innovative 1977 gallery which features 140 tons of intricately sculpted soil. *(141 Wooster Street, ☎ 473-8072. Wed-Sat: 12noon-3pm and 3.30pm-6pm. Sun-Tue: closed. Admission is free.)*

On Greene Street, between Canal and Grand Streets, from number 8 to number 34, is the longest stretch of cast-iron buildings in the world. Contained within the block at numbers 28-30 stands the so-called **Queen of Greene Street**. Her decorative features include columns, dormers, window arches and a tall mansard roof. Further up the block, at Numbers 72-76, stands the **King of Greene Street** – five stories tall, replete with Corinthian-style columns. Both were created by a master of cast-iron design, Isaac Duckworth. *(8-34 and 72-76 Greene Street.)*

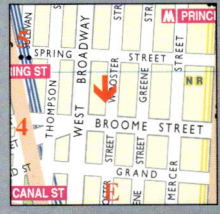

New York Earth Room

. . . Other Attractions

The recently refurbished **Haughwout Building**, known as the "Parthenon of cast iron", was constructed in 1857 for Edward Haughwout's fine china and glassware company. The exterior was inspired by a Venetian palazzo, while the interior boasted the world's

Police Building

first commercial passenger elevator, an invention which would later help make the skyscraper possible. *(488 Broadway.)*

The open doors of the **Eastern States Buddhist Temple of America** permit a glimpse of over 100 gold Buddhas glimmering amongst candles and incense. *(64b Mott Street, ☎ 966-6229. Mon-Sun: 9am-7pm.)*

St. Patrick's Old Cathedral, in Little Italy, was constructed in 1863 to replace the original building of 1809, which was destroyed by fire. In 1878, the archdiocese moved uptown to St. Patrick's Cathedral on Fifth Avenue (page 150). *(263 Mulberry Street, ☎ 226-8075. Open for mass only.)*

The **Police Building**, west of Mulberry on Center Street, is a gigantic structure that was built to house the police department in 1909. Today, underneath its impressive dome, some well-known celebrities and supermodels live in the building's luxury co-operative apartments. *(240 Center Street. Closed to the public.)*

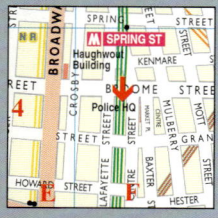

Police Building

Originally founded in 1899 to make kosher wines for the Jewish immigrants who populated the area, **Schapiro's Winery** still ferments and bottles over 30 different varieties of wine. You can tour the last remaining operational winery in New York City and taste this thick, sweet wine described as "extra heavy" on the bottles' labels. *(126 Rivington Street, ☎ 674-4404. Mon-Thu: 11am-5pm. Fri: 11am-2pm. Sun: 11am-4pm. Sat: closed. Free tours Sun: 11am-4pm.)*

Nearby, on Norfolk Street, the **Congregation Anshe Chesed** is New York's oldest synagogue building, though it is no longer used. Dating back to 1849, it was originally built to seat close to 1,500. *(172-176 Norfolk Street.)*

The **First Shearith Israel Graveyard** is the permanent home for a Jewish community dating back to the late 1600s. *(55-57 St. James Place.)*

Open Spaces

Washington Market Park *(Greenwich and Chambers Streets),* in west Tribeca, is an ideal children's park – complete with a playground and sandbox. A great time to visit is during the evening concerts held on the bandstand during the summer. A large variety of farm-fresh foods can be found at the greenmarket, which takes place in front of the park on Greenwich Street several times a week.

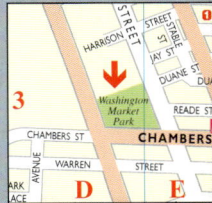

Washington Market Park

Rollerblade, bike or simply stroll along the riverside on a paved path that continues from Battery Park (page 64) all the way to 14th Street in the West Village. Benches line the pathway and provide a cool respite from the hustle of the city. Street vendors park along the route, hoping to tempt the scores of rollerbladers with an ice cream or a lemonade.

Columbus Park

In the heart of Chinatown, **Columbus Park** is the only open space you will find amongst the narrow windy roads which surround it. Early in the morning, residents practice Tai Chi here and all day long there are games of Chinese Mah Jong and palm-readers giving advice to superstitious customers. It is difficult to imagine that this quiet park was once a dangerous slum. In the 1800s, even the police avoided the area, where levels of crime were so high that a murder a day was not uncommon.

Washington Market Park

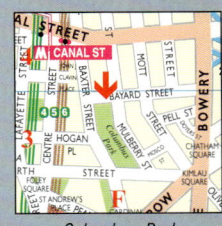

Columbus Park

Sara D. Roosevelt Park is less a park than a strip of green running north-south between Chrystie and Forsyth Streets, from Canal to Houston Streets.

Palm-readers in Columbus Park

This area can become dangerous at night, but is a good place to take a break from daytime sightseeing and shopping in Chinatown and the Lower East Side.

Eating and Drinking . . .

Both Soho and Tribeca have to their credit a number of excellent restaurants offering a wide range of international cuisine.

West Broadway, Soho's busiest street, is packed with

lively cafés and restaurants. One of the best, **Caffe Novecento** (page 86), gives a discount to *for less* cardholders.

Further south, in Tribeca, **Basset** (page 85) offers fresh coffee, desserts and homemade American cooking. For a very Southern taste, try the grits. In warm weather, outdoor seating allows you to people-watch on West Broadway.

Once the center of New York's poultry and dairy trades, Tribeca today is associated with a first-rate dining experience. It is home to some of the finest restaurants in the world, including **Chanterelle** *(2 Harrison Street, ☎ 966-6960)* and **Nobu** *(105 Hudson Street, ☎ 219-0500)*. You can also find Tribeca staples **Odeon**

Chinatown Shopping

(145 West Broadway, ☎ 233-0507) and **Tribeca Grill** *(375 Greenwich Street, ☎ 941-3900)*, the latter perhaps more famous for partner Robert DeNiro than for its fare.

New York diners mourned the loss of the city's top-ranked restaurant, **Bouley**, which closed after ten years on Duane Street, but were somewhat pacified with the re-opening in 1997 of a substitute around the corner on West Broadway. Today, the formal dining room and **Bouley Bakery** *(120 West Broadway, ☎ 964-2525)* are as busy as ever, though the atmosphere, some argue, is just not the same as the original.

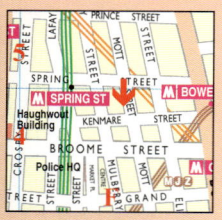

Mott Street

Chinatown offers a vast array of Asian cuisine at over 200 restaurants, including Szechuan, Hunan, Malaysian, Thai and Vietnamese. The main concentration of Chinese restaurants centers around **Mott Street**, while other Asian cuisines tend to be scattered along the surrounding streets.

Even the ice cream shops echo the neighborhood's ethnicity with flavors such as green tea, ginger and lychee making an appearance in cases normally stocked with vanilla and chocolate.

. . . Eating and Drinking

Chinatown markets draw residents from all over New York who come for the incredibly fresh seafood and vegetables, offered at remarkable prices.

Vegetarians will need to tread carefully in these parts, however, since restaurants serve genuine regional dishes which may be unfamiliar. A "vegetable" dish may arrive bathed in a meat sauce, unless you clearly specify (in your best Cantonese, of course). To be on the safe side, there are a few strictly vegetarian restaurants, including **Tiengarden** (page 88).

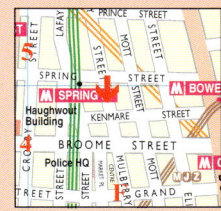

Mulberry Street

Little Italy's **Mulberry Street** is crammed with cafés, restaurants and specialty shops. Some of the most authentic restaurants, like **Rocky's** (page 88), are often a little off the beaten path. Sidewalk cafés offer a variety of coffee, incredible Italian desserts and pastries. Some of them, like **Sambuca's Cafe** (page 88), make everything fresh on the premises.

Italian Pastries at Sambuca's Cafe

On the Lower East Side, a number of trendy bistros have recently moved in beside long-established kosher delicatessens and restaurants. **Ratner's** *(138 Delancy Street, ☎ 677-5588)* was established in 1905 and remains one of the most famous kosher delis in New York.

There are also specialty stores which offer everything from wine and bialys to matzoh and knishes. Many of these have been around for decades.

![for less] Basset

American / Coffee & Tea Shop

123 West Broadway
☎ 349-1662

Average meal: $10-15
for less discount: 25%
AM/MC/VS/DC/DS

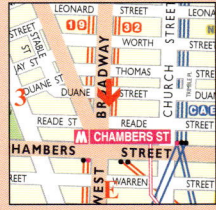

HOURS

Mon-Fri: 7.30am-10pm
Sat: 9am-6pm
Sun brunch: 11am-3pm

At this country café in Tribeca, you can have fresh coffee and desserts, or enjoy homemade American fare with a southern flavor. The shrimp and sausage jambalaya and daily soups are highly recommended.

HOURS

Mon-Sun: 12noon-
12midnight

Caffe Novecento

Continental / Argentinian

343 West Broadway
☎ 925-4706

Average meal: $20-25
for less discount: 25%
AM/MC/VS/DC

This chic, European-style restaurant is located in the heart of lively Soho. Enjoy dining and people-watching in this modern bi-level eatery. Chef's specialties include *empanadas* Novecento and *milanesa de carne*.

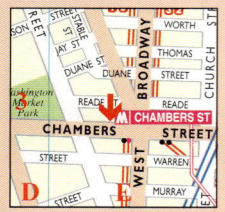

HOURS

Mon-Fri: 11am-11pm
Sat: 4pm-11pm
Sun: closed

Mao Mao

Chinese

143 Chambers Street
☎ 227-7399

Average meal: $15-20
for less discount: 25%
AM/MC/VS/DC

Mao-Mao is located on Chambers Street in lower Tribeca, not far from the World Trade Center. It serves authentic Szechuan vegetarian and non-vegetarian dishes. The butterfly shrimp and triple delight are recommended.

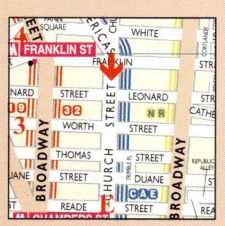

HOURS

Mon-Sat: 6pm-11pm
and Mon-Fri: 12noon-3pm
Sun: 6pm-10pm (in winter
only)

Barocco

Italian

301 Church Street
☎ 431-1445

Average meal: $20-25
for less discount: 25%
AM/MC/VS

Visit Barocco after sightseeing in bordering Soho, Chinatown or Tribeca. It serves modern Italian cuisine in a casually elegant atmosphere. Try the delicious *ravioli verdi* or the whole roast sea bass.

5&10 No Exaggeration

Continental / Cabaret

77 Greene Street
☎ **925-7414**

Average meal: $20-25
for less discount: 25%
AM/MC/VS/DC/DS

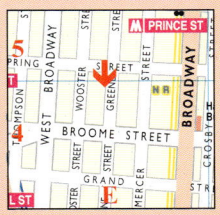

HOURS

Mon-Sun: 5pm-1am

5 & 10 No Exaggeration is a restaurant, bar, antique shop and performance studio. American and Continental cuisine is served, accompanied by live shows. 5 & 10 can be closed for private parties, so please call ahead.

 # P.J. Charlton's

American / Continental

549 Greenwich Street
☎ **924-9532**

Average meal: $15-20
for less discount: 25%
AM/DC

HOURS

Mon-Fri: 12noon-10pm
Sat-Sun: closed

For 20 years, this Tribeca bistro has been serving a wide selection of pastas, steaks and seafood at reasonable prices. The daily specials are based on items fresh from the day's market.

 # El Pollo

Peruvian

482 Broome Street
☎ **431-5666**

Average meal: $10-15
for less discount: 25%
AM/MC/VS/DC

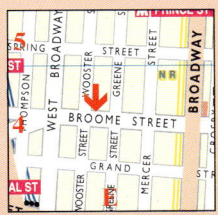

HOURS

Mon-Fri: 11.30am-10pm
Sat-Sun: 12.30pm-
11.30pm

El Pollo specializes in mouth-watering marinated and rotisserie chicken. Inside, antique furniture, carvings and oil paintings abound. As a side dish, try the sweet plantains or curly fried potatoes.

Rocky's

Italian

45 Spring Street
☎ 274-9756

Average meal: $15-20
for less discount: 25%
AM/MC/VS/DC/DS

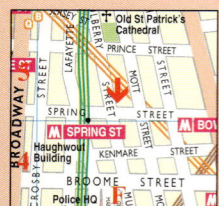

HOURS

Mon-Sun: 11am-10.30pm

Rocky's, a block from busy Mulberry Street, has been serving authentic, homecooked Italian cuisine for over 25 years. Try the tortellini with white prosciutto sauce and the delicious homemade cheesecake.

Sambuca's Cafe

Italian

105 Mulberry Street
☎ 431-0408

Average meal: $5-10
for less discount: 25%
AM/MC/VS

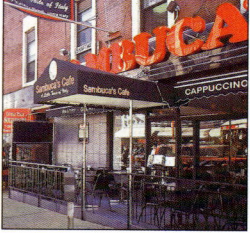

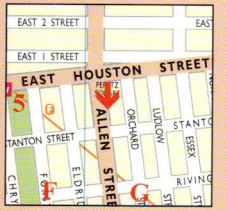

HOURS

Mon-Thu: 10am-2am
Fri-Sat: 10am-3am
Sun: 10am-2am

Sambuca's Cafe is located in the heart of Little Italy on Mulberry Street. It is perfect for Italian pastries, gourmet desserts and all types of coffee. The *tiramisu*, crafted by the owner himself, is made fresh every day.

Tiengarden

Vegetarian / Asian

170 Allen Street
☎ 388-1364

Average meal: $5-10
for less discount: 25%
Cash only

HOURS

Mon-Fri: 12noon-10pm
Sun: 12noon-10pm
Sat: closed

Tiengarden serves delicious vegetarian and vegan food near Chinatown. The vegetables are organically grown and all ingredients are natural. The "edible sculpture" *dim sum* has been featured in New York magazines.

Shopping . . .

Soho is a major New York City shopping district. From gourmet food markets to designer clothing, everything

here exudes style. Although the majority of storefronts display the chic and pricey contents you'll find inside, there are also a number of vintage clothing stores, specialty shops and street-side stands that

Spring Street Market

sell reasonably priced goods. Many of the more interesting Soho shops and boutiques offer a 20% discount to *for less* cardholders (pages 90-94).

For those fond of Flea Markets, visit the outdoor **Antiques Fair and Collectibles Market** *(Broadway and Grand Street, ☎ 682-2000. Sat-Sun: 9am-5pm)*. Also worth a look is the daily fair at the corner of Spring and Wooster Streets.

Another key commodity in the Soho shopping scene is art. **West Broadway**, in particular, is home to some of the world's best-known art galleries (see pages 80-81). Some of them have played a vital role in developing the careers of New York's best-known modern artists such as Andy Warhol and Roy Lichtenstein.

Canal Street, the dividing line between Soho and Tribeca, is a crowded shopping drag for inexpensive and imitation brand-name goods sprinkled amongst hardware and electrical supply stores. The eastern half of the street, which runs through Chinatown, contains mainly diamond and jewelry

stores.

Both **Chinatown** and **Little Italy**, however, are best known for their authentic food markets. In Little Italy, you can still find shops which specialize in one particular type of item, such as breads, meats or pasta. There are also plenty of pastry shops where you can taste another Little Italy specialty (see

Orchard Street

page 85).

Residents of all parts of Manhattan come to Chinatown for fresh produce and seafood at fair prices. The best-known of the Chinese markets is **Kam Man Food Products** *(200 Canal Street, ☎ 571-0330)* where you will find any Asian grocery item you can imagine.

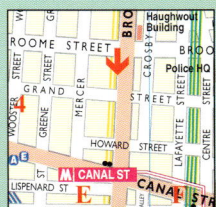

Antiques Fair and Collectibles Market

Shops in Soho

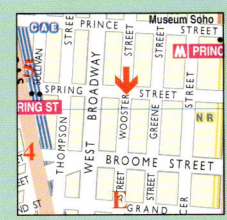

Spring Street Market

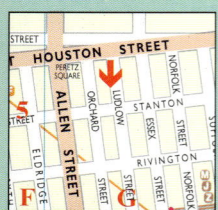

Bargain District

. . . Shopping

The **Lower East Side**, famous for its "**Bargain District**", which is centered around Orchard and Delancey Streets. On Sundays, **Orchard Street** is closed to traffic and becomes a bustling pedestrian mall. Before major discount stores moved into Manhattan, this area was the ultimate in bargain shopping. Today, prices are still competitive, though certainly not unrivaled. One advantage over discount chain shopping, however, is that there is sometimes room to "haggle" for a better price than that on the label.

A modern addition to the Lower East Side, **MarcoArt** (page 94) is an upbeat clothing boutique and art gallery north of the Bargain District, by Houston Street.

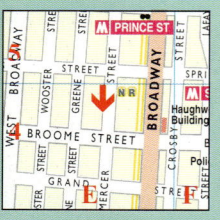

HOURS

Mon-Sun: 11am-7pm
Sun: 12noon-6pm

Enchanted Forest

Children & Gifts

85 Mercer Street
☎ **925-6677**

for less discount: 20%
AM/MC/VS/DC/DS

This magical store was chosen as "Best of New York" by *New York Magazine*. Classic, hand-crafted toys, puppets and stuffed animals can be found at this Soho shop, as well as a variety of books on fairy-tales and philosophy.

Alex Streeter

Original Jewelry

152 Prince Street
☎ **925-6496**

for less discount: 20%
AM

Alex Streeter has been selling art and designer jewelry for over 25 years. The artist designs each piece himself in a variety of unique styles and themes including archeological, science fiction and pop.

HOURS

Mon-Sat: 12noon-8pm
Sun: 1pm-6pm

 # A Uno

Women's Clothing

198 Spring Street
☎ **343-2040**

for less discount: 20%
AM/MC/VS

This European-style boutique offers clothing and accessories for women. Casual and sophisticated practical clothing is their specialty. Hats, scarves and jewelry are also available at reasonable prices.

 # Eastern Arts

Gifts & Crafts

107 Spring Street
☎ **966-4060**

for less discount: 20%
AM/MC/VS

This exotic shop brings a touch of Asia to Soho with its hand-crafted arts. Its impressive display of Indonesian art includes carvings, masks and jewelry. You can find many interesting gifts in this colorful store.

 # What Comes Around Goes Around

Vintage Clothing

351 West Broadway
☎ **343-9303**

for less discount: 20%
AM/MC/VS

This store carries collectibles and clothing from 1880-1980. Over 1,500 pairs of jeans makes it one of the largest collections of vintage denim in the country. Shoppers have included Bill Murray and Meg Ryan.

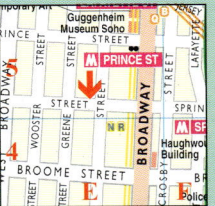

HOURS

Mon-Sat: 12noon-9pm
Sun: 12noon-7pm

HOURS

Mon-Sun: 11am-7pm

HOURS

Mon-Fri: 11am-7pm
Sat: 11am-7pm (until 1am in the summer)
Sun: 12noon-7pm

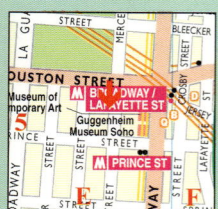

HOURS

Mon-Sun: 11am-7pm

After the Rain

Crafts, Gallery & Gifts

149 Mercer Street
☎ 431-1044

***for less* discount: 20%**
AM/MC/VS/DC/DS

After the Rain is an excellent place to purchase a high quality gift. It sells an extensive collection of jewelry, handblown glass and unusual books. There is also an interesting selection of kaleidoscopes and optical toys.

HOURS

Mon-Sun: 12noon-6pm

Margo Manhattan

Original Jewelry

100 Thompson Street
☎ 925-0735

***for less* discount: 20%**
AM/MC/VS

This modern boutique, which is owned by jewelry designer Margo Manhattan, features sterling silver and gold with semiprecious stones. A large, versatile collection of jewelry is available for both men and women.

HOURS

Mon-Sat: 11am-7pm
Sun: 12noon-6pm

Selima Optique

Optical Boutique

59 Wooster Street
☎ 343-9490

***for less* discount: 20%**
AM/MC/VS

Selima Optique is a chic and trendy optical shop located on a cobble-stoned street in historic Soho. It specializes in high-end designer and vintage eyewear and also carries stylish hats, scarves and bags.

1909 Company

Vintage Clothing

63 Thompson Street
☎ **343-1658**

for less discount: 20%
AM/VS/MC

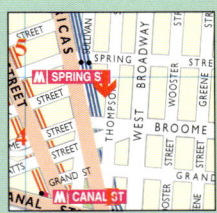

HOURS

Mon-Sun: 12noon-7pm

This shop sells quality vintage clothing and accessories from 1900-1970. Designer brands sold include Gucci, Missoni and Hermés. Winona Ryder, Julia Roberts and Molly Ringwald have all shopped here.

 # Evolution

Natural History

120 Spring Street
☎ **343-1114**

for less discount: 20%
AM/MC/VS/DS

HOURS

Mon-Sun: 11am-7pm

Evolution makes natural history a part of your Soho shopping experience. It stocks all kinds of curious items and collectibles. Some of the more unique items are butterflies, skulls, skeletons and fossils.

 # Alpana Bawa

Clothing

41 Grand Street
☎ **965-0559**

for less discount: 20%
AM/MC/VS

HOURS

Mon-Sat: 11am-7pm
(until 8pm in summer)
Sun: 12noon-6pm

Variety in colors, patterns and textures is Alpana Bawa's trademark. The designer combines items from her native India with modern designs. Handmade dresses have been bought by the likes of Helena Christiansen.

HOURS

Mon-Sat: 10am-7pm

MarcoArt

Clothing & Art

186 Orchard Street
☎ 253-1070

for less discount: 20%
AM/MC/VS

MarcoArt designs can be found on everything from Swatch watches to clothing. This shop is a colorful, lively boutique and art gallery. T-shirts, dresses and paintings are all designed by this well-known artist.

New York 911

Clothing & Gifts

263 1/2 Lafayette Street
☎ 219-3907

for less discount: 20%
AM/MC/VS

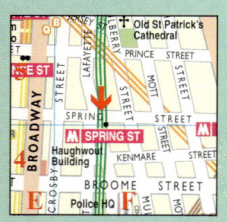

HOURS

Mon-Sat: 10am-6pm
Sun: closed

Bring home a truly unique gift from New York. T-shirts, collectibles, ball caps, patches and more are emblazoned with logos and phrases representing the NYC police and fire departments, hospitals and emergency units.

Hattitude

Hats, Gifts & Accessories

93 Reade Street
☎ 571-4558

for less discount: 20%
AM/MC/VS

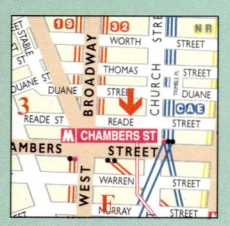

HOURS

Mon-Fri: 11am-7pm
Sat: 12noon-6pm
Sun: closed

Hattitude is located in a spacious Tribeca cast-iron building. The shop specializes in handmade hats and other interesting accessories. Also sold are unique decorative gifts and crafts.

Greenwich Village

Introduction . . .

Greenwich Village refers to the entire area between Houston and 14th Streets, but is usually more clearly defined as the East and West Villages, divided by Broadway. Also known as "the Village", it is comprised of charming townhouses and quaint, tree-lined streets.

Greenwich Village

The **West Village**'s main thoroughfare, **Bleecker Street**, is brimming over with restaurants, shops and sidewalk cafés that tempt you to sit all day, watching the crowds until the coffee runs dry.

If you happen to be in New York City on Halloween, the **Village Halloween Parade** is the place to be. If you can stand the crowds, you will undoubtedly enjoy the outrageous costumes and festivities which make it one of the best celebrations of the year.

Sheridan Square *(Intersection of Seventh Avenue, West 4th and Barrow Streets)*, was named after Civil War hero General Philip Sheridan whose statue stands in Christopher Park. In 1863, this was the site where a group of protesters, refusing to join the armed services, attempted to hang freed slaves, sparking the **Draft Riots**.

Halloween Parade

Since the 1960s, the West Village has become the center of the city's gay and lesbian community. A number of shops, bars and nightclubs in the area around Sheridan Square and along **Christopher Street** specifically cater to this market.

Washington Square Park (page 98), situated in the center of the Village, was a colonial cemetery and, during the Revolutionary War, a notorious hanging ground. When it was converted into a public park in the 1820s, however, the surrounding area became the center of New York's high society. Later, as the bohemian core of the city, many famous authors and artists lived and worked here – among them **Henry James**, **Edith Wharton**, **Mark Twain** and **Edna St. Vincent Millay**.

The imposing **Washington Memorial Arch** was built in 1889 to commemorate the 100th anniversary of the presidential inauguration of **George Washington**. Just above the arch, on the park's north side, is **The Row** – a series of distinctive Federal-style brick homes.

DON'T MISS

A stroll through the quiet tree-lined streets of the West Village. Just west of Seventh Avenue, streets such as Barrow, Bedford and Grove are good examples of West Village charm, and contain some of the oldest houses in the neighborhood.

. . . Introduction

New York University, the country's largest private university, is centered around Washington Square Park. The buildings on this urban campus are recognizable by the purple NYU flags that mark them.

New York University

Tucked away a block north of Washington Square Park, the cobble-stoned **Washington Mews** was originally built as stables for the homes facing the park. Converted into carriage houses around the turn of the century, they now serve as housing for New York University faculty.

Just east of Broadway, you can see the once fashionable homes known as **Colonnade Row** *(428-434 Lafayette Street)* built in 1833 by millionaires **John Jacob Astor** and **Cornelius Vanderbilt**. Nearby, the **Merchant's House Museum** (page 98) is the Village's only historic museum.

During the 1950s, artists migrated across Broadway to the inexpensive **East Village**. By the 1960s, beatnik philosophers **Jack Kerouac** and **Allen Ginsberg** were famous residents. Today, the tradition of the coffeehouse, with its music and poetry, is still an important part of the culture here, though new labels such as "spoken word" and "anti-folk" are used to categorize the evolution of these genres.

Unlike its western counterpart, the East Village is a little rough around the edges. Many of its residents consider it to be the last authentic bohemian neighborhood in the city, and it clings to its reputation as a haven for the creative and progressive.

The East Village has plenty of live music clubs and late-night bars. On **St. Mark's Place**, the East Village's main street, you will find a variety of cafés, bars, record stores and clothing boutiques. It is littered with live music flyers announcing the punk and rock shows which occur nightly. On the Bowery, legendary rock club **CBGB** *(315 Bowery, ☎ 982-4052)* has hosted famous bands like the Ramones and Talking Heads. Don't let the grubby exterior fool you, this place still books future stars. **Webster Hall** (page 210), one of the biggest nightclubs in New York, is a great place for dancing to the various types of music that are played on four different floors.

INSIDER'S TIP

For a night out at one of the East Village's best dance clubs, Webster Hall (page 210) gives a discount on admission to *for less* cardholders, as well as priority entrance and a glass of champagne. See page 206-210 for more information on New York City nightlife.

St. Mark's in the East Village

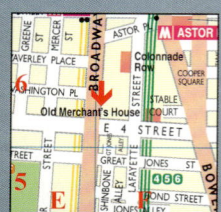

 # Merchant's House Museum

This landmark townhouse, built in 1832, is New York City's only family home preserved intact from the 19th century.

Located close to Washington Square Park, this was the home of a wealthy hardware merchant, **Seabury Tredwell**, and his family from 1835-1933. It became a museum in 1936 and is a fine example of the architecture which once dominated entire city blocks, as well as a fine representation of the lifestyle of an upper-middle-class 19th-century New York family.

Merchant's House Museum

When the house was built, it was equipped with all the modern-day conveniences and building technology available including pipes for gas lighting and a bell system for calling servants.

The exterior is constructed in a late Federal period architectural style. The most notable rooms of the Greek Revival-style interior are the elaborately crafted parlors, complete with free-standing Ionic columns and ornate fireplaces, doors and windows.

Parlor in the Merchant's House Museum

The ground floor is comprised of the original dining room and the kitchen. The dining room features an elegant black and gold marble mantle and a table set with porcelain from the Tredwell collection. The kitchen contains a beehive oven, a large fireplace and a soapstone sink into which water was pumped from a 4,000 gallon cistern in the garden.

On the main floor, the magnificent parlors are accompanied by two bedrooms and a study filled with the family's original furniture, clothing and memorabilia. These rooms provide a detailed look at life in the Tredwell household.

The top two floors were once servants' quarters and additional bedrooms for the eight Tredwell children.

Other Attractions . . .

Jefferson Market Library was built in 1865 as a volunteer firehouse. When it later became a courthouse, it was named after president Thomas Jefferson. Now part of the New York Public Library system, "Old Jeff", as it is affectionately known, features Venetian Gothic-style spires, a watchtower and bell. In 1877, it was voted one of the ten most beautiful buildings in the U.S. and is still considered an architectural treasure. *(425 Sixth Avenue, ☎ 243-4334. Mon and Thu: 10am-6pm. Tue and Fri: 12noon-6pm. Wed: 12noon-8pm. Sat: 10am-5pm. Sun: closed. Admission is free.)*

Jefferson Market Library

Just north of Washington Square Park, the **Salmagundi Club** was formed in 1870 by prestigious literary figures like Edith Wharton, Henry James and Herman Melville. Today, the club houses the American Artists' Professional League, the American Watercolor Society and the Greenwich Village Society for Historic Preservation. *(47 Fifth Avenue, ☎ 255-7740. Mon-Sun: 1pm-5pm. Admission is free.)*

Jefferson Market Library

Forbes Magazine Gallery contains the private collection of the late financial publisher Malcolm Forbes. The gallery displays thousands of antique toys, an outstanding collection of objects by Russian jeweler Peter Carl Fabergé (including the famous Fabergé eggs) and an autographed copy of President Abraham Lincoln's *Gettysburg Address*. *(62 Fifth Avenue, ☎ 206-5548. Tue-Wed and Fri-Sat: 10am-4pm. Thur: group tours by appointment only. Sun-Mon: closed. Admission is free.)*

Public Theater

The elegant **Grace Church** on Broadway was built by architect James Renwick Jr., who also designed St. Patrick's Cathedral (page 150). *(802 Broadway, ☎ 254-2000. Mon-Tue and Thu-Fri: 10am-5.30pm. Wed: 11.30am-5.30pm. Sat: 12noon-4pm. Sun: masses at 9am, 11am, 6pm.)*

The old **Astor Library**, built in 1849, is a beautiful red brick brownstone building that was saved from destruction and restored by Joseph Papp in 1965. Papp, who founded the New York Shakespeare Festival in 1954, later made the building home to the **Public Theater**. It is well-respected for its new American productions as well as the annual *Shakespeare in the Park* festival, which it stages every summer in Central Park (page 200). *(425 Lafayette Street, ☎ 239-6200 for tickets.)*

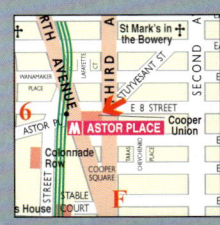
Cooper Union

. . . Other Attractions

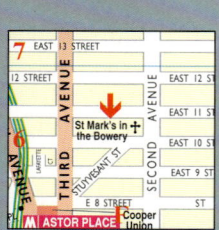

Founded by industrialist Peter Cooper in 1859, the **Cooper Union for the Advancement of Science and Art** was the city's first free, non-discriminatory college. The school still attracts talented young students and continues to produce notable contemporary artists. *(41 Cooper Square, ☎ 353-4100.)*

East Village street scene

Built in 1799, **St. Mark's-in-the-Bowery Church** is one of New York's oldest remaining churches. Situated on the former farm of Dutch colonial governor, Peter Stuyvesant, he and several generations of his descendants are buried here. *(131 East 10th Street, ☎ 674-6377. Mon-Sat: 10am-6pm. Sun: mass at 10.30am.)*

Anthology Film Archives (see nightlife, page 208) has two theaters which show new, classic and avant-garde films. There are also lectures and discussions on a variety of film-related topics. *(32 Second Avenue. Call the program info line on ☎ 505-5110 for schedule of screenings.)*

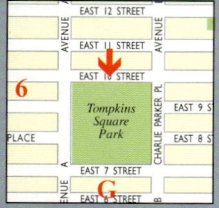

St. Mark's-in-the-Bowery

Open Spaces

On weekends, the former fountain in the middle of **Washington Square Park** (page 96) acts as a stage for street performers (from musicians to comedians to sword-swallowers) who draw an audience of interested passers-by and bored teenagers. If there are still remnants of bohemian culture in the Village, this park is where you are most likely to find them – amongst the acoustic guitars, African drums and amateur poetry.

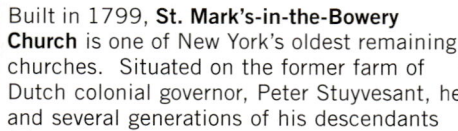

Tompkins Square Park

Houses on Washington Square

Once a favorite haunt of New York's high society, Washington Square Park fell into decline during the 1970s and early 1980s, and became infested with drug dealers. In the mid-80s, however, a massive clean-up program was initiated and the park is now a pleasant and lively place to visit.

In Alphabet City, just east of Avenue A, you will find **Tompkins Square Park**. Once a scene of social and political unrest, this park has recently become gentrified and is a good place to take a break after a shopping trip to the East Village.

Tompkins Square Park

Eating and Drinking

Greenwich Village is packed with inexpensive restaurants and cafés serving all types of cuisine (and, unfortunately in some cases, all levels of quality). In the West Village, Bleecker Street is particularly busy and is home to the excellent Indian restaurant **Mitali West** (page 102), which gives a discount to *for less* cardholders.

Barocco to Go's fresh baked goods

On a quiet block in the West Village, **Chumley's** *(86 Bedford Street, ☎ 675-4449)* is a former speakeasy which, during Prohibition, was a watering hole for some of New York's greatest writers, including John Steinbeck. You will have to look very closely for the entrance, though, as it is easy to miss.

On Sixth Avenue, **Balducci's** *(424 Sixth Avenue, ☎ 673-2600)* is an old-world Italian food market famous for the quality and variety of its products. It has one of the largest selections of cheeses in New York, and their excellence is vouched for by more than a few New York chefs who come here to make selections for their restaurants.

Balducci's market

Some of the least expensive dining in Manhattan can be found in the East Village, especially at some of the ethnic eateries. Sixth Street (between First and Second Avenues) is known as **Little India**. This row of Indian restaurants occupies nearly every storefront on the south side of the street. Many allow you to bring your own liquor. Around the corner, **Haveli** (page 104) is considered one of the best Indian restaurants in the city, and its prices are very reasonable.

The East Village is also home to an eclectic array of dining establishments. At **Roettele A.G.** (page 104), you can feel as if you have escaped to a retreat in the Swiss Alps. A warren of cozy rooms fills with the scent of home-made dishes, among them, the house specialty cheese fondue.

Friendly and warm, the staff at **Nice Guy Eddie's** (page 104) accept the *for less* card and serve tasty American dishes.

DON'T MISS

Outdoor dining in warm weather – Roettele A.G. and L'Oro di Napoli offer garden dining or sidewalk tables.

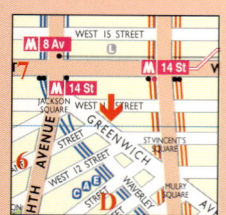

HOURS

Mon-Fri: 8am-8.30pm
Sat-Sun: 10am-6pm

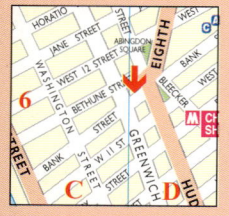

HOURS

Mon-Thu and Sun:
12noon-4pm, 5.30pm-
12midnight
Fri-Sat: 11am-4pm,
5.30pm-1am

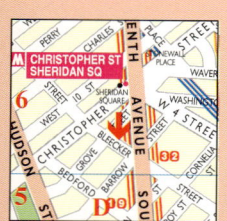

HOURS

Mon-Sun: 12noon-
12midnight

Barocco to Go *for less*

American / International

121 Greenwich Avenue
☎ 366-6110

Average meal: $10-15
for less discount: 25%
AM/MC/VS

Barocco to Go serves Tuscan-style fare in the West Village. Freshly made pizzas, salads, sandwiches and desserts are all prepared on the premises. This casual café is the perfect stop for a quick snack or a full meal.

Nadine's *for less*

International

99 Bank Street
☎ 924-3165

Average meal: $15-20
for less discount: 25%
AM/MC/VS

Chandeliers, candles and paintings create a romantic atmosphere at this West Village restaurant. An eclectic selection of dishes includes specialties like the cajun meatloaf or black bean pancakes.

Mitali West *for less*

Indian

296 Bleecker Street
☎ 989-1367

Average meal: $15-20
for less discount: 25%
AM/MC/VS

This spacious West Village restaurant serves fine Indian cuisine, offering an extensive choice of both vegetarian and non-vegetarian dishes. Favorites include the *chicken tikka* and vegetable curry.

Il Bocconcino

Italian

168 Sullivan Street
☎ **982-0329**

Average meal: $15-20
for less discount: 25%
AM/MC/VS/DC

Ideally located between Soho and Greenwich Village, Il Bocconcino serves hearty, Italian fare in a Romanesque setting. Dine on chef's specialties such as the pasta, veal or lobster dishes.

L'Oro di Napoli

Italian

206 Sullivan Street
☎ **598-4952**

Average meal: $20-25
for less discount: 25%
AM/MC/VS/DC/DS

L'Oro di Napoli is located in the West Village near Washington Square Park. The décor is rustic and the atmosphere is informal. Recommended dishes include the seafood and pasta specials.

La Belle Epoque

French / Creole

827 Broadway
☎ **254-6436**

Average meal: $25-30
for less discount: 25%
AM/MC/VS/DC/DS

Set in an elegant turn-of-the-century Parisian-style ballroom, La Belle Epoque serves French and Creole contemporary and traditional cuisine like *salmon buerre blanc*. The jazz brunch is recommended, reserve ahead.

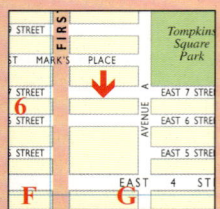

Tue-Sun lunch:
12noon-3pm
Tue-Thu: 5.30pm-11pm
Fri-Sat: 5.30pm-11.30pm
Sun: 5pm-10pm
Mon: closed

HOURS

Mon-Sun: 12noon-
12midnight

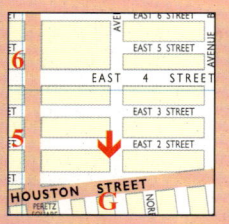

HOURS

Mon-Fri:12noon-2am
Sat-Sun: 12noon-2am

Roettele A.G.

German / Swiss

126 East 7th Street
☎ 674-4140

Average meal: $20-25
for less discount: 25%
AM/MC/VS/DC

Roettele A.G. serves German-Swiss cuisine with Italian and French accents. Inside, intimate rooms feature hardwood floors and a fireplace. In warm weather, enjoy specials like cheese fondue in the outdoor garden.

Haveli

Indian

100 Second Avenue
☎ 982-0533

Average meal: $15-20
for less discount: 25%
AM/MC/VS/DC/DS

Around the corner from Indian Row, Haveli is considered one of the city's best Indian restaurants. It successfully combines tradition with elegance. Try the *murgah tikka* or one of the flavorful vegetarian dishes.

Nice Guy Eddie's

American

5 Avenue A
☎ 539-0902

Average meal: $10-15
for less discount: 25%
AM/MC/VS

American southwestern cuisine and tasty Cajun dishes are served here. A 1970s rock jukebox adds to the laid-back, fun atmosphere. Try the apple cider-soaked chicken breast with Creole ratatouille.

Shopping

The scenic, winding streets of the West Village offer an ideal shopping experience. You can stick to the main thoroughfares like **Bleecker Street**, where you will find an assortment of stores selling everything from posters to New York City T-shirts, or you can explore the side streets to discover hidden treasures.

The Village has plenty of specialty shops like **Hudson Street Papers** (page 108), which has a unique selection of greeting cards and gifts. For something exotic, **Eastern Arts** (page 108) and **Truva** (page 106) import products from around the world.

Bleecker Street in the West Village

Stop in the **Village Chess Shop** (page 107) to play a friendly game of chess with the locals, or pick something up from their wide selection of chess and game-related items.

Broadway is crammed with stores that are perfect for purchasing basic items such as shoes and boots, jeans and casual clothing.

Because of the relatively low rents in the East Village, many independent artists and designers have come here to set up galleries and shops. The result is a neighborhood filled with an interesting collection of boutiques selling unusual and handmade items, generally at good prices. Shoppers can weave in and out of dozens of stores, each offering its own brand of unique merchandise.

Truva in the West Village

St. Mark's Place is the center of the area's shopping activity, with an abundance of vintage clothing boutiques, record stores and collectibles shops. You will also find a number of places on and around St. Mark's that offer a discount to **for less** cardholders. Tucked amongst vintage and specialty shops like **Garage Sale** (page 109), **Swish** (page 110) is one of the best skateshops in New York, selling all the top skateboard and streetwear brands.

Around the corner on East 7th Street, **Howdy-Do** (page 110) has a dazzling display of American kitsch and collectibles. It is virtually a museum of vintage Americana.

DON'T MISS

The collection of vintage lunch boxes at **Howdy-do** (page 110): from Wonder Woman to the Brady Bunch, this store stocks them all.

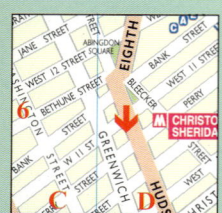

HOURS

Mon-Sun: 11am-6pm

Tootsie's

Children

555 Hudson Street
☎ **242-0182**

for less discount: 20%
AM/MC/VS/DC

Tootsie's sells classic and contemporary children's books and toys. Everything from games and puzzles to puppets can be found here, any of which would make a great children's gift or souvenir.

Whiskey Dust

Vintage Clothing & Western

526 Hudson Street
☎ **691-5576**

for less discount: 20%
AM/MC/VS/DS

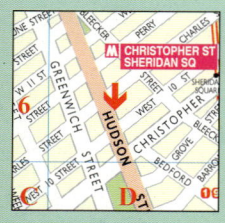

HOURS

Mon-Sat: 12.30pm-7pm
Sun: 1pm-6pm

Colorful and fun, Whiskey Dust is stocked with western memorabilia and merchandise. High quality, new and vintage western apparel includes an extensive collection of jeans, cowboy hats and boots for men and women.

Truva

Gifts & Crafts

58 Greenwich Avenue
☎ **462-4040**

for less discount: 20%
AM/MC/VS/DS

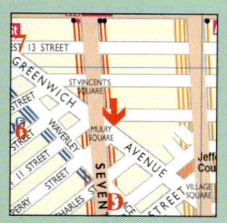

HOURS

Mon-Fri: 12noon-8pm
Sat: 11am-9pm
Sun: 12noon-7pm

Truva is an authentic Turkish gift shop, selling traditional goods like furniture and carpets. Picture frames, chess sets and copper items make great gifts. Ladies clothing and accessories are sold in the adjacent boutique.

Tah-Poozie

Children, Toys & Novelties

50 Greenwich Avenue
☎ 647-0668

for less discount: 20%
AM/MC/VS/DS

HOURS

Mon-Sun: 11pm-9pm
(longer hours in summer)

Tah-Poozie features curiosities of interest to both children and adults. It stocks a unique selection of toys, trinkets and novelties. You can also find postcards, world music CDs and New York mementos.

 # Village Chess Shop

Chess

230 Thompson Street
☎ 475-9580

for less discount: 20%
AM/MC/VS

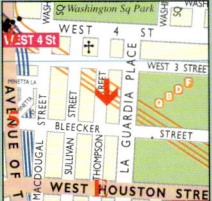

HOURS

Mon-Sun: 12noon-
12midnight

This famous chess shop stocks chess sets, boards, books and software. Chess players are welcome and there are tables set up for playing. You can also find checkers, dominoes, backgammon and other games.

 # Vision of Tibet

Gifts & Crafts

167 Thompson Street
☎ 995-9276

for less discount: 20%
AM/MC/VS

HOURS

Mon-Sun: 11am-7pm

Vision of Tibet stocks a multitude of Himalayan artifacts and crafts. Choose from exotic jewelry, clothing and other items. This is a great place to find an interesting, yet inexpensive, gift.

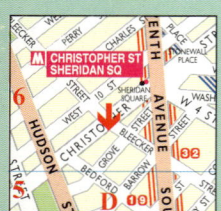

HOURS

Mon-Wed: 10am-7.45pm
Thu-Sat: 10am-8.45pm
Sun: 12noon-6.45pm

Village Army Navy

Army Navy & Clothing

328 Bleecker Street
☎ 242-6665

for less discount: 20%
AM/MC/VS

Village Army Navy is located in the heart of the West Village. It carries all the top brands and a wide selection of men's and women's clothing and accessories by Timberland, Levi's, Calvin Klein, Polo and more.

Eastern Arts

Gifts & Crafts

365 Bleecker Street
☎ 929-7460

for less discount: 20%
AM/MC/VS/DC

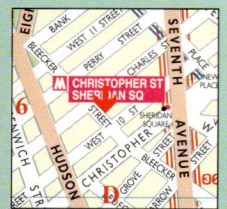

HOURS

Mon-Sun: 11am-8pm

This exotic, Asian-themed crafts shop has an impressive display of Indonesian art, including carvings, masks and jewelry. You can also obtain the discount at Eastern Arts' Soho location (page 91).

Hudson Street Papers

Gifts

357 Bleecker Street
☎ 229-1064

for less discount: 20%
AM/MC/VS

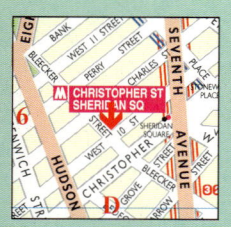

HOURS

Mon-Sat: 11am-8pm
Sun: 12noon-6pm

Hudson Street Papers carries an enormous selection of greeting cards, toys, jewelry and more. Decorative gifts such as candles and picture frames make great gifts and unusual souvenirs.

L'Uomo

Men's Clothing

383 Bleecker Street
☎ **206-1844**

for less discount: 20%
AM/MC/VS

L'Uomo sells classic and contemporary men's clothing and accessories. It stocks a complete range of styles and sizes in both casual and business wear. Top designer brands such as Hugo Boss and Rene Lezard are available.

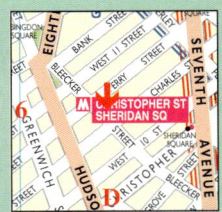

HOURS

Mon-Sat:
11am-7.30pm
Sun: 12noon-6pm

 ## Norman's Sound & Vision

Music

67 Cooper Square
☎ **473-6599**

for less discount: 20%
AM/MC/VS/DS

Located just off St. Mark's, Norman's sells both new and used CDs and videos. Their stock includes classical, country, rock, jazz, reggae and more. If you cannot find it, ask the knowledgeable staff who will surely help you.

HOURS

Mon-Fri: 10am-11pm
Sat: 10am-12midnight
Sun: 10am-10pm

 ## Garage Sale

Vintage & Collectibles

26 First Avenue
☎ **260-2269**

for less discount: 20%
AM/MC/VS

Garage Sale sells vintage clothing and accessories of every type. You can also find antiques and other collectibles such as handbags, jewelry and a unique collection of vintage lamps dating from the 1940s.

HOURS

Mon-Thu: 1pm-7pm
Fri-Sat: 1pm-8pm
Sun: 12noon-6pm

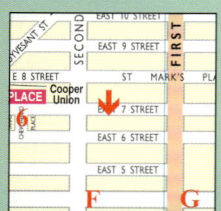

HOURS

Mon-Sat: 1pm-7pm
Sun: closed

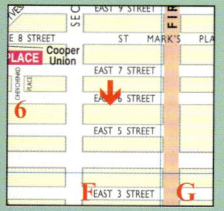

HOURS

Mon-Sun:
12noon-11.30pm

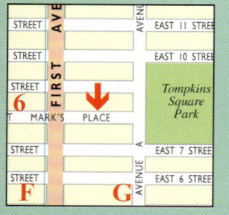

HOURS

Mon-Fri: 12noon-8pm
Sat: 12noon-9pm
Sun: 12noon-7.30pm

Howdy-Do

Vintage & Collectibles

72 East 7th Street
☎ **979-1618**

for less discount: 20%
AM/MC/VS

A myriad of kitsch items represent decades of American pop culture. Toy and television collectibles include dolls, lunch boxes and board games. Celebrities such as Boy George, Bjork and Rosie O'Donnell shop here.

Back from Guatemala

Gifts & Crafts

306 East 6th Street
☎ **260-7010**

for less discount: 20%
AM/MC/VS

Back from Guatemala has a unique collection of clothing, jewelry and artifacts from over 30 countries. It sells musical instruments from cultures around the world, and gifts such as picture frames and candles.

Swish

Skateshop & Clothing

115 St. Mark's Place
☎ **673-8629**

for less discount: 20%
AM/MC/VS/DC

Established in 1993, Swish is NYC's original skateshop. It continues to carry the best skateboard brands and streetwear for men and women. Also stocked are watches, sunglasses and other accessories.

Chelsea, Gramercy & the Flatiron District

Introduction . . .

During the 19th century, the construction of the elevated railroad helped transform **Chelsea** from farmland into a thriving commercial center. Carriages brought well-to-do women from around town to the stores which lined Broadway between Union Square and Madison Square, and it became

Annex Antiques Fair and Flea Market

known as "**Ladies' Mile**". As New York continued its expansion north, however, Chelsea was left behind as a warehouse district, while Herald Square and its new department store, **Macy's** (page 146), brought shoppers further uptown. Today, the retail industry has made a comeback in the area and you can now find national chains such as **Old Navy** (*610 Sixth Avenue,* ☎ *645-0663*), **Filene's Basement** (*620 Sixth Avenue,* ☎ *620-3100*) and **Loehmann's** (see page 124).

On weekends, one of the best things to do in Chelsea is to visit the **Annex Antiques Fair and Flea Market** (*Sixth Avenue, between 24th and 25th Streets*). This gigantic outdoor market has vintage clothing, antiques, furniture and more. Nearby, the **Chelsea Antiques Building** (*110 West 25th Street*) has 12 floors of antiques and collectibles. On the eighth floor, **Cafe Mozart** (page 121) is a good place for a light lunch after a day of antique and bargain hunting.

Recently, Chelsea has begun to acquire a reputation as an art center as more and more galleries are moving out of their longtime Soho homes and relocating into this less commercialized (and less expensive) area.

The Manhattan waterfront has recently been the focus of major development plans. In Chelsea, the abandoned docks, warehouses and decrepit piers have given way to the **Chelsea Piers Sports and Entertainment Complex** (page 116) – a prime example of the potential for other waterfront development projects.

Aerial view of Chelsea Piers

The **Flatiron District** is also known as the "Photo District" because of the abundance of photography

INSIDER'S TIP

The Empire State Building Observatory is one of the few attractions open late every evening and it makes a perfect place to visit after dinner when you can take in the illuminated Manhattan skyline from the 102nd floor.

. . . Introduction

studios, labs and modeling agencies. This area has recently become popular for its cutting-edge restaurants (see page 121) and nightlife.

Rich in architectural detail, the triangular **Flatiron Building** was the tallest building in the world when it was finished in 1902. The best place to view it is from the traffic island a block north. From this angle, the building really does appear to be flat.

Flatiron Building

A short walk along Fifth Avenue will take you to the **Empire State Building** (page 114-115) where you can go up to the Observatory for some of the best views of the city. On the second floor of the building, you can try out the **New York Skyride** (page 115) and take a cinematic sightseeing tour of New York City.

Located in a slightly shabby area, **Madison Square Garden** (page 117), known by sports fans as "the Garden", is home to the New York Knicks basketball team.

Theodore Roosevelt's Birthplace

Ivy-covered 19th-century townhouses remain on Irving Place and some of its neighboring streets. Of particular charm and beauty are those surrounding the private **Gramercy Park** (page 120). This area is rich with the history of its literary and artistic past. Just south of the park, in Pete's Tavern on Irving Place, O. Henry wrote his ironic tale *The Gift of the Magi*. Edwin Booth's theatrical **Players Club** and the **National Arts Club** (page 119) are located in Gramercy Park townhouses. Not far from here, the **Little Church Around the Corner** (page 119) has been known as a spiritual refuge for actors since the 19th century.

You can visit one of the area's brownstone houses at **Theodore Roosevelt's Birthplace** (page 118), which not only offers a glimpse of the former president's early childhood home, but also a chance to examine the architecture of these charming buildings up-close.

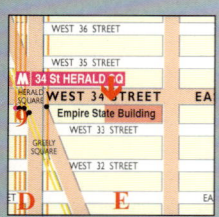

 # Empire State Building . . .

Dominating the skyline of midtown Manhattan, the Empire State Building rises to a height of 1,454 feet. Its fame began soon after talk of its construction, and it has since become a symbol of New York City which is recognized worldwide.

The building was completed on the site of the original Waldorf Astoria Hotel in 1931, in only one year and forty-five days – an amazing feat at the time. Although it came in under budget, it soon ran into financial trouble. In its early years, the effect of the 1929 stock market crash and the ensuing depression

Lit with the colors of Independence Day

made tenants hard to find, and for a while it was nicknamed the "Empty State Building".

Upon its completion, the Empire State became the world's tallest building, a title it retained until the World Trade Center was built in the 1970s. In 1955, the American Society of Civil Engineers honored the structure as one of the seven modern wonders of the western hemisphere.

The Empire State Building has appeared in more films than most Hollywood stars (over 100 in all) from *King Kong* to *Sleepless in Seattle* and *Independence Day*. In the 1960s, it was the subject of an Andy Warhol film which recorded the building for eight hours straight during which time the only thing that changed was the lighting.

View from the Observatory

The upper 30 floors of the building are illuminated nightly, from sunset to midnight, in a range of colors that reflect holidays and commemorate special events.

The Observatory offers panoramic views of Manhattan and beyond. High-speed elevators whisk passengers to the 86th floor where there are glass-enclosed viewing areas and outdoor promenades. There is also viewing from a second observatory on the 102nd Floor.

With the whole city laid out beneath you, you can see up to 80 miles on a clear day. Famous sights like the

ADDRESS

350 Fifth Avenue
☎ 736-3100

HOURS

Mon-Sun: 9.30am-12midnight, last elevator at 11.30pm.

GETTING THERE

Subway: 6 to 33rd Street, or B/D/F or N/R to 34th Street-Herald Square.
New York Apple Tours stop: Downtown/waterfront route stop #33, Empire State Building.

. . . Empire State Building

Chrysler Building, Yankee Stadium, Central Park, the
World Trade Center and the
Statue of Liberty are all
visible. You can also see the
surrounding boroughs and
the bridges that link them to
Manhattan.

At night, the city lights offer
an entirely different
experience from daytime
viewing. If you have the
time, one of the best things
to do is to go up to the
Observatory just before
sunset, when the lights from

Sunset view

the buildings are first visible, then leave after the sky
is completely dark. The skyline at sunset is
breathtaking, and many of the sights, the bridges in
particular, look best at this time.

The New York Skyride, located on the second
floor of the Empire State Building, offers a state-
of-the-art cinematic sightseeing tour of New York.

Star Trek's James Doohan, better known as Scotty, and
comedian Yakov Smirnoff are the pilots and guides on

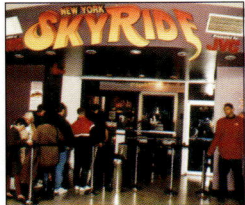

this 30-minute simulated
flight through the city. The
high-tech theater features a
specially designed platform
with hydraulic seats and wide
screens which are
synchronized to make you
feel as if you are actually
experiencing the ride.

New York Skyride

This unusual tour of Manhattan includes simulated
experiences such as a freefall off the top of the
Empire State Building, a high speed ride
between and over sights such as the
Brooklyn Bridge, the World Trade Center and
the Statue of Liberty and a chance to dodge
traffic in Times Square – without leaving
your seat. *(350 Fifth Avenue, Second Floor, ☎
564-2224. Mon-Sun: 10am-10pm.)*

**Important: to obtain your 20% discount, you
must present your *for less* card and
purchase the Combined Ticket before 10pm
from the Skyride ticket booth located up the
escalator on the 2nd floor, not from the ticket
booth downstairs on the concourse level.**

New York Skyride's high-tech theater

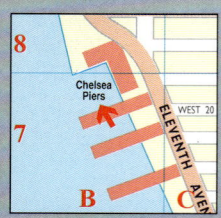

ADDRESS

17th-23rd Streets at the
Hudson River
☎ 336-6666

HOURS

Hours vary per activity.
Discount applies Mon-Fri:
opening time to 5pm.

PRICES

Golf: $15 for 68 balls and
up, club rental $2 each / 3
for $5.

Ice Skating: Adult $10.50,
Child $8 (plus rental $5)

Roller Skating: Adult $4,
Child $3 (plus rental:
Adult $10.00, Child $7)

Sports Center: $31 per day

DISCOUNT

General admission
(including golf, ice and
roller skating, as well as
day passes for the Sports
Center) are offered at a
20% discount to *for less*
cardholders (Mon-Fri:
opening until 5pm). A
20% discount at the
Chelsea Piers Store is also
available. Both offers
require the vouchers on
page 273.

 # Chelsea Piers

Chelsea Piers Sports and Entertainment Complex is a
30-acre waterfront sports village encompassing a golf
driving range, sports and fitness club, athletic
facilities, ice and roller skating rinks and a marina. It
is also the location
of **Silver Screen
Studios**, where
popular television
series such as *Law
and Order* and major
motion pictures
such as *City Hall*
with Al Pacino have
been filmed here.

Driving stalls at the Golf Club

The Golf Club is Manhattan's only year-round, outdoor
driving range. It has 52 covered and heated driving
stalls which overlook the Hudson River. Every golf ball
is mechanically retrieved
and lifted on its tee –
ready to be hit onto a
200-yard fairway.

The Sports Center offers
unparalleled opportunities
in a variety of sports and
has training facilities
which include the world's
longest indoor running track. You can take cross-
training to new heights, literally, on the largest rock
climbing wall in the northeastern U.S. An indoor arena
contains facilities for basketball, soccer, baseball plus
more unusual events like indoor sand volleyball. There
is also a 6-lane swimming pool, a boxing ring and
locker room facilities which include saunas, steam and
massage rooms.

Sky Rink

Sky Rink has the only
year-round indoor ice
skating facilities in
Manhattan. Although
it features two rinks,
it is often unavailable
for public skating in
the evenings because

Roller rinks at Chelsea Piers

of the many hockey leagues and professional
organizations that practice here.

In warm weather, the massive outdoor sun-deck at the
Sports Center is perfect for sunbathing and relaxing.
From the Chelsea Piers promenade there are great
views of the Hudson River.

Other Attractions . . .

Well-known for its roster of literary and musical guests, the **Chelsea Hotel** was made notorious in the late 1970s by the highly publicized death of punk rock star Sid Vicious' girlfriend Nancy Spungeon. The brass plaques on the building's facade list the names of some of the hotel's more illustrious former guests including Dylan Thomas, Tennessee Williams and Mark Twain. Today, the hotel continues to cater to an off-beat, artsy clientele. *(222 West 23rd Street, ☎ 243-3700.)*

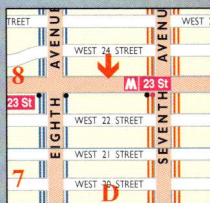
Chelsea Hotel

Joyce Theater

Housed in a former Art Deco cinema, the **Joyce Theater** (page 207) is a well-respected center for dance. Performances cover a tremendous range of styles from ballet to ballroom and everything in between. *(175 Eighth Avenue, ☎ 242-0800 for tickets.)*

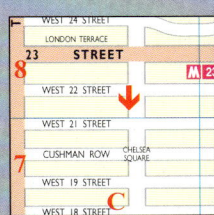
General Theological Seminary

Founded in 1817, the **General Theological Seminary** is a private facility for students preparing for the priesthood. Its beautiful grounds are a welcome oasis from the busy streets of Chelsea and guided tours are available during the summer. *(Ninth Avenue between 20th and 21st Streets, ☎ 243-5150. Mon-Fri: 12noon-3pm. Sat: 11am-3pm. Sun: closed.)*

Built in 1854, the **Marble Collegiate Church** is the oldest Reformed Church in the city. It is probably best known, however, for its former pastor-turned-author Norman Vincent Peale who wrote *The Power of Positive Thinking*. *(1 West 29th Street, ☎ 686-2770. Mon-Sat: 9am-12noon, 2pm-4pm. Sun: 9am-2pm.)*

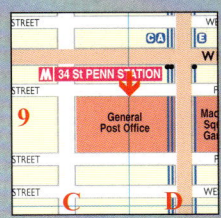
General Post Office

The **General Post Office** was created by the legendary New York architectural firm McKim, Mead and White in 1913. The colossal building is two city blocks long and is easily recognizable by its sweeping staircase and immense Corinthian columns. *(421 Eighth Avenue, ☎ 967-8585. Open 24 hours every day, including holidays.)*

General Post Office

Madison Square Garden is home to the New York Knicks basketball team and the New York Rangers hockey team. The 20,000-seat arena also hosts many other sporting and non-sporting events, including major rock and pop

. . . Other Attractions . . .

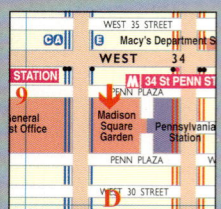

Madison Square Garden

concerts. Guided tours of the complex are available year round. *(4 Pennsylvania Plaza, ☎ 465-6741.)*

The Roman Catholic **St. John the Baptist Church** was founded in 1840 for German immigrants. The appearance of the exterior has become a little shabby, but the interior holds a variety of Gothic-style treasures, including marble arches and stained-glass windows. *(211 West 30th Street, ☎ 564-9070. Mon-Sun: 6am-6pm.)*

The busy **Appellate Division of the Supreme Court of the State of New York** hears appeals for civil and criminal cases from New York and the Bronx. Baseball great Babe Ruth, actor and dancer extraordinaire Fred Astaire and writer Edgar Allen Poe all participated in cases settled here. You can visit the building and see its elegant interior, but the court sessions are closed to the public. *(27 Madison Avenue, ☎ 340-0400. Mon-Fri: 9am-5pm. Sat-Sun: closed.)*

Parlor in Theodore Roosevelt's Birthplace

The **Metropolitan Life Insurance Company** became the tallest building in the world in 1909, surpassing its neighbor, the Flatiron Building. Its lighted 700-foot tower and four-faced clock are prominent features of the New York Skyline. *(1 Madison Avenue, ☎ 578-2211.)*

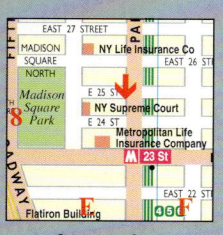

Supreme Court

Located in a Gramercy Park townhouse, **Theodore Roosevelt's Birthplace** has been reconstructed to represent the boyhood home of the 26th U.S. president. A national historic site, it includes period rooms, galleries and the largest selection of Teddy Roosevelt memorabilia anywhere. On Saturdays at 2pm, you can listen to chamber music concerts at no additional charge. *(28 East 20th Street, ☎ 260-1616. Adult $2, child (under 17) free, senior $2, student $2. Wed-Sun: 9am-5pm. Mon-Tue: closed. House tours on the hour, last tour at 4pm.)*

Metropolitan Life Insurance Building

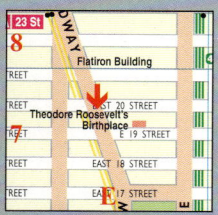

Theodore Roosevelt's Birthplace

. . . Other Attractions

The **National Arts Club** was designed in the early 1880s by one of the renowned architects of Central Park – Calvert Vaux. Members have included some of America's finest 19th and 20th century artists, many of whom contributed works that are still housed here. Although this is a private club, the collection is open to the public for viewing at various times throughout the year. *(15 Gramercy Park South, ☎ 475-3424. Call ahead for exhibition schedule.)*

National Arts Club

Next door, **The Players** is housed in the former home of actor Edwin Booth – famous not only for his profession, but also for his brother John Wilkes' assassination of President Lincoln. The theatrical club he began attracted the likes of Mark Twain and Winston Churchill as members. The only way to see the inside, however, is to arrange a group tour before you arrive. *(16 Gramercy Park South, ☎ 228-7610. Private club.)*

The **Episcopal Church of the Transfiguration**, better known as the **Little Church Around the Corner**, has been known as a spiritual refuge for actors since the late 1800s. The name stuck when an actor was refused burial at a nearby church because of his profession, and the preacher referred his friend to the "little church around the corner". Actress Sarah Bernhardt is said to have attended services here, and a window portrays actor Edwin Booth in his role as Hamlet. The church maintains a special relationship with the thespian community. *(1 East 29th Street, ☎ 684-6770. Sun only: 8am-1pm.)*

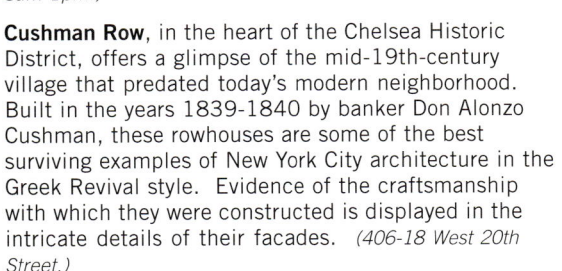
The Flower District

Little Church Around the Corner

Cushman Row, in the heart of the Chelsea Historic District, offers a glimpse of the mid-19th-century village that predated today's modern neighborhood. Built in the years 1839-1840 by banker Don Alonzo Cushman, these rowhouses are some of the best surviving examples of New York City architecture in the Greek Revival style. Evidence of the craftsmanship with which they were constructed is displayed in the intricate details of their facades. *(406-18 West 20th Street.)*

The Flower District is Manhattan's main source for plants and flowers – thousands of species are sold here and prices are generally better than elsewhere, thanks to the competition. *(Sixth Avenue at 27-29th Streets.)*

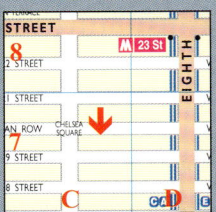
Cushman Row

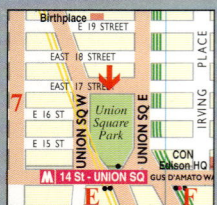

Union Square Park

Madison Square Park

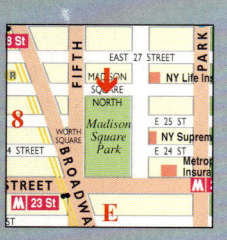

Madison Square Park

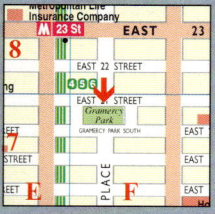

Gramercy Park

Open Spaces

The enormous sun-deck at **Chelsea Piers Sports and Entertainment Complex** (page 116) is a great place to soak up the sun in warm weather. A stroll along the piers themselves are another good way to enjoy the Manhattan waterfront.

Union Square Greenmarket

Union Square Park is a busy, open space wedged between Broadway and Fourth Avenues, just above 14th Street. Most of its daytime visitors are local workers who come here to eat their deli-bought lunches on the park benches. On the streets around the park, there are a variety of good restaurants and outdoor cafés, (see page121).

Union Square, however, is at its best on Wednesdays and Saturdays when the **Union Square Greenmarket** brings regional farmers to the park to peddle their harvests.

Once a busy entertainment district and the site of **P.T. Barnum's Hippodrome**, **Madison Square** is now a tranquil park where, despite the nearby traffic, you can enjoy a little peace and quiet. A pleasant half hour can be spent examining the 19th-century statues and monuments situated throughout the grounds, and enjoying the view of the nearby Flatiron Building. Surrounding the park, other early 20th-century buildings, such as the **New York Life Insurance Company** and **Metropolitan Life Insurance Company** (page 118), add to the scenery. At night, the buildings are lit in a variety of colors which change with the seasons.

Organized baseball is said to have grown out of the famous **Knickerbocker Club**, formed in 1845, by a group of baseball enthusiasts who played regularly in the park.

Gramercy Park

Modeled after a London square, **Gramercy Park** is one of the quietest, most peaceful places in the city. The surrounding townhouses are stately and beautiful, but (to the dismay of everyone else) their residents are the only ones who possess keys to this private oasis.

Eating and Drinking

With the recent influx of stylish restaurants, the Flatiron District and the area around Union Square has become one of the city's prime eating and drinking destinations. Top restaurants like **Gramercy Tavern** *(42 East 20th Street, ☎ 477-0777)* and **Union Square Cafe** *(21 East 16th Street, ☎ 243-4020)* have set the pace for fresh newcomers seeking to please an audience of discriminating diners.

Several excellent restaurants in this area offer a discount to **for less** cardholders. **Portfolio** (page 122) and **Caffe Bondi** (page 123), for example, provide top-notch food and service at moderate prices.

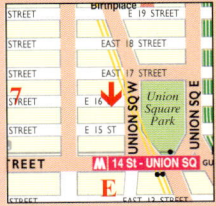

Union Square

Portfolio in the Flatiron District

Around the square, **Heartland Brewery** (page 122) makes their own beers on the premises, serves hearty food to complement the brews and is lively and fun. Across the square, **Barocco Kitchen** (page 122) is a great place to enjoy a light lunch in a chic setting.

When visiting the Empire State Building, feast on an over-stuffed sandwich at **Mendy's East** (page 123), a kosher, deli-style restaurant and steakhouse just a block away on 34th Street.

Cafe Mozart

Café

110 West 25th Street
☎ 807-8763

Average meal: $5-10
for less discount: 25%
No credit cards

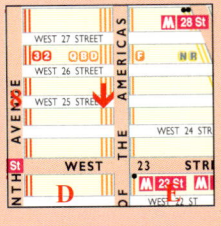

HOURS

Tue-Sun: 11am-6pm
Mon: closed

On the eighth floor of the Chelsea Antiques Center, Cafe Mozart serves a variety of coffees, teas and fresh-baked goods. The soups and sandwiches are great at lunchtime, after browsing the many antique shops in the building.

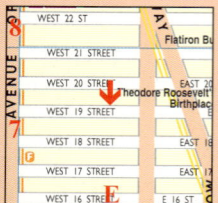

HOURS

Mon-Thu: 11am-11pm
Fri-Sat: 11am-12midnight
Sun: 11am-10pm

Portfolio

Italian

4 West 19th Street
☎ **691-3845**

Average meal: $20-25
for less discount: 25%
AM/MC/VS/DC

This charming restaurant offers high quality food and service at great prices. The décor is chic and the limited edition artwork on the walls is for sale. Portfolio's homemade pasta dishes and daily specials are superb.

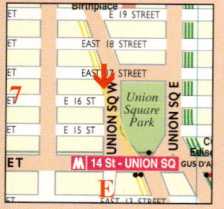

HOURS

Mon-Thu: 11pm-11pm
Fri-Sat: 11pm-12midnight
Sun: 12noon-10pm

Heartland Brewery

American / Brewery

35 Union Square West
☎ **645-3400**

Average meal: $15-20
for less discount: 25%
AM/MC/VS/DC

Heartland is located in an historic building with an on-site brewhouse. The setting is a spacious loft with hand-painted murals and wooden booths. An informal menu compliments the wide spectrum of beers available.

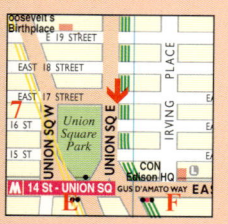

HOURS

Mon-Thurs: 7am-6pm
Fri: 7am-5pm
Sat: 10am-5pm
Sun: closed

Barocco Kitchen

American / International

42 Union Square East
☎ **254-6777**

Average meal: $10-15
for less discount: 25%
AM/MC/VS

On Union Square, Barocco Kitchen serves a variety of freshly made international dishes in a modern café setting. House specialties include vegetable and meat lasagna and fresh salads.

Cafe Bondi

Italian

7 West 20th Street
☎ **691-8136**

Average meal: $25-30
for less discount: 25%
AM/MC/VS/DC

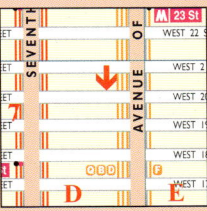

HOURS

Mon-Sat: 12noon-10pm
Sun: 12noon-9.30pm

Sicilian cuisine is the specialty at this elegant, romantic restaurant. A cozy dining room and an airy garden enhance the dining experience. *Pasta con sarde* and *calamaretti alla griglia* are both excellent dishes.

Mendy's East

Delicatessen / Kosher

61 East 34th Street
☎ **576-1010**

Average meal: $15-20
for less discount: 25%
AM/MC/VS/DC/DS

HOURS

Mon-Thu, Sun:
11am-10pm
Fri: 11am-3pm
Sat: closed

Mendy's East is located near the Empire State Building. It is an ideal place to enjoy lunch or dinner after visiting the attraction. This kosher restaurant serves a full range of tasty steaks and sandwiches and deli items.

Cafe Inferno

Californian / Mediterranean

165 Eighth Avenue
☎ **989-2330**

Average meal: $15-20
for less discount: 25%
AM/MC/VS

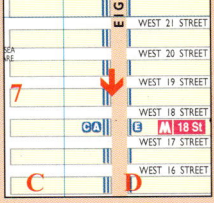

HOURS

Mon-Wed: 12noon-1am
Thu-Sat: 11am-2am
Sun: 11am-12midnight

This cozy bistro serves excellent Californian/ Mediterranean cuisine. Cafe Inferno features a gourmet wood-burning brick oven. One of the recommended specialities is the vanilla-marinated lobster tail.

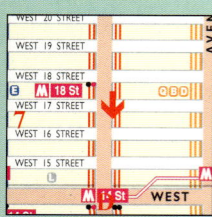

Loehmann's

Shopping

Chelsea is well-known as a retail destination. Discount superstore **Loehmann's** *(101 Seventh Avenue, ☎ 352-0856)* can be found here as well as smaller clothing and gift boutiques, which carry designer clothing and home furnishings. For sportswear and casual clothing, **Starting Line** (see below) and **Chelsea Army and Navy** (page 126) sell all the major brands.

Around the corner from **Emporio Armani** *(110 Fifth Avenue, ☎ 727-3240)*, **Carapan** (page 126) is a quiet retreat which has a choice selection of bath, body and hair care products. A great place to buy an unusual gift is Gramercy Park's **Recherché** (page 125) – a favorite stop for young Hollywood actresses visiting New York City.

Starting Line

Clothing & Athletic Wear

180 Eighth Avenue
☎ 691-4729

for less discount: 20%
AM/MC/VS/DS

Starting Line offers stylish designer clothing for men and women, including a wide variety of jeans, jackets, shoes and bags. Popular brands like Adidas, French Connection and Puma are all stocked.

Avenue A Cards

Posters, Gifts & Cards

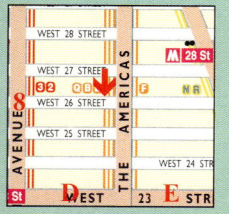

117 West 26th Street
☎ 352-3110

for less discount: 20%
AM/MC/VS/DS

Located near the Annex Antiques Fair and Flea Market (see page 112), this shop offers an enormous selection of music, movie and art posters, cards and gifts. Vintage European and American reprints are also available.

HOURS

Mon-Thu: 11am-9pm
Fri-Sat: 11am-10pm
Sun: 12noon-7pm

HOURS

Mon-Sun: 10am-7pm

Recherché

Gifts

171 Third Avenue
☎ 979-1415

for less discount: 20%
AM/MC/VS

This elegant shop is the perfect place to find a unique gift. Items range from one-of-a-kind handmade objects to antique collectibles. Jewelry, pillows and specialty items are available, many made by local artisans.

 ## Decor Art Gallery

Art Gallery & Poster Shop

158 Seventh Avenue
☎ 604-9864

for less discount: 20%
AM/MC/VS

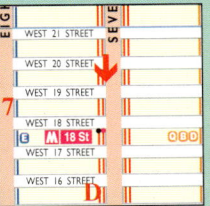

This shop carries a large selection of posters and art covering many subjects. The *for less* discount also applies at the other Decor Art Galleries located at 353 Third Avenue and 333 Park Avenue.

 ## Cambridge Camera Shop

Cameras & Electronics

119 West 17th Street
☎ 675-8600

for less discount: 20%
AM/MC/VS/DS

For 35 years, this shop has provided excellent prices and helpful service. It carries new and used photographic and electronic equipment. Rental, repair and film developing are also offered.

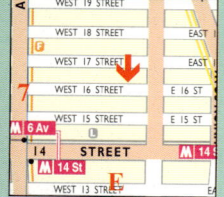

Sat-Wed: 10am-6.45pm
Thu-Fri: 10am-7.45pm
Sun: 12noon-5.30pm

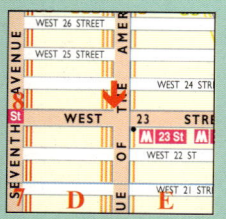

HOURS

Mon-Sun: 10am-9.30pm

HOURS

Mon-Fri: 9am-5pm
Sun: 10am-7pm
Sat: closed

Chelsea Army and Navy

Army Navy & Clothing

111 Eighth Avenue
☎ 645-7420

for less discount: 20%
AM/MC/VS/DS

Chelsea Army and Navy offers sports apparel and army navy gear, including a large range of jackets, shoes and boots. A solid selection of well-known brands includes clothing and accessories for both men and women.

Carapan

Gifts

5 West 16th Street
☎ 633-6220

for less discount: 20%
AM/MC/VS

Carapan sells a fine selection of natural bath, body and hair care products. Cards, candles, incense and oils are also available. There are various Native American items including "dreamcatchers" and decorations.

Galaxy Army & Navy

Army Navy & Clothing

859 Sixth Avenue
☎ 736-1166

for less discount: 20%
AM/MC/VS/DS

Galaxy Army and Navy stocks a full range of outdoor and military gear. Apparel includes jeans, jackets, boots, camping equipment and accessories. Brand names include Lee, Levi's and Timberland.

Midtown West

Introduction . . .

Midtown West is the area which best exemplifies the busy streets of New York City seen on television and in the movies. The area is essentially commercial – filled with tall office buildings and notorious for its "midtown traffic".

Busy midtown streets

Entering the lower midtown from Chelsea, you will easily be able to identify your entrance into the **Garment District** (page 142) by the delivery trucks holding up traffic and the clothing trolleys delaying pedestrians along Seventh Avenue – known here as "**Fashion Avenue**".

Before the late 19th century, **Herald Square**, named after the defunct Herald newspaper, was one of the seedier areas of New York. After the giant **Macy's** department store (page 142) was established in the late 1800s, however, it became a popular commercial and shopping district, a character that it retains to this day.

For visitors, Midtown West is best known for its **Theater District**. Although the majority of commercial theaters here are actually located on the side streets *off* Broadway, the term "Broadway" has come to collectively represent all the major theaters in the area.

Broadway at 34th Street, ca. 1910

This neighborhood has shown signs of becoming a center for New York theaters since the latter half of the 19th century. When the *New York Times* built their offices above what was known as Longacre Square, at the beginning of the 20th century, the newly named "**Times Square**" was connected to the subway system and quickly brought the hub of the Theater District to its present location.

Of the 40 or so active theaters, 22 of them have been designated historical landmarks. **The Lyceum** is the oldest and has operated continuously since it was built in 1903. The nearby **Shubert Theatre** welcomed an unknown Barbra Streisand in her 1962 Broadway debut.

Today, Times Square sees one-and-a-half million people pass through every day. It is famous for its

DON'T MISS

If you visit New York in early December, you might catch the annual lighting of the Christmas Tree at Rockefeller Center. The enormous tree is lit with over 20,000 bulbs and the ceremony has become a New York tradition.

. . . Introduction

colossal neon signs, giant billboards and the neon apple that falls annually to ring in the New Year.

Recently, an aggressive make-over campaign has focused on shaking Times Square's grimy reputation. The closing of "adult" film theaters and shops along 42nd Street, coupled with major corporate openings like the **Virgin Megastore**, **All-Star Cafe** and **Disney Store** have literally changed the face of the area.

Times Square

Bryant Park (page 137), the only major park in Midtown Manhattan, was the site of the 1853 World's Fair. It had endured a long period of decay in this century before being closed in 1989 for a complete make-over. Today, this tree-lined grassy expanse, with its neatly manicured lawns, is a great place to retreat from the hectic midtown sidewalks.

The **International Center of Photography Midtown** (page 135) mounts some excellent photographic exhibits, often focusing on a particular genre or artist. Further north, you can experience three major New York City museums in just a few short blocks – the **Museum of Modern Art**, known as MoMA (page 130-131), the **American Craft Museum** (page 134) and **The Museum of Television and Radio** (page 132).

One of New York's most popular tourist attractions, **Rockefeller Center** (page 135) is great to visit all year round. The best time to come here, however, is during the holidays when the giant Christmas tree is lit in front of the GE Building and ice skaters fill the rink below.

Around the corner, the legendary **Radio City Music Hall** is famous for its quality productions, and its *Christmas Spectacular*, which continues to draw the crowds year after year. The **Grand Tour** (page 133) provides a fascinating look behind-the-scenes at this landmark Art Deco building.

Along the Hudson River, you can visit the aircraft carrier ***USS Intrepid*** which is now the centerpiece of the **Intrepid Sea-Air-Space Museum** (page 134). Once a year, sailors from the U.S. Navy gather here for "Fleet Week". Although this is not an event that most New Yorkers take part in, they are reminded of its existence when they suddenly notice packs of uniformed sailors filling the streets.

Christmas Tree at Rockefeller Center

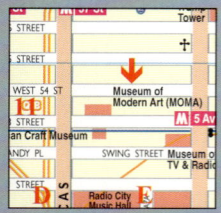

ADDRESS

Museum and MoMA Book Store:
11 West 53rd Street
☎ 708-9400

MoMA Design Store:
44 West 53rd Street
☎ 708-9669

HOURS

Museum:
Sat-Tue and Thu:
10.30am-6pm
Fri: 10.30am-8:30pm
Wed: closed

MoMA Book Store:
Sat-Tue: 11am-6.30pm
Thu-Fri: 11am-9pm
Wed: closed

MoMA Design Store:
Sat-Wed: 10am-8pm
Thu-Fri: 10am-9pm

 # The Museum of Modern Art . . .

The Museum of Modern Art holds the world's premier collection of modern art. Its unrivaled selection of 20th-century artists ranges from **Picasso** to **Warhol**, **Monet** to **Matisse**. Even if you're not very familiar with modern art, you will recognize many works here.

Girl with Ball (1961) by Roy Lichtenstein

The Museum of Modern Art opened its first exhibition in 1929, displaying Post-Impressionist artists such as **Cézanne**, **Gauguin**, **Seurat** and Van Gogh who were hardly known in the United States at the time.

This new museum generated an immediate response from an appreciative public who were eager to learn more about the art of their day. In the first ten years of its life, the museum outgrew four temporary homes before moving into its current building.

Since its founding, the collection has grown to include approximately 100,000 paintings, sculptures, drawings, architectural models and plans, prints, photographs and design objects. The museum now receives over one-and-a-half million visitors each year.

Among the museum's finest (and most famous) paintings are Claude Monet's *Water Lilies*; Pablo Picasso's *Les Demoiselles d'Avignon*; Henri Matisse's *Dance*; **René Magritte**'s *The False Mirror*; Salvador Dali's *The Persistence of Memory* and Andy Warhol's *Gold Marilyn Monroe*. Perhaps the best known and most treasured painting is **Vincent Van Gogh**'s *The Starry Night*.

Sculpture Garden at MoMA

You will probably want to start your visit to the museum in the **Painting and Sculpture** galleries, situated on the second and third floors. There you will find major artists and movements from **Post-Impressionism** to **Pop Art**, including the majority of the museum's most famous works.

The second floor also houses the **Drawings** galleries, featuring works on paper by **Paul Klee**, Henri Matisse, **Georgia O'Keeffe** and **Robert Rauschenberg** as well as drawings that focus on a particular movement such as **Surrealism** and **Dada**.

The **Photography** galleries, on the second floor, span

. . . The Museum of Modern Art

the entire history of the medium, including works by
Cartier-Bresson and **Stieglitz**.

On the third floor, the **Prints and Illustrated Books
Collection** covers artists from over 60 countries,
including an impressive selection of works by Picasso.
Diverse and expansive, it features lithographs,
etchings, screenprints and woodcuts.

One of the most unusual collections is that of
Architecture and Design, located on the fourth floor.
Architectural models and plans are featured alongside
design objects which range from household appliances
and furniture to high-tech equipment such as a
Bell helicopter and a Formula One race car.

The Museum of Modern Art was the first
museum to recognize the motion picture as an
art form. Since 1935, it has been collecting
and preserving important films. It now
possesses some ten thousand films as well as
four million film stills from all periods and
genres. Screenings are held daily in two
theaters, and video exhibitions are scheduled
on a regular basis.

In addition to its permanent collection, MoMA
also mounts large temporary exhibitions.
Indeed, of the 87,000 square feet of gallery
space, 20,000 is reserved for temporary
exhibitions that display works and retrospective
studies of modern and contemporary artists.

The museum's renowned publishing program
has produced more than 500 books on the
visual arts including exhibition catalogues,
books on modern art, books that illustrate the
museum's collections and an annual journal called
Studies in Modern Art. Many of these can be
purchased at The MoMA Stores, which offer a discount
to *for less* cardholders.

The Museum of Modern Art was the first New York City
museum to offer a random-access **digital audio guide**
for their permanent collection. It allows you to
explore the museum's painting and sculpture galleries
at your own pace. You can select up to three hours of
commentary by the museum's director and top
curators, who provide fresh insights and information
about the works and the artists who created them.
With the vouchers at the back of the book, you can
obtain a discount on admission *and* two audio tours for
the price of one, as well as a 10% discount in the
MoMA stores.

PRICES

Adult $9.50
Child (under 16) free
Senior $6.50
Student $6.50

*Number 10 (1950)
by Mark Rothko*

DISCOUNT

$1 off admission with
voucher on page 273.

2 audio guides for the
price of 1 with
voucher on page 275.

10% discount in the
MoMA stores with
voucher on page 275.

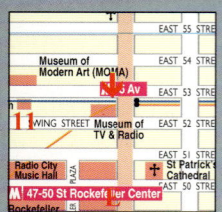

ADDRESS

25 West 52nd Street
☎ 621-6800

HOURS

Mon: closed
Tue-Wed and Sat-Sun:
12noon-6pm
Thu: 12noon-8pm
Fri: 12noon-6pm, theater
open until 9pm

PRICES

Suggested admission:
Adult $6
Child $3
Senior $4
Student $4

DISCOUNT

20% discount at the
museum shop with
voucher on page 275.

DON'T MISS

An individual screening of
your past favorite TV or
radio program or
advertisement.

 # The Museum of TV & Radio

Founded by **William S. Paley**, former head of the giant
CBS network, The Museum of Television & Radio is a
unique museum experience. It gives you the
opportunity to enjoy television and radio programs
spanning the entire history of the media.

Today, the museum possesses some 75,000 programs
from more than 75 years of television and radio
history. The programs include everything from news
and public affairs to documentaries and performing

arts. There are also
children's programs,
sports, comedy,
variety shows and
even commercial
advertising. You can
watch or listen to
everything from news
coverage of World
War II to **The Beatles**,
playing on the **Ed
Sullivan Show**.

The entire collection
is catalogued in a
computerized library
database which
allows you to
privately screen or
listen to a program of
your choice. By

The Museum of TV and Radio

making a reservation at the front desk when you arrive,
you can select up to six programs at a time. You then
go to an individual television and radio console where
you can watch or listen to your selections.

Exhibitions, a screening and listening series, seminars
and education classes are offered throughout the year.
Every day, the museum presents programs in the two
main theaters and two screening rooms. Copies of the
daily schedule are available at the lobby front desk.

The seminars consist of in-person discussions with
prominent writers, producers, directors, actors and
others recognized for their work in programming.
There are also galleries with exhibits relating to
television and radio.

The museum's shop is located on the main floor and
offers T-shirts, posters, cassettes, postcards and other
gift items. There are also books on subjects related to
television and radio. With the voucher on page 275,
you can receive a 20% discount off all goods.

Radio City Music Hall Grand Tour

Radio City Music Hall, one of New York City's premier entertainment venues, is a landmark Art Deco building situated around the corner from Rockefeller Center. Opened in 1932, it escaped demolition in 1979 and

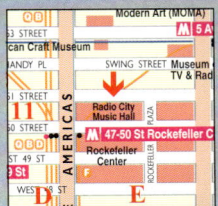

Radio City Music Hall

has since been beautifully restored.

Radio City is probably most famous for its Rockettes – the dance troupe that draws over a million spectators to its annual *Radio City Christmas Spectacular*, a 90-minute holiday show in which Santa Claus makes a cameo appearance. The *Radio City Spring Spectacular* is also very popular, especially with children. The theater also hosts first-rate live music acts and special events throughout the year.

Professional guides lead you through the one-hour **Grand Tour** offering behind-the-scene views of the theater's remarkable history and Art Deco architectural splendor.

You will meet one of the **Radio City Rockettes**, visit the costume shop and see 60 years worth of history-making fabrics, patterns and costume sketches. You can also explore the celebrated Art Deco interior with its block-long **Grand Foyer**, 24-carat gold leaf ceiling, sweeping staircase and pair of two-ton glass chandeliers.

You see first-hand the incredible technology involved in creating these productions, including "curtains" that create steam and rain, a **Wurlitzer organ** that weighs 5 tons and has pipes ranging in size from a few inches to 32 feet. You will learn about a stage elevator system so sophisticated that its design was borrowed by the U.S. Navy for aircraft carriers during World War II.

The Art Deco interior of Radio City Music Hall

Tours depart approximately every half hour from Radio City Music Hall's main lobby at the corner of Sixth Avenue and 50th Street. With the *for less* voucher on page 275, you receive a free tour for every one purchased.

ADDRESS

1260 Avenue of the Americas
☎ 632-4041

HOURS

Mon-Sat: 10am-5pm
Sun: 11am-5pm
Tours depart approximately every half hour.

PRICES

Adult $13.75
Child $9
Senior $13.75
Student $13.75

DISCOUNT

2 tours for the price of 1 with voucher on page 275.

Intrepid Sea-Air-Space Museum

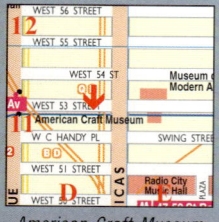

American Craft Museum

Other Attractions . . .

The Intrepid Sea-Air-Space Museum is housed aboard the aircraft carrier *USS Intrepid*. Docked on the Hudson River, a short distance from Midtown Manhattan, this World War II vessel has weathered bombs, kamikazes and torpedoes. It was designated a National Historic Landmark and, after 37 years of active duty, it is now the world's largest naval museum. It offers a complete history of naval aviation, space and undersea exploration.

In addition to the *Intrepid*, other painstakingly restored historic ships include the guided nuclear missile submarine *Growler* and the large fleet destroyer *Edson*. Also part of the flotilla are the Coast Guard cutter *Tamaroa*, which sits next to another World War II veteran, the destroyer escort *Slater* and the operational school ship *Elizabeth M. Fisher*. Touring these ships gives you a first-hand look at life at sea.

Exhibits focus on subjects such as World War II, the history of undersea and space exploration, aircraft and ship design and satellite communication. You can also see the world's fastest plane, a CIA spy plane, the *Lockheed A-12 Blackbird*, as well as a Russian *MIG 21*.

The SR-2 simulator takes visitors through a series of fast-moving maneuvers in less than seven minutes. This is a great place for children and, with *New York for less*, all admission prices are reduced 20%. *(Hudson River at 46th Street, ☎ 245-2533. Mon-Sat: 10am-5pm. Sun: 10am-6pm (summer). Wed-Sun: 10am-5pm. Mon-Tue: closed (winter). Adult $10, child (12-17) $7.50, child (6-11) $5, child (2-5) $1, senior and veteran $7.50, student $7.50. 20% off admission with voucher on page 275.)*

The interior of the American Craft Museum

The American Craft Museum recently celebrated its 40th year as America's most significant resource for 20th-century craft objects. Its mission is to collect, exhibit and preserve contemporary crafts and interpret their evolution over the course of the 20th century.

Since it opened in 1956, the museum has showcased the work of American craftspeople whose handmade

. . . Other Attractions . . .

objects are not only appreciated for their beauty, but also recognized for their spirit in a world of machine-made products.

The museum's extensive collection dates from 1900 and contains an interesting and innovative mix of furniture and crafts.

Over the years, there have been numerous major exhibitions ranging from the simple to the unusual. Two examples of previous exhibits are *The Ideal Home: 1900-1920* and *"Edible Drawings" by John Cage*. The museum also organizes exhibitions that tour the nation.

American Craft Museum

Artists represented here have worked in a variety of media including ceramics, glass, metal, wood and plastic – often using the materials in unconventional

ways. You can see the results of modern techniques upon traditional crafts such as the updated art of gold and silversmithing.

Educational programs strive to enhance public awareness of

ICP Midtown

contemporary crafts, while workshops teach craftmaking techniques. *(40 West 53rd Street, ☎ 956-3535. Tue-Wed and Fri-Sun: 10am-6pm. Thu: 10am-8pm. Mon: closed. Adult $5, child free, senior $2.50, student $2.50. 50% off admission with the voucher on page 275.)*

The International Center of Photography Midtown is one of the few museums in the world devoted solely to photography. The main ICP (page 186) is located on Museum Mile. The midtown branch of this renowned photographic institution is housed in a modern building a block away from Bryant Park. Exhibits generally highlight a particular genre or photographer. *(1133 Sixth Avenue, ☎ 768-4680. Tue-Thu: 10am-5pm. Fri: 10am-8pm. Sat-Sun: 10am-6pm. Mon: closed. Adult $6, child $1, senior $4, student $4. 50% off admission with voucher on page 277.)*

Built between 1931 and 1940 by oil tycoon John D. Rockefeller, **Rockefeller Center** was originally comprised of 14 buildings. Today, it occupies almost three city blocks. A total of 19 buildings are within the complex, including Radio City Music Hall (page 133). The tallest building and centerpiece of the complex is the 70-story **GE Building** *(30 Rockefeller*

INSIDER'S TIP

On Tuesdays, from 6pm-8pm, ICP Midtown has a pay-what-you-wish admission policy.

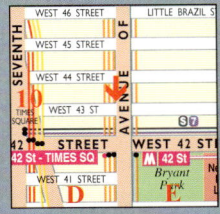

International Center of Photography

. . . Other Attractions . . .

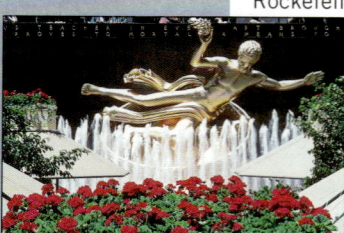
Rockefeller Center

Plaza), the headquarters of America's largest company. Rockefeller Center was declared a landmark in 1985 and is the largest privately owned business and entertainment center in the world. *(47th-50th Streets, between Fifth and Sixth Avenues.)*

At Rockefeller Plaza, **NBC Studios** currently opens three shows to guests: *Saturday Night Live*, *The Rosie O'Donnell Show* and *Late Night with Conan O'Brien*. For most shows, you must write for tickets months in advance, but for *Late Night with Conan O' Brien*, a limited number of tickets are given out Tuesday through Friday, at 9am in NBC's main lobby, on the day of the show. Call 664-4000 for more information or to make a reservation. *(30 Rockefeller Plaza, ☎ 664-4000. Hours vary.)*

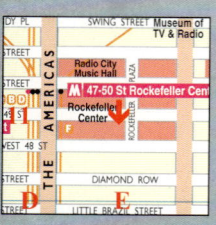
30 Rockefeller Plaza

Ed Sullivan Theater

The **Late Show with David Letterman**, which was once based in the GE Building at Rockefeller Plaza, is now taped at the **Ed Sullivan Theater**. *(1697 Broadway, ☎ 975-1003 for ticket information.)*

New York Public Library

The New York Public Library is New York City's main public research center. The interior is just as grand as the impressive facade where granite lions guard the entrance. The library hosts various exhibits and offers free one-hour tours Monday through Saturday at 11am and 2pm starting from the "friends desk" in Astor Hall. *(Fifth Avenue and 42nd Street, ☎ 661-7220. Mon, Wed and Fri: 10am-6pm. Tue and Thu: 11am-7.30pm. Sun: closed.)*

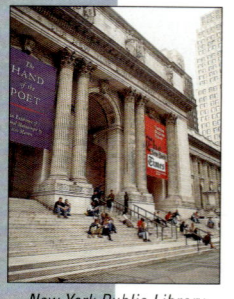
New York Public Library

Jacob K. Javits Convention Center, which opened in 1986, is a 15-story glass building on the Hudson River which was designed for large-scale expositions and conventions. *(655 West 34th Street, ☎ 216-2000.)*

Shubert Alley, named after theater legend Sam S. Shubert, describes those theaters located west of Broadway on 44th and 45th Streets. The 1913 **Shubert Theater** is where *A Chorus Line* broke records as one of the longest running shows in Broadway history. Also of historical and architectural interest is **The Booth Theater**, built in the same year. *(Shubert Alley: West 44th-45th Streets. Shubert Theater: 221 West 45th Street. Booth Theater: 22 West 45th Street.)*

. . . Other Attractions

Built in 1924, the **City Center of Music and Drama** is a magnificently detailed Moorish-style Masonic Shriners' Temple that later became home to the New York City Opera and Ballet. Today, no longer affiliated with the opera or ballet, the exquisitely restored City Center is still an important venue for dance performances. *(131 West 55th Street, ☎ 581-7909.)*

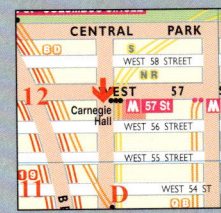

Carnegie Hall

Carnegie Hall, New York's first and most prestigious concert hall, was financed by steel magnate Andrew Carnegie. Tchaikovsky conducted the opening performance in 1891. After being saved from destruction in the late 1950s, the building was declared a landmark. A refurbishment in 1986 restored the hall to its former glory. In 1991, Carnegie Hall opened an exhibit celebrating its first 100 years. Top American and international artists still perform here regularly. *(57th Street and Seventh Avenue, ☎ 247-7800.)*

Carnegie Hall at night

Open Spaces

Nestling behind the New York Public Library, **Bryant Park** seems like it would be more at home in Paris than in New York City. Its shady perimeter consists of a stone path where, in warm weather, folding chairs are set out for the hordes of office workers who descend upon the park at lunchtime.

Bryant Park

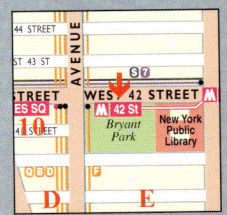

Bryant Park

A few years ago, it was chosen as the location for New York's **semi-annual fashion shows**. These shows attract huge crowds and have helped lend a more sophisticated image to what was, not long ago, a run-down and dangerous park.

Throughout the summer, the park holds a variety of free cultural events including concerts and outdoor movies shown on a giant screen at sunset.

Channel Gardens at Rockefeller Center is set between the British Empire Building and La Maison Française. It is a great place to relax after a busy day of sightseeing and shopping. The mermaid and dolphin fountains are surrounded by fresh flowers, making a great background for photo-taking.

Channel Gardens at Rockefeller Center

Eating and Drinking . . .

Until recently, Times Square was not only packed with traffic but also with over-priced, fast food restaurants of the worst quality. New Yorkers generally skipped this area altogether and headed to the side streets instead.

Today, the revitalization of Times Square has brought the quality of its restaurants to a new level, and many theme restaurants have found a home here as well. The **Official All Star Cafe** *(1540 Broadway (at 45th Street),* ☎ *840-8326)* is a tribute to the world of sports. Celebrity sports stars and stockholders such as Andre Agassi, Shaquille O'Neal and Tiger Woods make frequent appearances.

Planet Hollywood *(140 West 57th Street,* ☎ *333-7827)* also capitalizes on celebrity stockholders. In this case they happen to be some of the world's most famous movie stars – Arnold Schwarzenegger, Sylvester Stallone, Bruce Willis and Demi Moore are just a few of the recognizable faces occasionally spotted in Planet Hollywood.

Planet Hollywood

Also on 57th Street are the music-based theme restaurants **Hard Rock Cafe** *(221 West 57th Street,* ☎ *489-6565)* and **Motown Cafe** *(104 West 57th Street,* ☎ *581-8030)*. Motown Cafe takes its theme a step further by providing live entertainment. The "Motown Moments" take the stage every hour to perform some of Motown's greatest hits live. You can check out memorabilia including costumes and props used by legendary acts, or climb a stairway made of gold records acheived by Motown artists.

Motown Cafe

Despite the fact that jaded New Yorkers would never admit it, theme restaurants actually *can* be fun to visit and the food is of surprisingly good quality.

The legendary **"21" Club** *(21 West 52nd Street,* ☎ *582-7200)* first gained its famous reputation as a speakeasy. A secret door leads to the wine cellar, located in the basement of an adjoining building. During prohibition raids, the police would search the

. . . Eating and Drinking

entire building, never realizing that the goods weren't actually in the building at all. This brownstone landmark building (still flanked by its trademark jockey statues) retains the clublike atmosphere it had in bygone days, though a new executive chef has brought a fresh perspective on its classic cuisine.

Hardrock Cafe

More than 50,000 bottles, including many tagged with the names of their celebrity owners, make its wine cellar one of the world's largest.

Many of the restaurants on the following pages, all of which give a discount to *for less* cardholders, are in, or near, the Theater District.

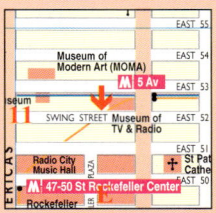

The "21" Club

At **Commonwealth Brewery** (see below) you can take a break from sightseeing to enjoy fine food and home-brewed beer at Rockefeller Center.

If outdoor dining is on your agenda, or you simply crave some good Italian fare, **Zi Teresa** (page 140) would be a good choice. Other Italian options where you can use your *for less* card are **Maristella** (page 140) and **Il Brunello** (page 140).

For good food in a casual and lively atmosphere, you can dine at **Mike's American Bar and Grill** (page 140).

 Commonwealth Brewing Company

International / Brewery

35 West 48th Street
☎ **977-2269**

Average meal: $20-25
for less discount: 25%
AM/MC/VS/DC/DS

At Rockefeller Center, this spacious brew-pub serves interesting international dishes and a variety of carefully crafted beers in an upbeat atmosphere. Try the Bavarian butcher's skillet or the CBNY charbroiled angus burger.

HOURS

Mon-Sat: 11.30am-11pm
Sun: 12noon-7pm

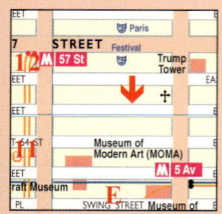

HOURS

Mon-Fri: 11.30am-
10.30pm
Sat: 4.30pm-10.30pm
Sun: closed

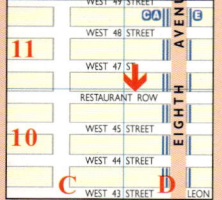

HOURS

Mon-Sun: 12noon-
12midnight

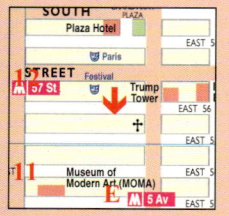

HOURS

Mon-Sun:
11.30am-10.30pm

Maristella

Italian

69 West 55th Street
☎ 489-7655

Average meal: $15-20
for less discount: 25%
AM/MC/VS/DC/DS

Maristella serves Italian fare in a comfortable, modern setting. The homemade ravioli and seafood dishes are recommended. Open at 11.30am, Maristella is a good choice for pre-theater lunch or dinner.

Broadway Joe's Steakhouse

American / Steakhouse

315 West 46th Street
☎ 246-6513

Average meal: $20-25
for less discount: 25%
AM/MC/VS/DC/DS

This landmark restaurant is a favorite with sports and theater celebrities. It has been serving the best in prime meats and seafood for 50 years. A "Wall of Fame" pictorial reflects the surrounding Broadway theaters.

Il Brunello

Italian

56 West 56th Street
☎ 247-2779

Average meal: $15-20
for less discount: 25%
AM/MC/VS/DC

This friendly family-run restaurant offers good northern Italian fare. Il Brunello is convenient to midtown shopping and the Broadway theaters. Try any of the pasta dishes or the veal and chicken combination.

Mike's American Bar and Grill

American

650 Tenth Avenue
☎ **246-4115**

Average meal: $15-20
for less discount: 25%
AM/MC/VS

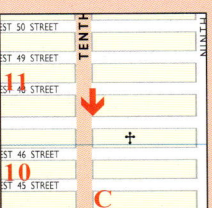

HOURS

Sun-Mon: 5pm-11pm
Tue-Sat: 5.30pm-
12midnight
Sat-Sun (brunch):
11am-4pm

Mike's is a casual, theme restaurant a short walk from the Theater District. Previous themes include musicals, TV shows and movies like *Star Wars*. You can enjoy hearty dishes like grilled pork chops and pastas.

MK Restaurant

Continental

440 Ninth Avenue
☎ **629-0744**

Average meal: $15-20
for less discount: 25%
AM/MC/VS/DC/DS

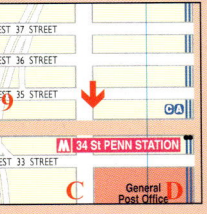

HOURS

Mon-Fri: 11.30am-3pm,
5pm-9.30pm
Sat-Sun: closed

MK has been serving continental cuisine at reasonable prices for over 15 years. The décor is modern and the atmosphere is warm and friendly. Recommended dishes are breast of chicken Dijon and beef stroganoff.

Zi Teresa

Italian

417 Ninth Avenue
☎ **563-0708**

Average meal: $15-20
for less discount: 25%
AM/MC/VS

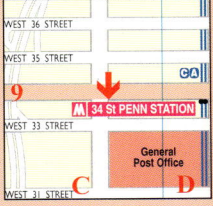

HOURS

Mon-Fri: 11.30am-9.30pm
Sat: 5pm-10pm
Sun: closed

This friendly, casual restaurant serves tasty Italian cuisine. Zi Teresa offers seating in the outdoor garden in warm weather. Recommended dishes include *pollo zi teresa* and *vitello castelli*.

Shopping . . .

The Garment District *(Seventh Avenue between 34th and 42nd Streets)* is the heart of the fashion industry. Top designers and their expensive creations are tucked away in showrooms high above Seventh Avenue, which is known here as "**Fashion Avenue**".

Lord & Taylor

Practically a local phenomenon, "sample sales" are more akin to a sport than a pleasant diversion as women play tug-of-war with designer threads at incredibly reduced prices. Finding these sales is also something of a sport, since they are generally unadvertised and only last several hours or, at best, several days. Your best bet is to look out for leaflets which are often distributed on the streets in the Garment District announcing these sales.

On **Diamond Row** *(47th Street between Fifth and Sixth Avenues)* practically every shop window sparkles with diamonds and gold. The area became a center for the jewelry trade early in the century, when Jewish diamond merchants emigrated from Amsterdam.

Diamond Row

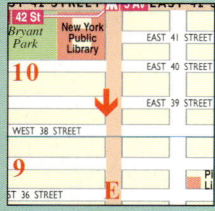
Lord & Taylor

Times Square is a mecca for electronic and souvenir shops. **Santino Photos** (page 144) carries souvenirs as well as photographic and electronic equipment. Nearby, **Triton Gallery** (page 144), in the Theater District, specializes in Broadway-themed posters and prints.

Midtown West is home to many of New York's big department stores including **Macy's** *(Herald Square at 34th Street, ☎ 695-4400)*, the world's largest. Its annual televised **Thanksgiving Day Parade** faithfully entertains the nation with gigantic character balloons, which float down Fifth Avenue. Across the street, **Manhattan Mall** *(Sixth Avenue and 33rd Street)* is a suburban shopping mall in the middle of Manhattan.

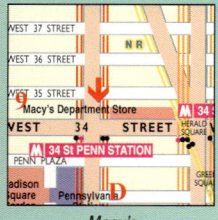
Macy's

On Fifth Avenue, **Lord & Taylor** *(424 Fifth Avenue, ☎ 391-3344)* is best known for its classic American styles. During its winter sales, you can find timeless items like cashmere sweaters at substantial savings. **Bergdorf**

. . . Shopping

Goodman *(754 Fifth Avenue, ☎ 753-7300)* and **Henri Bendel** *(712 Fifth Avenue, ☎ 247-1100)* tend to be quite expensive, though the quality of their merchandise is outstanding.

Many designer boutiques line Fifth Avenue (see also Midtown East shopping, page 155) including famous (as in famously expensive) jeweler **Harry Winston** *(718 Fifth Avenue, ☎ 245-2000)*. Even Hollywood stars who wear Winston's jewels to the Academy

Macy's at Herald Square

Awards *borrow* them. This is exactly what makes this museum-like store worth a peek.

MASH Army and Navy

Army Navy & Clothing

721 Eighth Avenue
☎ **765-1500**

for less discount: 20%
AM/MC/VS/DS

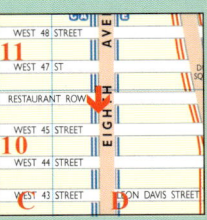

HOURS

Sun-Thu: 10am-8pm
Fri: 9am-4pm
Sat: closed

MASH specializes in outdoor and casual items. Military surplus, camping gear, work shoes and boots are all available, as well as casual shirts, shoes, boots and jeans in a variety of name-brands.

Authentic New York

Clothing

433 Fifth Avenue
☎ **686-0778**

for less discount: 20%
VS/MC/DC/DS

HOURS

Mon-Sat: 9am-8pm
Sun: 10am-7pm

A huge stock of denim includes Calvin Klein, Guess and Levi's 501. Ralph Lauren clothing and Schott's leather can also be found. You can also find T-shirts, sweat shirts and other casual clothing, as well as accesories.

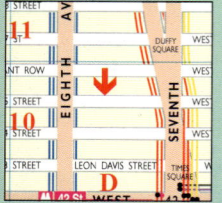

HOURS

Mon-Fri: 7.30am-6.30pm
Sat: 10am-4.30pm
Sun: closed

HOURS

Mon-Sat: 10am-6pm
Sun: 1pm-6pm

HOURS

Mon-Sun: 8am-8pm

Fromex 1 Hour Photo

Film Developing

1369 Sixth Avenue
☎ 307-1848

for less discount: 20% off
color film developing
AM/MC/VS/DS

One-hour photo developing allows you to see your vacation photos before you leave New York. With **New York for less**, you can save 20% when you have your color film developed at this and other Fromex locations.

Triton Gallery

Art Gallery & Posters

323 West 45th Street
☎ 765-2472

for less discount: 20%
AM/MC/VS/DC/DS

Triton carries a large selection of posters and art. Subjects range from classical art works and Broadway musicals to modern designs. You can also bring in your own poster to which they can custom fit a frame.

Santino Photos

Electronics & Souvenirs

1693 Broadway
☎ 397-6062

for less discount: 20%
AM/MC/VS

Santino Photos is stocked with a full range of high quality equipment. You can find laptop computers, video equipment, cameras and more. Top brands available include Sony, Canon, JVC and Panasonic.

Midtown East

Introduction . . .

Midtown East is synonymous with skyscrapers, mega-corporations and Fifth Avenue. From outside Manhattan, you can see the mountainous peaks created by the enormous buildings located here, rising

Grand Central Terminal

like steps to the Empire State Building (pages 114-115) at 34th Street.

What distinguishes Midtown East from New York's other commercial districts is the architectural grandeur of many of its buildings. The 1920s construction boom led to the creation of skyscrapers such as the Empire State Building and the **Chrysler Building** (page 149). Both emerged as permanent fixtures of the Manhattan skyline and both bear the architectural details of the Art Deco era. With its stainless steel gargoyles and shiny hubcap decoration, the Chrysler Building is probably the quintessential example of the Art Deco style. The **Chanin Building** *(122 East 42nd Street)*, the area's first skyscraper, and the **News Building** (page 150) are also notable.

More recently, corporate America's gleaming towers have adopted a simpler style, but have retained the ability to impress with a grandeur all their own. When **Lever House** *(390 Park Avenue)* was built in 1952, it was the first of its kind – sheer faces of glass and steel stood in stark contrast to the stone high-rises which surrounded it. Though Lever House set an architectural precedent, it now stands in the shadow of more modern (and much bigger) skyscrapers like the 1970s Citicorp Center, the IBM Building and the **Sony Building** *(550 Madison Avenue,* ☎ *833-8100)* whose ground floor is filled with interactive workstations, a retail store and hundreds of high-tech toys and games.

The **Met-Life Building** stands astride Park Avenue, dividing it in half, north to south. Cars must actually drive through and around the building in order to cross 42nd Street. Adjacent to it, **Grand Central Terminal** (page 149) is one of the most important transportation hubs in the city. From here, trains carry commuters to and from the nearby New York and Connecticut suburbs. A major renovation inside the main concourse has kept most of the interior under wraps for some time, but the

DON'T MISS

An architectural tour of Midtown East's famous skyscrapers – starting with the Municipal Art Society's free tour of Grand Central Terminal every Wednesday at 12.30pm (page 149).

Art Deco subway station

. . . Introduction

recent unveiling shows a stunning restoration. Future plans include retail space and additional dining throughout the concourse.

Waldorf-Astoria Hotel

Along Park Avenue, block-long residential buildings echo the grand scale of their commercial neighbors. One tribute to turn-of-the-century extravagance is the stunning **Villard Houses** (page 151).

On East 42nd Street, **Tudor City** was developed in the 1920s as a middle-class housing project constructed on an immense scale. Included within the 12 buildings are 3,000 apartments, a hotel, restaurants, shops and parks. The complex even has its own post office.

Murray Hill, situated in the East 30s, is named after the estate that once stood on the site. This residential neighborhood began as an enclave for turn-of-the-century New Yorkers wealthy enough to escape the crowded city downtown. Evidence of their lavish lifestyles can still be seen at the **Pierpont Morgan Library** (page 148), which was founded from J.P. Morgan's private collection. The area's brownstone homes and quiet streets continue to make it one of Manhattan's most desirable residential districts.

The former tradition of the "grand hotel" can still be seen at landmarks such as the **Waldorf-Astoria** (page 42 and 151) and **The Plaza** (page 151) on Central Park South.

Fifth Avenue, the dividing line between Midtown East and Midtown West, is one of the most popular tourist destinations in town. With **Rockefeller Center** (page 135) on one side of the street, **St. Patrick's Cathedral** (page 150) and **Saks Fifth Avenue** (page 155) on the other, and just about every designer shop you could imagine in between, this is one of New York's best shopping and sightseeing areas.

Flags at the United Nations

On the East River, the **United Nations** building (page 149) is recognizable by the huge array of flags flying in front – one for each member nation. Interestingly, the area around the building is international territory and is not subject to United States law.

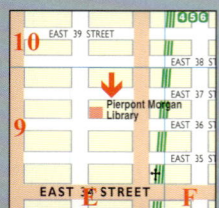

ADDRESS

29 East 36th Street
☎ 685-0610

HOURS

Tue-Thu: 10.30am-5pm
Fri: 10.30am-8pm
Sat: 10.30am-6pm
Sun: 12noon-6pm
Mon: closed
Bookshop closes 15
minutes before galleries.

PRICES

Suggested admission:
Adult $7
Child $3
Senior $5
Student $5

DISCOUNT

10% discount
in the museum
shop with the voucher
on page 277.

DON'T MISS

The autographed
manuscript of Charles
Dickens' *A Christmas
Carol*, the *Gutenberg Bible*
and *The Hours of
Catherine Cleves*.

for less Pierpont Morgan Library

The Pierpont Morgan Library was founded in 1906 by legendary banker **J.P. Morgan** (1837-1913), who wanted to create an American institution for the arts and humanities to rival the great libraries of Europe.

The magnificent result, housed in a Renaissance-style palazzo, is a museum, research library and historic landmark. It is now recognized as one of the world's premier artistic, literary and historical collections. The library's focus is the history, art and literature of Western civilization from the Middle Ages to the 20th century.

After purchasing the 9th-century *Lindau Gospels* in 1899, Morgan went on to acquire nearly 600 medieval and Renaissance manuscripts, many other rare books

Pierpont Morgan Library

and bindings and a number of autographed manuscripts from English and American literary greats such as **Austen**, **Dickens**, **Thoreau** and **Twain**.

His collection also included more than 9,000 drawings and prints from the major French, German, Italian and Dutch schools as well as the country's largest and finest collection of **Rembrandt** etchings. There are also autographed music manuscripts (including Mozart's *Haffner Symphony*), a selection of Islamic manuscripts and roughly 1,200 Mesopotamian cylinder seals. Highlights of the collection are a rare vellum copy of the **Gutenberg Bible**, the medieval Dutch masterpiece *The Hours of Catherine Cleves*, Dürer's *Adam and Eve* and a letter from President George Washington to James Madison.

Following Morgan's death, his son, J.P. Morgan, Jr., increased the library's holdings and, in 1924, helped establish it as a public museum and research institution. Since this time, the collection has continued to grow.

There are tours of the library at 12noon from Tuesday to Friday. The adjacent shop, located in J.P. Morgan, Jr.'s former townhouse, offers items based on the museum's collection and grants a 10% discount to *for less* cardholders.

Other Attractions . . .

Founded in 1945, the **United Nations** is an organization of nations that have banded together to promote world peace. New York was chosen as its

United Nations

headquarters and an $8.5 million donation from John D. Rockefeller, Jr. was used to purchase the site. All of the member nations are represented in the General Assembly, while additional councils are represented by selected delegates from various member nations. The Security Council is the most powerful, and the one most often spotlighted in the media. It is the body that deals with international security and crises, negotiating cease-fires, imposing economic sanctions and deploying military troops. Guided tours of the Security Council Chamber and General Assembly Hall are given daily, and are available in several foreign languages. In the lobby, you can see art and gifts given by various countries, including a chunk of moon rock given by the U.S. and a model of *Sputnik 1* from the Soviet Union. *(First Avenue at 46th Street, ☎ 963-7713. Mon-Sun: 9.15am-4.45pm (Mar-Dec). Mon-Fri: 9.15am-4.45pm. Sat-Sun: closed (Jan-Feb).)*

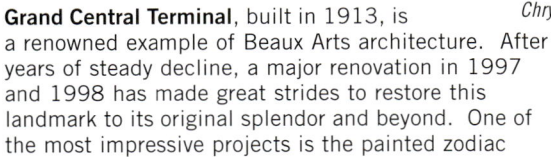
United Nations

Completed in 1930, the 77-story **Chrysler Building** is recognizable by its shining 7-story chrome top. Designed for automobile pioneer Walter P. Chrysler, the building's brilliantly restored lobby once served as a car showroom and the Art Deco tower was designed to look like a car's radiator grill. *(405 Lexington Avenue, ☎ 682-3070. Mon-Fri: 8am-6pm. Sat-Sun: closed.)*

Chrysler Building

Chrysler Building

Grand Central Terminal, built in 1913, is a renowned example of Beaux Arts architecture. After years of steady decline, a major renovation in 1997 and 1998 has made great strides to restore this landmark to its original splendor and beyond. One of the most impressive projects is the painted zodiac

. . . Other Attractions . . .

and constellation design on the turquoise blue ceiling, which has looked gray for years. All throughout Grand Central, the marble sparkles and the lighting fixtures shine. There have also been some practical changes as well, as new retail shops and restaurants are slowly being added throughout the terminal. A food market, newsstands and the legendary Oyster Bar seafood restaurant (page 153) can also be found within the building. The four-faced clock above the information booth is a well-known rendezvous spot in the middle of the enormous concourse. The Municipal Art Society, which was largely responsible for preserving Grand Central as a national landmark, provides free tours every Wednesday at 12.30pm (see page 218). *(East 42nd Street, at Park Avenue, ☎ 935-3960 for tours.)*

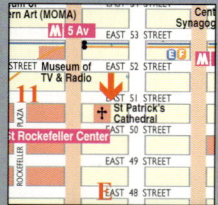

Grand Central Terminal

Across the street, on the ground floor of the Philip Morris Building, there is a branch of the **Whitney Museum** (page 183). Viewing of the 20th-century art exhibits is enhanced by quiet tables and a coffee bar. *(120 Park Avenue, ☎ (917) 663-2550. Mon-Wed and Fri: 11am-6pm. Thu: 11am-7.30pm. Sat-Sun: closed. Admission is free.)*

Grand Central Station

Built in 1931, the **News Building** is home to the *Daily News*, one of New York City's most popular papers, which was founded in 1919. Its lobby contains the largest interior globe in the world and is best known for its role as the home of the *Daily Planet* in the movie *Superman*. *(220 East 42nd Street. Mon-Fri: 8am-6pm. Sat-Sun: closed.)*

St. Patrick's Cathedral

Directly across from Rockefeller Center, **St. Patrick's Cathedral** is the largest and most famous Catholic cathedral in the United States, dedicated to the patron saint of the Irish. Built to seat 2,500 people, it was completed in 1878, but its massive spires, which rise 330 feet into the air, were added seven years later. A well-known New York image consists of these spires juxtaposed with the stark black Olympic Tower next door. As impressive inside as out, some of the

. . . Other Attractions . . .

cathedral's best features include the tremendous Rose Window, the Great Organ and the enormous bronze

doors at the entrance. The parish was moved to its grand Fifth Avenue site from the original downtown St. Patrick's (page 82) which remains in Little Italy. *(5th Avenue and 50th Street, ☎ 753-2261. Mon-Sun: 7.30am-8.30pm. Masses also held daily.)*

St. Patrick's Cathedral

Located behind St. Patrick's, the historic **Villard Houses** are a series of six townhouses designed by architects McKim, Mead & White during the late 19th century. Commissioned by Henry Villard, railroad industrialist and publisher of the *New York Evening Post*, the Italianate houses and elegant courtyard were intended to be residences but later became part of the New York Palace Hotel (page 42). *(457 Madison Avenue.)*

Built in 1931, the world-famous **Waldorf-Astoria Hotel** (page 42) is worth a look just for its elegant lobby. This is the hotel where kings, queens, ambassadors and U.S. presidents stay while visiting New York City. Cole Porter wrote some of his most famous tunes on the piano he kept in his suite. You can still listen to it being played today in the hotel's lobby. *(301 Park Avenue, ☎ 355-3000.)*

Another famous hotel is the 1907 landmark **Plaza Hotel** located in Grand Army Plaza, just on Central Park. Designed by the same architect who did the grand Dakota apartment building (page 158) on the Upper West Side. It has had famous associations throughout its history, including starring in several films such as *Plaza Suite*, *Home Alone 2*, *Scent of a Woman* and Hitchcock's *North by Northwest*. It has also served as the location for the

Waldorf-Astoria Hotel

Villard Houses

Waldorf-Astoria Hotel

. . . Other Attractions

The Plaza Hotel

1960's Black and White Ball thrown by Truman Capote, and the over-the-top wedding of Marla Maples and the Plaza's owner Donald Trump. *(Fifth Avenue, at 59th Street ☎ 759-3000.)*

Created in 1907, the **Japan Society** has inhabited its present building since 1971. A sleek gallery hosts exhibitions spotlighting Japanese art and culture, and changes frequently. Call ahead for the most updated schedule. The society's traditional Japanese garden is a pleasant place to relax. *(333 East 47th Street, ☎ 832-1155. Mon-Sun: 11am-5pm. Suggested admission $5.)*

Open Spaces

Opened in 1991, the **Garden Court** at the Pierpont-Morgan Library (page 148) is located beside J.P. Morgan, Jr.'s former townhouse. This three-story enclosed atrium, which is filled with trees and plants, even has its own café.

Paley Park, located on 53rd Street between Madison and Fifth Avenues, is known as the "vest pocket park". This small grassy nook is a good place to bring a picnic lunch. Another small park, between Second and Third Avenues at 51st Street, is **Greenacre Park**.

At 43rd Street between First and Second Avenues, **Tudor Park** is a quaint European-style park featuring

Tudor Park

gravel paths and an intricately decorated fence. After descending a flight of stairs from Tudor Park, you will arrive at the **Ralph J. Bunch Park** which is situated directly in front of the United Nations.

There are several acres of park land and sculpture gardens surrounding the

Peace Gardens at the United Nations

United Nations. They provide great views of the East River and nice places to relax in warm weather.

Eating and Drinking

Since restaurants in Midtown East compete for the lunch and dinner business of nearby corporations, their quality tends to be quite high, as do their prices.

Some New York classics can be found here, including legendary steakhouse **Smith & Wollensky** *(797 Third Avenue, ☎ 753-1530)* and the **Oyster Bar** *(Grand Central, lower level, ☎ 490-6650)* recently re-opened after a fire.

For the ultimate "power" scene, dine at the **Four Seasons** *(99 East 52nd Street, ☎ 754-9494)* and witness the spectacle that is lunch – where the media elite shower each other with air-kisses and hold meetings between courses. Of course, entertainment like this comes with a steep price tag. Even the pre-theater menu approaches the $50 mark.

Across the street from the exclusive auction house Christie's, **Akbar** (see below) serves fine Indian cuisine in an elegant setting at surprisingly reasonable prices.

After shopping for a suit at Armani (or maybe only browsing), stop in the slightly more affordable **Armani Cafe** *(601 Madison Avenue, ☎ 715-0500)*, located below Emporio Armani. You can dine on pastas, risottos and other Italian specialties, including a daily salad option.

Ottomanelli's (page 154) offers family dining at great prices and offers a discount to *for less* cardholders.

For light, mediterranean fare head to **Cafe Soleil** (page 154) where you will find a fantastic array of salads, *mezze* and traditional Turkish and middle-eastern dishes. This is also a great place to pick up a picnic lunch in warm weather (see Open Spaces, page 152).

INSIDER'S TIP

Restaurants close to the midtown sights (especially around Fifth Avenue) tend to be quite expensive. A better bet would be to head east towards First, Second or Third Avenues where you will find many dining options at more reasonable prices.

Akbar

Indian

475 Park Avenue
☎ 838-1717

Average meal: $20-25
for less discount: 25%
AM/MC/VS/DC/DS

HOURS

Mon-Fri: 11.30am-3pm
5.30pm-11pm
Sun: 5.30pm-11pm

On elegant Park Avenue, Akbar serves fine Indian cuisine in a palatial atmosphere at modest prices. Chef's specialties include lamb chops, chicken ginger and tandoori fish.

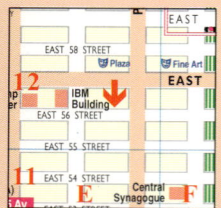

HOURS

Mon-Fri: 7am-8pm
Sat: 9am-6pm
Sun: closed

Cafe Soleil

Mediterranean

135 East 56th Street
☎ **832-0199**

Average meal: $10-15
for less discount: 25%
No credit cards.

This cozy Mediterranean café is a good place to enjoy flavorful, traditional dishes in a casual, café atmosphere. Specialties include Turkish meatballs, *shish-kababs* and an assortment of salads.

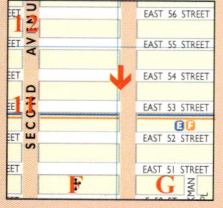

HOURS

Mon-Sun: 11.30am-11pm

Panda

Chinese

987 First Avenue
☎ **752-8822**

Average meal: $10-15
for less discount: 25%
AM/MC/VS/DC

This modern restaurant offers a vast selection of traditional Chinese dishes. Enjoy the rice and noodle specialities, or try the Peking duck. A friendly atmosphere complements the high quality food.

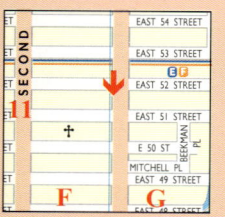

HOURS

Mon-Sun: 12noon-10pm

Ottomanelli's

Italian / American

951 First Avenue
☎ **758-3725**

Average meal: $10-15
for less discount: 25%
AM/MC/VS/DC/DS

A great family restaurant, Ottomanelli's has a wide range of Italian and American favorites, like pastas, pizzas and burgers, at excellent prices. Checked tablecloths and hardwood floors add to the rustic atmosphere.

Shopping . . .

From **Saks Fifth Avenue** *(611 Fifth Avenue, ☎ 753-4000)* department store to the scores of designer shops, Fifth Avenue is New York's best-known (and most expensive) shopping thoroughfare.

The exquisite jeweler **Cartier** *(653 Fifth Avenue, ☎ 446-3400)* is housed in one of the few remaining mansions which lined this street around the turn-of-the-century. Nearby, **Fortunoff** *(681 Fifth Avenue, ☎ 758-6660)* sells jewelry and fine housewares at less stratospheric prices.

Cartier

Takashimaya New York *(693 Fifth Avenue, ☎ 350-0100)* is the New York outpost of Japan's largest department store. The impressive building features a sleek architectural style, complete with a garden atrium. The store's goods have a decidedly Asian feel, as does the tearoom which provides a quiet respite from the bustle of Fifth Avenue.

Tiffany & Co.

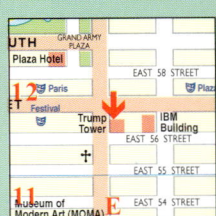

Tiffany & Co.

Gaze in the window of **Tiffany & Co.** *(727 Fifth Avenue, ☎ 755-8000)* as Audrey Hepburn did in the 1961 classic *Breakfast at Tiffany's* (no, you can't actually eat there). Better yet, go inside where you will find ten floors of practical and luxury items. Visitors are often surprised to find that, in Tiffany's, not everything is incredibly expensive. Of course, very big stones have very big price tags, but there are many items which cost less than $50 and, no matter what you buy, you can still take home one of their famous "Tiffany blue" bags.

Next door, the ostentatious lobby of **Trump Tower** *(725 Fifth Avenue, ☎ 832-2000)* contains a 6-story atrium loaded with marble, brass, mirrors and a waterfall. Upstairs, the luxurious apartments are home to the rich and famous, like Donald Trump himself.

Saks Fifth Avenue

F.A.O. Schwartz *(767 Fifth Avenue, ☎ 644-9400)* is a one-of-a-kind toy store made famous in the Tom Hanks film

Introduction . . .

The **Upper West Side** is bordered by **Central Park** to the east and **Riverside Park** and the Hudson River to the west. Like the Upper East Side, it has its share of opulence and wealth, but the Upper West Side possesses a very different character. The many actors, directors and artistic types who reside in its 19th-century apartment buildings and brownstone houses have helped to

The Dakota

impart a creative, liberal character to this neighborhood that makes it quite distinct from its conservative east side counterpart.

The main avenues (Broadway, Columbus and Amsterdam) are a shoppers paradise by day (see page 173) and are crowded with revelers by night. Turn off the busy avenues, however, and you will find the quiet residential side streets for which the area is best known.

The Upper West Side first became a desirable residential neighborhood in the late 19th century. Uptown migration was partly due to the creation of Central Park and partly to the rising real estate prices in midtown Manhattan. The advent of elevated trains, and eventually the subway, made commuting inexpensive and easy.

Broadway street scene and the 72nd Street subway station

In 1884, after four years of construction, New York City's first luxury residential apartment building, the **Dakota**, was completed. Nearly a hundred years later, one of the its most famous residents, John Lennon, was murdered in front of the building. Across the street, in Central Park, **Strawberry Fields** (page 204) has been created to honor his memory.

Other luxury apartment buildings followed the Dakota along Central Park West and charming brownstone buildings were erected on the cross streets during the 1890s. Completed in 1931, the **San Remo** (page 166) is one of the most magnificent residences in the

INSIDER'S TIP

At 72nd Street and Broadway, you can still catch a glimpse of the original subway buildings which once punctuated the train lines at street level.

. . . Introduction

city. Nearby, the Beaux Arts **Ansonia** (page 166) is also worth a stop for architecture buffs.

For visitors, the Upper West Side is best known for the performing arts. **Lincoln Center** (page 162) was built in the 1950s on the site of the slum area depicted in the musical *West Side Story*. Today, this single complex draws close to 5 million visitors a year and the surrounding streets are lined with shops, restaurants and expensive real estate.

On Central Park West, the enormous **American Museum of Natural History** (page 160-161) is one of New York City's most impressive museums and the only major museum on the Upper West Side. The recent addition of the dinosaur halls have proven to be extremely popular.

To the north-west of Central Park, **Morningside Heights** is home to **Columbia University**

Lincoln Center

(page 166). Here, the streets reflect the needs of the students who frequent the many bookstores, coffeeshops and inexpensive eateries that abound (see page 170).

A little further north, centered around 125th Street, Harlem has been pivotal to the development of

Brownstones on the Upper West Side

African-American culture throughout this century. The 1920s "Harlem Renaissance" produced some of the best-known jazz musicians in the world. Artists such as Cab Calloway and Duke Ellington performed at venues like the **Apollo Theater** (page 168) and the **Cotton Club**.

Recently, Harlem has begun to show signs of another kind of renaissance. A new generation of residents, respectful of Harlem's past and tradition, are finding new ways to improve it for the future. Many young, successful African-Americans are returning to Harlem, refurbishing its beautiful brownstone houses and becoming new leaders in the community.

American Museum of Natural History . .

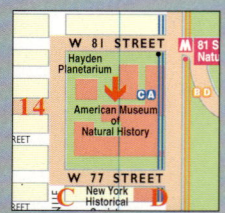

Founded in 1869 by Albert S. Bickmore and supporters such as Theodore Roosevelt, Sr. and J.P. Morgan, the American Museum of Natural History has a long tradition of attracting and educating visitors from around the world.

The museum focuses upon a broad range of subjects, from insects to dinosaurs, from marine life to planetary science. Comprising 23 adjoining buildings, the American Museum of Natural History houses more than 30 million specimens and cultural artifacts.

Main entrance to the museum

ADDRESS

Central Park West at 79th Street
☎ 769-5100

HOURS

Sun-Thu: 10am-5.45pm
Fri-Sat: 10am-8.45pm

There are 40 grand exhibition halls, numerous laboratories and teaching facilities and the largest natural history library in the western hemisphere. The scientific departments conduct research in anthropology, earth and planetary sciences, biology and paleontology.

Allosaurus

Since 1887, the museum has also sponsored and supported thousands of scientific expeditions to every corner of the world. Two of the most noteworthy were the 1921-25 **Central Asiatic Expeditions to Mongolia**, which unearthed the first dinosaur eggs and a variety of new fossil mammals, and the 1897 **Jesup North Pacific Expedition**, led by Franz Boas, who later became famous for his theory that all cultures are intrinsically equal.

PRICES

There is no required admission to the museum, though the suggested admission is as follows:
Adult $8
Child $4.50
Senior $6
Student $6

Between 1994 and 1996, six new fossil halls were opened to display the museum's vast collection of dinosaurs and fossil vertebrates –
recognized as the largest and most scientifically important in the world. The museum is now able to display more than 6,000 specimens, 85% of which are real fossils rather than the cast reproductions used at the majority of new museum exhibitions.

Dinosaurs in the Rotunda

Computer stations in these halls provide visitors with a hands-on account of the most current and innovative

. . . American Museum of Natural History

scientific information. The **Miriam and Ira D. Wallach Orientation Center** provides an overview of the fossil halls and is a good place to start a tour of them.

The new dinosaur halls – the **Hall of Saurischian Dinosaurs** and the **Hall of Ornithischian Dinosaurs** – which opened in 1995, feature close to 100 fossil specimens. Included are two of the museum's best-known dinosaurs: *Tyrannosaurus Rex* and *Apotosaurus* (formerly called *Brontosaurus*) both of which have been remounted in light of contemporary understanding of these animals.

A herd of African Elephants

The **Lila Acheson Wallace Wing of Mammals and Their Extinct Relatives**, which opened in 1994, contains the most significant selection of fossil mammals ever assembled. The **Hall of Vertebrate Origins** examines the history of the physical development of vertebrates. Other museum highlights include the **Hall of Human Biology and Evolution**, the only permanent exhibit in

the U.S. which documents the evolution of human life.

You can acquire a better understanding of how animals live within their environment at the **Hall of North American Mammals**, **Hall of**

77th Street Facade

African Mammals and **Hall of North American Birds**, where specimens are displayed in their natural surroundings.

The other permanent exhibition halls focus on a wide range of subjects, including meteorites, gems, ocean life, reptiles and amphibians. The cultural history of the people of various nations and continents is also documented.

"Audio expeditions" are designed to help you better explore the museum's enormous collections. Another way to enhance your visit here is to take advantage of the **IMAX theater** which features thrilling and informative cinematic adventures.

Presently, the **Hall of Life's Diversity** is under development and is due to open soon. The **Hayden Planetarium** is undergoing a major transformation and will be reopened by the year 2000.

DON'T MISS

The "touch fossils" which allow you to feel the actual fossilized remains of dinosaurs.

The amazing Star of India sapphire in the Hall of Gems.

INSIDER'S TIP

The museum is a great place to visit on Fridays and Saturdays when it's open late.

GETTING THERE

Subway: B/C to 81st Street-Museum of Natural History, or 1/9 to 79th or 86th Street. *New York Apple Tours stop*: Uptown route to stop #5, American Museum of Natural History .

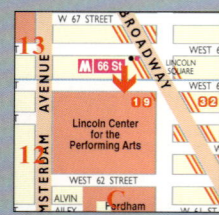

ADDRESS

Lincoln Center
Broadway from 62nd to
66th Streets
☎ 875-5350

HOURS

Classic Tour:
Mon-Sun:9.30am-4.30pm

PRICES

Classic Tour:
Adult $9.50
Child $4.50, free under 6
Senior $8
Student $8

DISCOUNT

50% discount on
classic tour with
voucher on page 277.

GETTING THERE

Subway: 1/9 to 66th
Street-Lincoln Center.
New York Apple Tours stop:
Uptown route to stop #3,
Lincoln Center.

 # Lincoln Center

Lincoln Center is one of the world's leading performing arts centers. It is home to 12 resident companies dedicated to music, dance and theater including the **Metropolitan Opera**, **New York Philharmonic**, **New York City Ballet** and **New York City Opera** which gives a discount to *for less* cardholders (page 207).

The enormous plaza, with its centerpiece fountain is a bustling hub when performances are taking place, or in the summer when a temporary stage attracts passers-

by with free entertainment.

Behind the fountain, looms the grand **Metropolitan Opera House** with its soaring glass windows. On

Metropolitan Opera House and Lincoln Center

either side of the opera house lie the **New York State Theater** and **Avery Fisher Hall**.

Through the plaza, you will find **Damrosch Park** and the **Guggenheim Bandshell** (see Open Spaces, page 169).

Also on the campus is the distinguished **Juilliard School of Music**, **New York Public Library for the Performing Arts** and the **Vivian Beaumont Theater**, as well as Lincoln Center's newest constituent – **Jazz at Lincoln Center**.

At any one time, almost 20,000 spectators can be accommodated in the various halls and concert venues at Lincoln Center.

Every day, backstage tours are offered in order to provide a behind-the-scenes look at the history, artistry and architecture of this impressive arts center. Your *for less* card entitles you to a discount on the Classic Lincoln Center Tour.

This one-hour tour allows you to experience the main stages at Lincoln center – the **Metropolitan Opera House**, **Avery Fisher Hall** and the **New York State Theater**. You will hear stories about some of the artists who have appeared here and you may even catch a rehearsal in progress.

Tours originate at the tour desk located on the concourse level of Lincoln Center, which you can access through the Metropolitan Opera House.

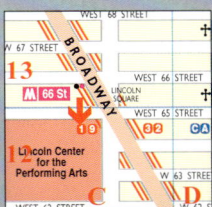 Sony IMAX Theatre

The Sony IMAX Theatre presents a truly unique film experience – combining 3D sight and sound technology with an 8-story screen in a plush, futuristic theater.

IMAX is the largest film format available. Each frame of film is ten times the size of 35 millimeter film, and is projected

Sony IMAX Theatre

onto a silver screen 80 feet high and 100 feet wide - the largest in the world to present IMAX 3D.

High-tech headsets with liquid crystal lenses receive infra-red signals from the IMAX projector, creating the 3D visual effects. Built-in speakers "move" the sound from the front of the headset to the back so that the sound can come from behind you, or from anywhere in the room. The personal sound system overlaps with the speakers of the main system which are distributed around the room. This theater is the first in the world to use this type of advanced sound technology.

Because film schedules change fairly often, it is advisable to call ahead for a listing of current films and show times.

Past films have included *Wings of Courage*, a film which tells the true story of two aviation pioneers, starring **Val Kilmer** and **Tom Hulce**. The IMAX format allows you to experience the film in a truly unique way, such as "flying" over the Andes Mountains.

L5: First City in Space uses 3D computer-generated imagery, actual footage taken in space and data from NASA to simulate life on a floating station orbiting the earth.

New York 3D: Across the Sea of Time is the story of a young Russian boy who travels to New York on a quest for an ancestor who emigrated to America almost a hundred years ago. Filmed entirely on location in New

L5: First City in Space

York City, it mixes 3D black and white images of the early 20th-century with present-day New York.

ADDRESS

1998 Broadway
☎ 336-5000

HOURS

Mon-Sun: 10am-12midnight

PRICES

Adult $9.50
Child $6
Senior $7.50
Student $6

DISCOUNT

2 admissions for the price of 1 for any IMAX feature with voucher on page 277.

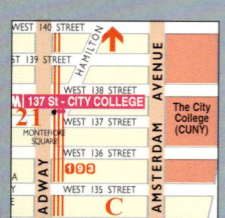

ADDRESS

65 Jumel Terrace
☎ 923-8008

HOURS

Wed-Sun: 10am-4pm
Mon-Tue: closed

Dining room in the mansion

PRICES

Adult $3
Child $2
Senior $2
Student $2

DISCOUNT

50% discount on
admission with
voucher on page 279.

Morris-Jumel Mansion

The Morris-Jumel Mansion is Manhattan's oldest remaining colonial residence. It is listed on the National Register of Historic Places and has been designated a New York City landmark.

Morris-Jumel Mansion

This 1765 mansion was built in the Georgian style and its design was based on a similar one by 16th-century Italian architect **Andrea Palladio**. The restored exterior of the house, with its double-height portico, grand columns and triangular pediment, is an excellent example of colonial architecture.

The mansion was originally built as a summer residence for British Colonel **Roger Morris** and his American wife Mary Philipse Morris. At the outbreak of the Revolutionary War in 1776, the Morrises fled to England, abandoning the house. During the war, General George Washington used the mansion as his headquarters during the **Battle of Harlem Heights**.

In 1810, **Stephen Jumel**, a wealthy French emigrant merchant, and his wife Eliza Bowen bought the house. A year after her husband died in 1832, Eliza Jumel married former Vice President **Aaron Burr** in the front parlor of the house. She divorced Burr only three years later. Considered one of the wealthiest women in New York, she remained in the mansion until her death in 1865.

In 1906, the **Washington Headquarters Association** undertook the responsibility to preserve and operate the mansion as a museum.

Bedroom at the Morris-Jumel Mansion

Guided and self-guided tours illuminate specific people and events that have contributed to the history of the house. In terms of its age, architecture and historical importance, the Morris-Jumel Mansion is perhaps the greatest house in Manhattan.

Other Attractions . . .

for less Founded in 1973, the **Children's Museum of Manhattan** is dedicated to teaching and inspiring children with playful interactive programs and exhibits. Emphasis is placed on literacy, arts and the sciences,

Children's Museum of Manhattan

and the activities are both educational and fun. The museum's activities include *Music to My Ear* - a 3,100 square foot playground with an emphasis on hearing. Children can touch, bang and jump on ear-themed props including an ear drum trampoline. The Warner Media Center provides children with the opportunity to interact with a camera, create special effects, then edit and watch the tape they have made. *(212 West 83rd Street, ☎ 721-1234. Wed-Sun: 10am-5pm. Mon-Tue: closed. Adult $5, child $5 (under 1 year free), senior $2.50, student $5. 50% discount on admission with voucher on page 279.)*

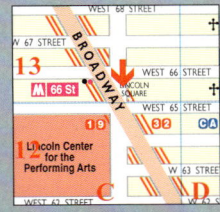

Museum of American Folk Art

Opened in 1989, the **Museum of American Folk Art** exhibits everything from Native American art and carvings to traditional American crafts like quilts and rugs. The museum hosts temporary exhibits in addition to its permanent display. It is small enough to visit in an hour or so. The museum also sponsors events for children and craft demonstrations. *(2 Lincoln Square, ☎ 595-9533. Tue-Sun: 11.30am-7.30pm. Mon: closed. Suggested admission $3.)*

Columbia University's Low Library

Founded in 1804, the **New York Historical Society** is the oldest museum in New York City. The society has a variety of paintings and furniture dating from the 17th century. *(2 West 77th Street, ☎ 873-3400. Library open Tue-Sat: 11am-5pm. Sun-Mon: closed. Adult $5, child free, senior $3, student $3.)*

The **Beacon Theater**, once a movie palace, is now a regular concert venue which hosts top performers. The opulent interior is a designated landmark. *(2214 Broadway at 74th Street, ☎ 496-7070.)*

. . . Other Attractions . . .

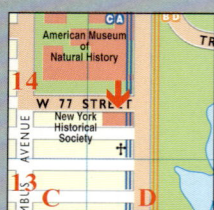

New York Historical Society

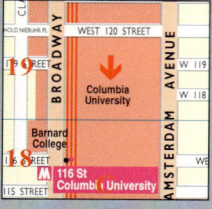

Columbia University

The beautiful Beaux Arts **Ansonia** is now a condominium apartment building, but its original function was as an all-suite hotel. Famous past residents include Babe Ruth, Enrico Caruso and Arturo Toscanini. The fireproof walls created sound-proof rooms havens which were apparently quite attractive to the music-minded who bunked there. *(2019 Broadway, between 73rd and 74th Streets.)*

Grant's Tomb

When the **Dakota** was built in 1884, it was practically in the suburbs of New York. Today its Central Park location is ideal and right in the heart of the Upper West Side's residential area. Although its most famous resident was undoubtedly John Lennon, other famous past-residents include Rudolf Nureyev, Lauren Bacall and Mia Farrow, who also starred in the horror film *Rosemary's Baby* which was filmed here. *(1 West 72nd Street, at Central Park West.)*

St. John the Divine

Nearby, the 1931 landmark **San Remo**, with its signature twin towers, has seen its share of celebrity residents as well. Marilyn Monroe, Paul Simon and Dustin Hoffman have all called the San Remo home. Rising high above the trees, the building is visible from much of Central Park. *(145-146 Central Park West.)*

Founded in 1754 in Lower Manhattan as King's College, **Columbia University** is New York City's contribution to the Ivy League. In the 1960s it was the site of numerous demonstrations and protests concerning the Vietnam War, racial and gender equality and other controversial issues. This urban campus has a series of architecturally impressive buildings including the Low Library, which was designed by architects McKim, Mead and White and is located in the university's central courtyard. Built in 1904, St. Paul's Chapel (☎ 854-6625) has a beautifully crafted brick interior and an impressive pipe organ. *(West*

. . . Other Attractions . . .

114th-120th Streets, between Broadway and Morningside Drive, ☎ 854-1754.)

In Morningside Heights, not far from Columbia University, **Grant's Tomb** contains the remains of Civil War commanding General Ulysses S. Grant and his

Hamilton Grange

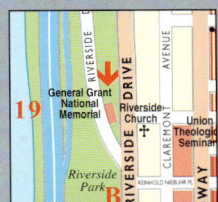

Grant's Tomb

wife. After winning the Civil War, General Grant went on to become the 18th president of the United States of America. In 1885, after Grant died, the American people honored him by raising over $600,000 to build this massive monument. The interior was inspired by the tomb of Napoleon. You can visit the two exhibit rooms which document the life and career of Ulysses S. Grant. *(West 122nd Street and Riverside Drive, ☎ 666-1640. Mon-Sun: 9am-5pm.)*

Begun in 1892, the Neo-Gothic-style **Cathedral of St. John the Divine** is the largest church in the United States and is intended to be the largest cathedral in the world when it is finally finished. Presently, only about two-thirds of the cathedral is complete, the rest is scheduled to be finished sometime late in the 21st century. Its towers, nave, buttresses and windows are exquisitely designed. The facade resembles Notre Dame in Paris, with a large bronze door in the center cast in Paris by M. Barbedienne, the same man who cast the Statue of Liberty. The cathedral hosts cultural events such as concerts, plays and exhibitions. *(Amsterdam Avenue at 112th Street, ☎ 316-7540.)*

The Unicorn Tapestries (ca. 1500) at The Cloisters

The Cloisters, the medieval branch of the Metropolitan Museum of Art, is perched high atop a hill overlooking the Hudson River, from northern Manhattan's Fort Trynon Park. Housed in a reconstructed medieval-style monastery, the setting is perfectly suited for the

. . . Other Attractions

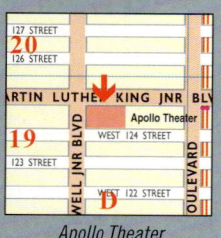

Cathedral of St. John the Divine

outstanding collection it contains. Cloistered walkways, courtyards, exhibition halls and galleries complement medieval art, sculpture, tapestries, illuminated manuscripts and more. Even the gardens continue the medieval theme with plant varieties typically grown at that time. *(Fort Trynon Park at 190th Street, ☎ 923-3700. Mar-Oct: Tue-Sun: 9.30am-5.15pm. Mon: closed. Nov-Feb: Tue-Sun: 9.30am-4.45pm. Mon: closed. Suggested admission: adult $8, child free (under 12), senior $4, student $4 includes same day admission to The Met (pages 178-179).)*

Hamilton Grange National Memorial is the 1802 home of Alexander Hamilton, co-author of the *Federalist Papers* and the first Secretary of the U.S. Treasury. Hamilton lived here with his family until he was killed in a gun duel with Vice-President Aaron Burr in 1804. The interior is not open to the public. *(Convent Avenue at 141st Street, ☎ 283-5144.)*

Apollo Theater in Harlem

The **Apollo Theater** was founded in 1914 as an opera house for a strictly white audience. In 1934, it was opened to all races and evolved into a premier black entertainment venue. Top African-American artists such as Billie Holiday, Ella Fitzgerald, Duke Ellington, Michael Jackson and comedian Sinbad have all performed here. Wednesday night is "Showtime at the Apollo", a televised amateur night, where fresh talents sing and dance in the hope of being discovered. *(253 West 125th Street, ☎ 864-0372.)*

Built in 1891, the **St. Nicholas Historic District** is comprised of elegant townhouses designed by some of the leading architects of the day. Harlem residents nick-named the houses "Strivers' Row" because of the successful African-Americans who resided in them. *(West 138th and West 139th Streets, between Seventh and Eighth Avenues.)*

Opened in 1991, the **Schomburg Center for Research into Black Culture** is the nation's largest research, educational and cultural center for African-American and African culture and history. Its massive holdings were collected by the late curator and black intellectual, Arthur Schomburg and include rare books, manuscripts and art. *(135th Street and Malcolm X Boulevard, ☎ 491-2200. Mon-Wed: 12noon-8pm. Thu-Sat: 10am-6pm. Sun: 1pm-5pm.)*

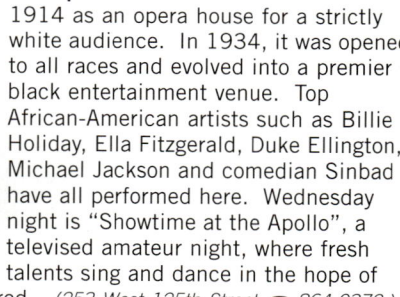

Apollo Theater

Open Spaces

Created by Frederick Law Olmstead, who also designed Central Park, **Riverside Park** *(Hudson River, between 72nd and 145th Streets)* is a sliver of green space running alongside the river. It is an extremely popular spot with Upper West Siders who walk their dogs, jog and cycle along the banks of the Hudson while enjoying the spectacular views. Within the park, at 89th Street, the **Soldiers and Sailors Monument** commemorates those who fought and died in the Civil War.

Established in the last century, **Claremont Riding Academy** *(175 West 89th Street, ☎ 724-5100)* is the only remaining stable in Manhattan. It offers horseback-riding lessons and rentals which allow you to ride indoors, or to enjoy Central Park on horseback.

Riverside Park

Set in the southeast corner of Lincoln Center, **Damrosch Park** is home to the annual Big Apple Circus. Throughout the summer, it also hosts free outdoor concerts and performances at the **Guggenheim Bandshell**. Across from Lincoln Center, **Dante Park** was designed in 1921 to honor the 600th anniversary of the author's death. This small, open area is marked by a bronze statue in his likeness.

Soldiers' and Sailors' Monument

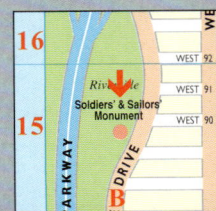
Soldiers' and Sailors' Monument

Next to the Cathedral of St. John the Divine (page 167), the **Children's Sculpture Garden** has an assortment of flowers and benches for resting as well as small plaques engraved with "words of wisdom". The garden also has a gigantic water-filled fountain with a winged hero battling with evil beasts. Surrounding the fountain, the *Ring of Freedom* features sculptures created by children.

A pleasant spot to relax amidst an array of beautiful flowers is the **Lotus Garden** *(97th Street, between Broadway and West End Avenue)*.

Nearby, **Morningside Park** is a wooded area extending from 110th to 123rd Streets. Further north, the medieval gardens and courtyards at **The Cloisters** (page 167) provide a unique place to relax.

Peace Garden at St. John the Divine

Eating and Drinking

The majority of restaurants on the Upper West Side are concentrated along Broadway, Amsterdam and Columbus Avenues. From wholesome American to Cuban-Chinese, you can find every type of cuisine imaginable.

The area is a good place for "bar hopping" among the restaurants and bars crammed onto every block. Mainly attracting a college crowd, "happy hours" (with excellent deals on drinks) are the specialty here. Announced on giant chalk boards placed on the sidewalk, a typical offer is two drinks for the price of one. Another favorite is "Ladies Night" where women drink for free for a few hours. For those with the patience and ability to balance a drink while wedged between the bar and an enormous football player, these evenings can be very economical and even fun.

A good place to watch televised sports events and enjoy traditional American food is **Boomer's Sports Club** (page 171). At one of the city's top comedy clubs, **Stand Up New York** (page 210), your *for less* card entitles you to a discount on admission to the club *and* on dinner. You can also visit **Mendy's** (below), one of comedian Jerry Seinfeld's favorites.

Zabar's *(2245 Broadway, ☎ 787-2000)*, one of the best known gourmet markets in New York, stockpiles prepared foods, imported items, fresh-baked goods and even housewares – all of the best quality.

In Harlem see a show at the Apollo Theater (page 168) before dining at **Sylvia's** *(328 Lenox Avenue, ☎ 996-0660)* which is, if not the best "soul food" in town, then at least the most famous.

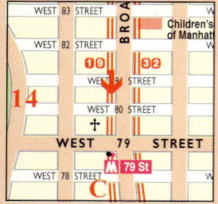

Zabar's

Mendy's West

Delicatessen / Kosher

210 West 70th Street
☎ 877-6787

Average meal: $15-20
***for less* discount: 25%**
AM/MC/VS/DC

HOURS

Mon-Thu:1pm-12midnight
Sat: 6.30am-2am
Sun: 1pm-12midnight
Fri: closed

This friendly restaurant and sports bar serves great food at reasonable prices. Mendy's friendly staff will point out interesting sports memorabilia. The veal chops and pastrami sandwich are particularly recommended.

Cafe Mozart

Viennese

154 West 70th Street
☎ 595-9797

Average meal: $10-15
for less discount: 25%
AM/MC/VS/DC/DS

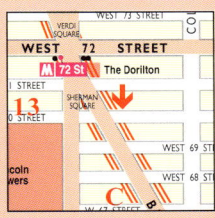

HOURS

Mon-Thu: 8am-1am
Fri: 8am-3am
Sat: 10am-3am
Sun: 10am-1am

Cafe Mozart serves European cuisine in an Old Viennese-style atmosphere. Try the Viennese chicken *schnitzel* or one of the 50 varieties of dessert. Relax while listening to the live classical music which is performed nightly.

 # Mingala West

Burmese

325 Amsterdam Avenue
☎ 873-0787

Average meal: $15-20
for less discount: 25%
AM/MC/VS/DC/DS

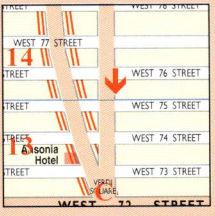

HOURS

Mon-Thu: 10.30am-11.pm
Fri-Sat: 12noon-
12midnight
Sun: 12noon-11.30pm

Mingala West offers traditional Burmese cuisine in an exotic setting. Specialties include red curry shrimp and scallops with string beans. A wide variety of salads and noodle dishes is also available.

Boomer's Sports Club

American

349 Amsterdam Avenue
☎ 362-5400

Average meal: $10-15
for less discount: 25%
AM/MC/VS/DC

HOURS

Mon-Thu: 5pm-1am
Fri: 5pm-2am
Sat: 11.30am-2am
Sun: 11.30am-12midnight

This traditional American sports bar is fun, casual and friendly. It shows all kinds of sports games and events on 25 televisions. Boomers is known for its delicious chicken wings.

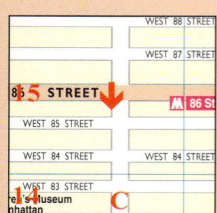

HOURS

Mon-Sun: 12noon-
12midnight

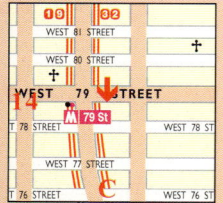

HOURS

Mon-Sat: 11.30am-
12midnight
Sun: 12noon-12midnight

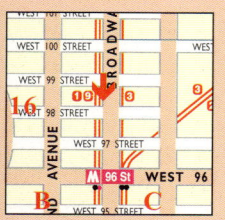

HOURS

Mon-Thu and Sun:
12noon-1am
Fri-Sat: 12noon-1.30am

Firehouse

American

522 Columbus Avenue
☎ 787-3473

Average meal: $15-20
for less discount: 25%
AM/MC/VS/DC

This casual American restaurant serves inexpensive and
tasty food. It is located in an antique firehouse filled with
interesting memorabilia. Choose from ribs, chicken
wings, gourmet pizzas, salads and more.

Miss Elle's

American

226 West 79th Street
☎ 595-4350

Average meal: $15-20
for less discount: 25%
AM/MC/VS/DC/DS

Miss Elle's is housed in a landmark brownstone building
with an enclosed garden atrium. The décor is romantic
and the fare is American with an Italian influence. Try
the hearty pot roast and mashed potatoes or the lasagna.

Hunan Balcony

Chinese

2596 Broadway
☎ 865-0400

Average meal: $10-15
for less discount: 25%
AM/MC/VS/DC

Hunan Balcony offers vegetarian and non-vegetarian
Chinese dishes. Chef's specialties include the vegetarian
paradise and pineapple chicken. Floor-to-ceiling
windows offer great views of Upper Broadway.

Shopping

Although the Upper West Side is as filled with standard chain stores like **The Gap** and **Banana Republic**, there are also quite a few independent shops and boutiques

Creating your own pottery at Our Name is Mud

which are worth investigating.

At **Our Name is Mud** (page 174) you can choose from a variety of objects which you can then design and paint to your liking. There are also items for sale which have been crafted either by local artists or on the premises.

The funky designs at **Betsey Johnson** *(248 Columbus Avenue, ☎ 362-3364)* can be found nearby. **Allan and Suzi** *(416 Amsterdam, ☎ 724-7445)* sells everything from platform shoes and feather boas to slightly worn designer wear.

Filene's Basement *(2222 Broadway, ☎ 873-8000)* is a discount superstore which carries brand-name clothing at good prices.

The book shop and café, **Barnes and Noble** *(2289 Broadway, ☎ 362-8835)* is gigantic, as are the music superstores **Tower Records** *(2107 Broadway, ☎ 799-2500)* and **HMV** *(2081 Broadway, ☎ 721-5900)*, both of which are open late.

Zabar's food shop (page 170) has been a New York favorite for years, having evolved from its origins as a kosher deli in the 1930s. Its quality, selection and prices are among the best in the city.

The Columbus Avenue Street Fair

(Columbus Avenue between 76th and 77th Streets) is held at P.S. (public school) 44 on Sundays. In addition to arts, crafts and antiques, there are goods imported from other countries, basic sportswear and even a small greenmarket.

Shopping on the Upper West Side

Have all your fabulous New York pictures ready to take home, developed in under an hour at **Fromex 1 Hour Photo** (page 174).

INSIDER'S TIP

After a tiring day shopping, head to Barnes and Noble where you can relax in a comfortable armchair with a cup of coffee and a good book.

Our Name is Mud

Crafts & Gifts

506 Amsterdam Avenue
☎ 579-5575

for less discount: 20%
AM/MC/VS

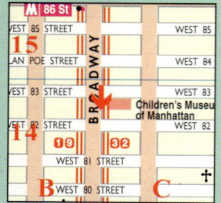

Handmade crafts and gifts are available in this lively shop and bright art studio. It sells pottery, scented candles and other creations. Visitors can observe artists at work or create their own art at the paint bar.

Metro Art

Posters & Framing

2341 Broadway
☎ 595-1615

for less discount: 20%
AM/MC/VS

HOURS

Mon-Sat: 10am-8pm
Sun: 11am-6pm

Metro Art has a large collection of fine art prints of famous artwork, landscapes and modern themes. Choose from posters and lithographs (either with or without frames) or have a frame customized for you.

Fromex 1 Hour Photo

Film Developing

2041 Broadway
☎ 580-8181

for less discount: 20% off
1 hour color film developing
AM/MC/VS/DC/DS

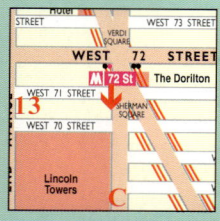

HOURS

Mon-Fri: 7:30am-9pm
Sat: 11am-6pm
Sun: 11am-5pm

Your *for less* card entitles you to receive 20% off one-hour color film processing. The discount also applies at the other Upper West Side Fromex location *(2151 Broadway, ☎ 496-2211)*.

Upper East Side

GUGGENHE

Introduction . . .

After the Civil War, the **Upper East Side** became a summer vacation spot for members of New York City's high society who had permanent residences downtown.

Metropolitan Museum of Art

However, the building of elevated trains and the creation of Central Park in the 1870s led to the real development of the neighborhood. The wealthy built mansions on Fifth and Park Avenues near the salubrious setting of the park, while working class Europeans created ethnic enclaves on First, Second and Third Avenues.

Along Fifth Avenue's former **Millionaire's Row**, some of the old mansions have been converted into museums and galleries, and the area is now referred to as the **Museum Mile**. The **Frick Collection** (page 182) and the **Cooper-Hewitt** (page 188) were once the homes of 19th-century entrepreneurs Henry Clay Frick and Andrew Carnegie, respectively. The Frick Collection maintains the feeling of a private residence while displaying works by artists such as Rembrandt and Renoir.

Guggenheim Museum (page 180-181) is an architectural anomaly on this row of classically-designed structures. Designed by Frank Lloyd Wright, the museum's modern exterior mirrors the works within it, including major pieces by Picasso and Matisse.

It would literally take weeks to view all of the treasures displayed in the imposing structures along this stretch of Fifth Avenue. Indeed, you could easily spend a couple of days at **The Metropolitan Museum of Art** (page 178-179), the largest museum in the western hemisphere, and only begin to scratch the surface. Although it is unlikely that anyone would

INSIDER'S TIP

Many museums offer free or pay-what-you-wish admission one day a week, during special hours: Cooper-Hewitt (Tue: 5pm-9pm), The Jewish Museum (Tue: 5pm-8pm), Whitney (Thu: 6pm-8pm), Guggenheim (Fri: 6pm-8pm), National Academy Museum (Fri: 5pm-6pm)

spend their entire time in Manhattan visiting museums, Museum Mile is a must-see, even if just for an afternoon.

The proximity of the museums to each other makes sampling a select few in one day a viable

The Frick Collection

possibility. On the following pages you will find information that will help you decide which ones best suit your interest. The majority of museums on Museum Mile offer a discount to *for less* cardholders.

. . . Introduction

Today, the Upper East Side, particularly the area close to Central Park and along Park Avenue, is still synonymous with old wealth. Posh apartment houses subject applicants to rigorous screening processes that have occasionally been a subject of controversy. Even wealthy celebrities have been known to be barred from living in some of these buildings.

On quiet streets in the East 60s, many of New York's exclusive clubs can be found (page 189-190). Catering to members only, many of these have survived almost unchanged from the end of the 19th century.

The **Whitney Museum of American Art** (page 183), on Madison Avenue, resembles an upside-down pyramid

and exhibits modern works by prominent American artists such as Georgia O'Keeffe, Jasper Johns and Frank Stella.

Madison Avenue was once the name generically applied to the scores of advertising agencies that made their homes here. Since most of them have relocated, Madison Avenue and

Christie's on Park Avenue

its exclusive shops (see page 195) have come to symbolize the wealth and extravagance of the Upper East Side. A short walk from here, you will find **Christie's** *(502 Park Avenue, ☎ 546-1000)* one of the best-known auction houses in the world.

At the northernmost point of the Museum Mile, the **Museo del Barrio** (page 188) has Latino culture as its focus, and its location marks the beginning of Spanish Harlem. This mainly Puerto Rican enclave is known to its residents as "El Barrio", meaning "the neighborhood". It has the largest Spanish-speaking population in New York City.

Roosevelt Island (page 190) is situated in the East River between Manhattan and Queens. Stretching the equivalent of more than 30 city blocks, it runs parallel to Manhattan from the United Nations (page 149) in Midtown East to **Carl Schurz Park** (page 191) on the Upper East Side. The island is a good place to view the river and the city, but the best part is getting there. Although the subway stops on Roosevelt Island, the aerial tram provides a unique mode of transportation which is much more fun.

DON'T MISS

The Whitney Biennial – the only continuous series of exhibitions spotlighting achievements and developments in American art by artists who have not yet achieved "official recognition".

Summer Days (1936) by Georgia O'Keeffe at the Whitney

The Metropolitan Museum of Art ..

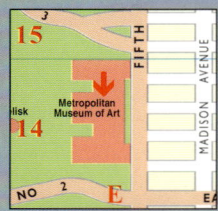

ADDRESS

Fifth Avenue and 82nd
Street
☎ 879-5500

HOURS

Tue-Thu: 9.30am-5.15pm
Fri-Sat: 9.30am-8.45pm
Sun: 9.30am-5.15pm
Mon: closed

Founded in 1870 by a group of American businessmen, artists and scholars, the museum's original collection consisted of 174 paintings from three private European collections. More than a century later The Metropolitan Museum of Art, known simply as "The Met", has grown to include more than two million works of art, spanning 5,000 years of culture, from prehistoric times to modern day.

Caroll and Milton Petrie Sculpture Court

From the first glimpse of the museum's Fifth Avenue entrance with its Neo-Classical facade, you know you are about to embark upon an unforgettable journey in the world of art. Inside, there are over two million square-feet of space exhibiting one of the world's largest and most impressive collections of paintings, sculptures,

The American Wing of The Metropolitan Museum of Art

photographs, decorative arts, costumes, drawings, musical instruments and much more.

The Met has three enormous floors and is ever-changing in both size and configuration. The Greek and Roman galleries have recently been renovated with the addition of the **Robert A. and Renee E. Belfer Court**.

The galleries are arranged as 20 different collections which range in content from Egyptian art to 20th-century art (including works by **Kandinsky, Pollock** and **Warhol**). Some of the world's finest and most recognizable pieces of French Impressionist, Post-Impressionist, Romantic and Barbizon works can be found in the **European Paintings Collection**, located on the second floor.

PRICES

There is no required admission charge, though the suggested admission is as follows:
Adult: $8
Child: free when accompanied by an adult
Senior: $4
Student: $4

The **Charles Engelhard Court**, a glass-enclosed garden containing sculptures and paintings by American artists, is one of the more popular attractions in the museum. Located on all three floors, the **American Wing** includes 25 furnished period rooms that are accentuated by Chippendale furniture and Tiffany & Co. silver settings.

. . . The Metropolitan Museum of Art

The Met has one of the most comprehensive collections of Egyptian art and archaeological findings in the world. Of the nearly 35,000 pieces in the collection, the most impressive are the **Tomb of Perneb** and the **Temple of Dendur**, which are housed in a spectacular glass-enclosed gallery overlooking Central Park.

Other impressive collections are the **Arms and Armor** gallery, the **Arts of Africa**, **Oceania and the Americas** galleries and the **Medieval Arts** gallery, all located on the first floor. The second floor houses a wide range of art from Asia, including a Chinese art collection and a suite of galleries displaying the arts of **South and Southeast Asia**. Also situated on the second floor is an exhibit focusing on the Islamic-influenced art of Morocco, Central Asia and India. The Islamic galleries are introduced by the **Nur ad-Din Room** from Syria. Complete with a marble fountain, wood-panelled reception area and stained-glass windows, the room is a representation of Ottoman wealth.

Temple of Dendur

The **Costume Institute** features everything from traditional folk costumes to 18th-century ball gowns and modern designs by the likes of Halston and Balenciaga. Exhibition openings are gala events that draw New York's luminaries, with the media in tow.

Seeing everything that The Met has to offer would literally take weeks. Therefore, the best thing to do is

Caroll and Milton Petrie European Sculpture Court

to visit one of the information desks located in the **Great Hall**, on the first floor. There you can pick up maps and brochures and sign up for one of the free multilingual tours provided by members of the staff. Museum policy stipulates that photographs can be taken for non-commercial use only (without a flash or tripod) and video cameras are prohibited.

To view more of the museum's medieval collection, visit **The Cloisters** (page 167) in northern Manhattan.

Solomon R. Guggenheim Museum . . .

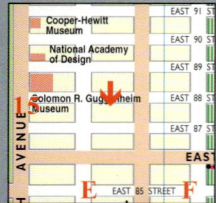

ADDRESS

1071 Fifth Avenue
☎ 423-3500

HOURS

Sun-Wed: 10am-6pm
Fri-Sat: 10am-8pm
Thu: closed

PRICES

Adult $12
Child free
Senior $7
Student $7

Founded by the wealthy Solomon R. Guggenheim in 1937, his eponymous museum has now expanded far beyond his initial collection of European abstract art.

Dedicated to collecting, preserving and exhibiting modern and contemporary art. Some of the better known pieces in its permanent collection are by **Picasso**, **Kandinksy**, **Klee**, **Van Gogh** and **Cezanne**.

Unlike most of the world's museums, Solomon R. Guggenheim's vision of a "temple of non-objective painting" is perhaps as well-known for its physical structure as it is for the works of art that are housed within it.

Frank Lloyd Wright rotunda

Designed by Frank Lloyd Wright, the building was completed in 1959, after both his and Guggenheim's deaths. Its most notable feature is the six-story rotunda, which represents Wright's interpretation of ancient Mesopotamian ziggurats and provides the main gallery space.

Guggenheim above Fifth Avenue

Guggenheim was a wealthy industrialist who made his money in copper and silver mining. He began by collecting Old Masters more as an investment than a personal passion. However, after a 1929 meeting with artist **Vasily Kandinsky**, at which he purchased several of his paintings, Guggenheim began taking an interest in modern art that soon became a full-time passion.

He gradually amassed a collection of works by other contemporary artists including **Marc Chagall**, **Jackson Pollock** and **Willem de Koonig** which grew to overwhelming proportions and led to the formation of the Solomon R. Guggenheim Foundation.

. . . Solomon R. Guggenheim Museum

After loaning his collection to various museums, Guggenheim commissioned Wright to build it a permanent home. The museum, which was Wright's only major New York commission, was to be named 'The Museum of Non-Objective Painting'. The resulting structure was initially criticized by commentators who seemed more interested in its design than the works within it. However, while it is true that the curves that make-up the rotunda's exterior do seem out of place beside an otherwise vertical Upper East Side, the Guggenheim has become one of New York's most photographed and best loved buildings. Indeed, in 1990 it became the youngest building ever to be designated a city landmark.

Wright's internal design deviates from the traditional gallery approach of housing works in a room-by-room format. Rather, Wright designed a spiralling walkway that constitutes the six-story rotunda. The walkway provides a quarter-mile of, what seems to be, endless

works of art. The glass dome, which covers the museum's round top, provides natural light for the changing exhibits that line the walls.

Since the museum's opening, both its physical structure and its original collection of European abstract art have expanded. A major renovation that took place in the early 1990s left the

Rotunda at the Guggenheim

exterior refurbished and the interior with much-needed additional space. More recently still, new Guggenheims have opened in Soho (page 78) and, as the first step of an international expansion program, in Spain.

From the original exhibition, which included two ramps devoted to Kandinsky's work, to more recent exhibitions including the works of Max Beckman, Robert Maplethorpe and an exhibit devoted to the art of Africa, the museum has proven that its interests reach beyond the limitations of more classical museums.

"Let every man practice the art he knows" was inscribed by Wright on the entrance floor to the museum. Perhaps no better words have been written to describe the structure or the art within.

DISCOUNT

$2 off admission with voucher on page 279.

GETTING THERE

Subway: 4/5/6 to 86th Street
New York Apple Tours stop: Uptown route to stop #5, Guggenheim Museum.

INSIDERS' TIP

The best way to see the exhibits in the rotunda is to ride the elevator to the top, then work your way down the spiraling ramp.

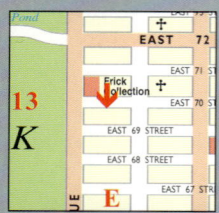

ADDRESS

1 East 70th Street
☎ 288-0700

HOURS

Tue-Sat: 10am-6pm
Sun: 1pm-6pm
Mon: closed

The Frick Collection

Opened to the public in 1935, the Frick Collection is housed in the former residence of steel baron **Henry Clay Frick** (1849-1919). Designed by the architects **Carrère and Hastings**, architects of the New York Public Library on Fifth Avenue, this mansion was built in 1914.

The Frick Collection

One of its most delightful architectural features is the Garden Court located in the center of the museum. It provides a pleasant environment in which to relax and take in the magnificence of this former private home.

Frick stated in his will that the Frick Collection was founded "to encourage and develop the study of fine arts, and advance the knowledge of kindred subjects."

Courtyard at the Frick

The breadth of his private collection is astounding, but nearly one-third of the paintings have been added since his death.

The collection contains impressive works of Western art, dating from the early Renaissance to the late 19th century. Particularly notable are its Old Master paintings, Renaissance bronzes and French sculpture from the 18th century.

Masterpieces by artists such as **Rembrandt**, **Renoir**, **Vermeer**, **El Greco**, **Goya**, **Titian** and many more are on display here. Highlights include Rembrandt's S*elf Portrait*, Vermeer's *Mistress and Maid*, Titian's *Man in a Red Cap*, **Holbein**'s *Sir Thomas More* and **Thomas Gainsborough**'s *Mall in St. James's Park*.

PRICES

Adult $7
Children under ten are not permitted in the galleries
Senior $5
Student $5

DISCOUNT

50% discount on admission with voucher on page 279.

The museum is exceptional because the works are displayed in an untraditional, whimsical manner which combines historical periods in the intimate setting of a private home without typical museum features like ropes and descriptive placards. The furniture, decorative art works and porcelain are as remarkable as the paintings and sculptures.

Because of the unique nature of the museum, and the vulnerability of the objects on display, children under ten years of age are not permitted in the galleries.

Whitney Museum of American Art

Early 20th century sculptor and wealthy arts patron Gertrude Vanderbilt Whitney acquired a substantial studio collection during her lifetime. In 1930, after the Metropolitan Museum of Art rejected the

The Whitney

collection she had amassed, the Whitney Museum of American Art was founded.

The inverted pyramid, a minimalist building designed by Marcel Breuer (a member of the Bauhaus school), became the Whitney's current home in 1966. It is located on exclusive Madison Avenue.

The Whitney is dedicated to the gathering and exhibiting of 20th-century American art, with a particular emphasis on the work of living artists. The permanent collection includes 11,000 paintings, sculptures, prints, drawings and photographs representing over 1,700 artists. It is best known for its impressive showing of American artists like **Georgia O'Keeffe**, **Jasper Johns**, **Roy Lichtenstein** and the complete artistic estate of **Edward Hopper** - comprising approximately 2,000 pieces. Highlights include **Alexander Calder**'s *Calder's Circus*, Jasper John's *Three Flags*, Roy Lichtenstein's *Little Big Painting*, Edward Hoppers's *Early Sunday Morning*, Georgia O'Keeffe's *The White Calico Flower* and **Andy Warhol**'s *Green Coca Cola Bottles*.

Early Sunday Morning (1930) by Edward Hopper

In 1991 a photographic collection was assembled with important acquisitions including **Gerald Murphy**'s *Cocktail* and **Agnes Martin**'s *The Islands*, a series of 12 photographs believed to be her most significant work.

Poker Night (1948) by Thomas Hart Benton, 1948

Founded in 1970, the **New American Film and Video Series** shows the works of independent, non-commercial American filmmakers and video artists. Their innovative and provocative works are shown in the film and video gallery.

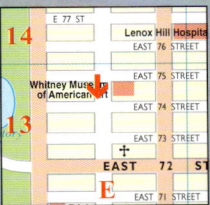

ADDRESS

945 Madison Avenue
☎ 570-3676

HOURS

Wed: 11am-6pm
Thu: 1pm-8pm
Fri-Sun: 11am-6pm
Mon-Tue: closed

PRICES

Adult $9
Child free
Senior $7
Student $7

DISCOUNT

50% discount on admission with voucher on page 279.

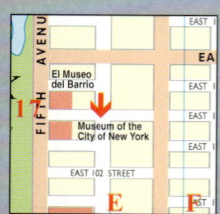

Museum of the City of New York

America's first city museum was founded in 1923 as a place to assemble and permanently display material associated with the fascinating history of New York City and its people.

Museum of the City of New York

Its treasury contains more than 1.5 million paintings, prints, photographs, costumes, manuscripts, memorabilia and sculptures. Highlights include gowns worn at George Washington's Inaugural Ball, a massive silver collection dating from 1678, the city's earliest fire engines and Jacob Riis' photographs of urban poverty.

The museum possesses one of America's most renowned **photographic archives** with more than half a million images documenting New York City since the advent of photography itself.

An impressive display of period rooms taken from actual homes represents life in New York from the colonial period through the 20th century. A collection of **toys, dollhouses and miniatures** dating from 1769, meticulous in detail, provides its own commentary on New York social life.

The museum also has a fascinating exhibition of various artifacts relating to the history and culture of New York City. One of the most remarkable is a section of the B-25 bomber that crashed into the Empire State Building in 1945.

As part of its "Museum for a New Century" program,

John D. Rockefeller's bedroom at the Museum of the City of New York

renovation and expansion will eventually allow the museum to more than double its exhibition galleries while continuing to serve as an outstanding educational resource and a major cultural attraction for New Yorkers and visitors alike.

The museum gift shop offers a 10% discount on all purchases. Present the voucher on page 279 to obtain the discount.

ADDRESS

1220 Fifth Avenue
☎ 534-1672

HOURS

Tue: Group tours by appointment only
Wed-Sat: 10am-5pm
Sun: 12noon-5pm
Mon: closed

PRICES

Suggested admission:
Adult $5
Child $4
Senior $4
Student $4
Family $10

DON'T MISS

The display of period rooms, the collection of silver or the incredible photographic archives.

DISCOUNT

10% discount in museum shop with the voucher on page 279.

National Academy Museum

The National Academy of Design was founded by a group of successful artists in 1825 "to sustain an association of artists for the purpose of instruction and exhibition." The academy is located in a handsome 19th-century Beaux Arts townhouse on Fifth Avenue, donated in 1940 by art patron Archer

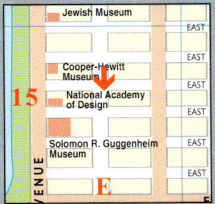

Huntington and his wife, sculptor Anna Hyatt. As you enter the academy, notice Anna Hyatt Huntington's *Statue of Diana* which is located in the foyer at the bottom of the grand spiral staircase.

National Academy of Design

The National Academy of Design is an artist-run organization that consists of the museum, the **School of Fine Arts** and an honorary association of artists. Many of America's finest architects, painters, sculptors and printmakers were among its founding members. These included Thomas Cole, Rembrandt Peale and the National Academy's first president Samuel F. B. Morse.

Each elected member was required to donate a self-portrait along with another piece of representative work. This practice resulted in the acquisition of an impressive collection of **19th- and 20th-century American art** that includes more than 8,000 paintings, drawings, architectural models, engravings and sculptures. Well-known artists and architects including **Winslow Homer**, **Frank Lloyd Wright** and **John Singer Sargent** are all represented.

Modeled after London's Royal Academy, the **National Academy of Design's School of Fine Arts**, which is the oldest art school in New York, offers courses specializing in painting, drawing, sculpture, anatomy, perspective and printmaking. It is dedicated to educating, training and exhibiting accomplished artists as well as young and unrecognized talents.

Exhibitions, tours, lectures and educational programs, which are held regularly, focus on American and European art. The Annual Exhibition displays new work from contemporary artists.

ADDRESS

1083 Fifth Avenue
☎ 369-4880

HOURS

Wed-Thu, Sat-Sun:
12noon-5pm
Fri: 10am-6pm
Mon-Tue: closed

PRICES

Adult $8
Child $4.25
Senior $4.25
Student $4.25

DISCOUNT

50% discount on admission with voucher on page 281.

INSIDER'S TIP

On Fridays from 5pm-6pm, admission to the museum is free.

International Center of Photography

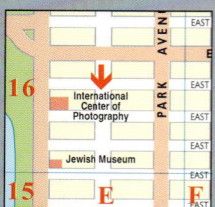

ADDRESS

1130 Fifth Avenue
☎ 860-1777

HOURS

Tue-Thur: 10am-5pm
Fri: 10am-8pm
Sat-Sun: 10am-6pm

PRICES

Adult $6
Child $1
Senior $4
Student $4

DISCOUNT

50% discount on admission with voucher on page 281.

GETTING THERE

Subway: 6 to 96th Street.
New York Apple Tours stop: Uptown route to stop #13, Jewish Museum / Cooper Hewitt / International Center of Photography.

Founded in 1974, the International Center of Photography (ICP) is the only museum in New York City (and one of the few museums world-wide) devoted solely to photography.

Housed in a landmark Federal-style mansion, its mission is to collect, preserve and present all aspects of photography. ICP has a second exhibition gallery (ICP Midtown, page 135) which opened in 1989 and is located on Avenue of the Americas at 43rd Street. *New York for less* entitles you to discounts at both locations.

Over 20 exhibitions are mounted at the ICP each year. Subjects include everything from photojournalism to experimental, cutting-edge photography. Many of the exhibitions feature film or video presentations which are shown in the ICP screening room.

Since its foundation, ICP has shown the work of over 2,000 photographers from around the world. Among the many outstanding photographers who have been featured are Harry Callahan, Man Ray, Ansel Adams and Annie Leibowitz.

ICP's Traveling Exhibitions program is the largest in the United States. It circulates photographic exhibits around museums, galleries and other art and educational institutions both in the U.S. and abroad.

International Center of Photography

The ICP library contains over 8,000 volumes on photography, 7,000 biographical files on photographers and 10,000 magazines and journals.

In addition, ICP maintains the largest full-time photography education program in the world. Courses, lectures and workshops are given by reputable photographers and cover a full range of photography-related topics. Interactive guided tours are available from Tuesday to Friday from 10am to 2pm.

The Jewish Museum

In 1904, Judge Mayer Sulzberger contributed his library and art collection to **The Jewish Theological Seminary of America** as an initial offering and foundation for a museum. In 1947, Mrs. Felix M. Warburg, a board member of the seminary, donated her 1908 chateau-style mansion on Fifth Avenue as the site for The Jewish Museum.

The scope and diversity of Jewish culture over the last 4,000 years is illustrated through a permanent collection of more than 27,000 paintings, sculptures, photographs, archeological artifacts and ceremonial items.

Goldfish Vendor (1928) by Reuven Rubin

The focal point of the museum is the permanent exhibit *Culture and Continuity: The Jewish Journey*, which conveys Jewish ideas, values and culture as they have developed from ancient to modern times. Situated on two floors, this 11,000-square-foot exhibition contains 17 galleries with four main themes: *Forging an Identity*, *Interpreting a Tradition*, *Confronting Modernity* and *Realizing a Future*. Each section features a range of Jewish-related art and artifacts, including a space devoted to the Holocaust.

The exhibit also features a replica of an ancient synagogue complete with original artifacts taken from various synagogues throughout the Mediterranean.

Perhaps the most impressive gallery examines **Sephardi**, **Ashkenazi** and **Eastern Jewish** culture. It contains ceremonial art including exquisitely crafted Torah arks and beautifully embroidered textiles.

The museum also holds temporary exhibitions covering topics ranging from historical events to individual interpretation of Jewish culture by prestigious contemporary artists. One recent exhibit featured the well-known Jewish artist **Marc Chagall**.

You can also visit the **Goodkind Resource Center** which offers books and periodicals as well as video and audio programming from the museum's vast archives.

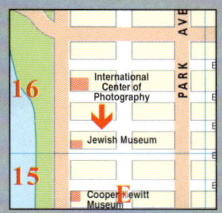

ADDRESS

1109 Fifth Avenue
☎ 423-3200

HOURS

Tue: 11am-8pm
Wed-Thu and Sun-Mon:
11am-5.45pm
Fri-Sat: closed

PRICES

Adult $8
Child free
Senior $5.50
Student $5.50

DISCOUNT

2 admissions for the price of 1 with voucher on page 281.

The Jewish Museum

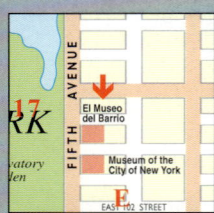

Museo del Barrio

Other Attractions . . .

The **Museo del Barrio**, founded in 1969, is the only museum in the United States showcasing Latin-American Art. The museum's permanent collection consists of over 200 wooden carvings of santos (saints) as well as Latin-related paintings, crafts, artifacts and sculpture. Temporary exhibits feature Latino artists and examine the Hispanic-American community. *(1230 Fifth Avenue, ☎ 831-7272. Wed-Sun: 11am-5pm. Mon-Tue: closed. Suggested admission: Adult $4, child free, senior $2, student $2.)*

The **Cooper-Hewitt National Design Museum** is located

Cooper-Hewitt National Design Museum

in a 64-room Georgian mansion, dating from 1901, which was once the home of industrialist Andrew Carnegie. More than 250,000 items make it one of the largest design collections in the world. Started in 1897 at the Cooper Union School for the Advancement of Science and Art, the collection was donated to the Smithsonian Institution in 1967 when it was moved to its current location. Its holdings include drawings, prints, textiles and ceramic art. *(2 East 91st Street, ☎ 849-8300. Tue: 10am-9pm. Wed-Sat: 10am-5pm. Sun: 12noon-5pm. Mon: closed. Adult $5, child free, senior $3, student $3.)*

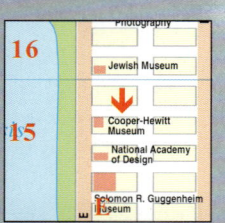

Cooper-Hewitt Museum

Goethe House is located across the street from the Metropolitan Museum of Art. Lectures and films focus on German culture and current events. Goethe House also sponsors German films, complete with English subtitles, at various locations throughout the city. Call for ticket information and prices. *(1014 Fifth Avenue, ☎ 439-8700. Tue and Thu: 12noon-7pm. Wed and Fri-Sat: 12noon-5pm. Sun-Mon: closed. Admission is free.)*

Henderson Place Historic District comprises a surviving row of more than 20 Queen Anne-style houses, built during the 1880s. Details such as gabled roofs, dormer windows and corner turrets enhance the brick and stone facades. The fine craftsmanship with which they were constructed is a vivid reminder of the architectural grandeur of the late 19th century. *(East End Avenue at 86th Street.)*

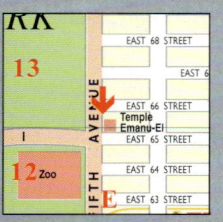

Temple Emanu-El

Built in 1929, **Temple Emanu-El** ("God is with us") is the largest synagogue in America, seating a congregation of over 2,500. The design of the temple

. . . Other Attractions . . .

is a mixture of Romanesque and Byzantine styles. *(1 East 65th Street, ☎ 744-1400. Sun-Fri: 10am-4.45pm. Sat: service at 10.30am.)*

Gracie Mansion was built by Archibald Gracie, an affluent merchant, in 1799 and has been the official home of New York's mayor since 1942. The mansion's Federal-style architecture is one of the best-preserved in the city. Guided tours are available on Wednesdays only and must be reserved ahead. *(East End Avenue at 88th Street, ☎ 570-4751. Wed: 10am-2pm (Apr-Nov). Adult $4, child $4, senior $3, student $4.)*

Gracie Mansion

Founded in 1956 by John D. Rockefeller III, the **Asia Society** was created to promote an understanding of Asian culture. The society is housed in an eight-story building and has maintained three galleries, one of which displays Rockefeller's personal collection. Events and activities include exhibitions, lectures, films and music. *(725 Park Avenue, ☎ 288-6400. Tue-Wed and Fri-Sat: 11am-6pm. Thu: 11am-8pm. Sun: 12noon-5pm. Adult $4, child free, senior $2, student $2.)*

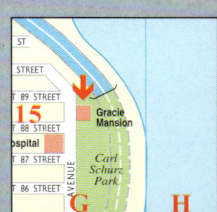
Gracie Mansion

Built in 1880, the **Seventh Regiment Armory** was used in every United States war from the War of 1812 to the Second World War. Behind the imposing exterior is an opulent setting filled with 19th-century furnishings. Designed by Louis Comfort Tiffany, the Veterans' Room and adjoining library are particularly impressive. The Armory remains an active military unit and also hosts cultural events. *(643 Park Avenue, ☎ 744-8180. Mon-Fri: open for tours by appointment only. Sat-Sun: closed.)*

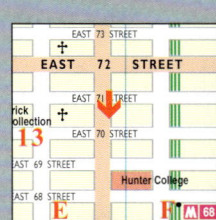
Asia Society

The Abigail Adams Smith Museum, built in 1799, was named after the daughter of President John Adams. This Federal-style building was once the carriage house belonging to the Adams family, who resided in a nearby estate. It was later converted to an inn. In 1924, it was purchased by the Colonial Dames of America who restored it and made it into a museum.

Asia Society

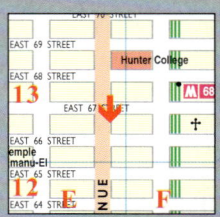
Seventh Regiment Army

. . . Other Attractions

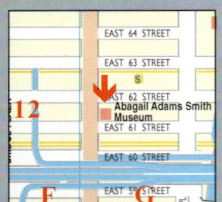

*Abigail Adams
Smith Museum*

The nine-room house displays a collection which includes Federal furnishings and a letter from George Washington. *(421 East 61st Street, ☎ 838-6878. Tue-Sun: 11am-4pm. (Jun-Jul also Tue: 11am-9pm). Mon: closed. Aug: closed. Adult $ 3, child free, senior $2, student $2.)*

Built in 1917, the exclusive and sophisticated **Grolier Club** was where the wealthy men of the early 20th century once wheeled and dealed. The club is dedicated to the art of bookmaking, and houses a research library and an exhibition room. *(47 East 60th Street, ☎ 838-6690. Library and exhibition room open by appointment only.)*

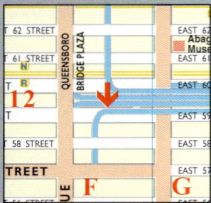

Tram to Roosevelt Island

The **Gagosian Gallery** has a collection of famous artists such as Andy Warhol, Willem de Kooning and Jackson Pollack. In Soho, there is also a downtown location of this gallery (see page 81). *(980 Madison Avenue, ☎ 744-2313. Tue-Sat: 10am-6pm. Sun-Mon: closed.)*

At the **Society of Illustrators**, you will find a unique collection of illustrations, ranging from advertisements and cartoons to war-time propaganda. The collection has a broad appeal and interests not only illustration buffs, but also offers something for everyone. *(128 East 63rd Street, ☎ 838-2560. Wed-Fri: 10am-5pm. Tue: 10am-8pm. Sat: 12noon-4pm. Sun-Mon: closed. Admission is free.)*

Roosevelt Island

Roosevelt Island is located in the East River between the Upper East Side of Manhattan and Queens. Originally inhabited by the Canarsie Indians, it was later sold to the Dutch. Known as Welfare Island, it was the site of a prison and a number of hospitals and asylums during the 19th century. In 1969 it was transformed into a residential community and, in 1986, its name was officially changed to Roosevelt Island in honor of President Franklin D. Roosevelt. Today, it is a prosperous suburb filled with beautiful parks and stunning views, only minutes from the busy streets of Manhattan. To get there, take either the Q or B subway trains or the Q102 bus. Better still, the Roosevelt Island tram car takes visitors on a scenic journey to and from the island. *(East River. Tram to Roosevelt Island: Second Avenue at 60th Street, ☎ 832-4540. Tram cars run every 15 minutes, Sun-Thu: 6am-2am. Fri-Sat: 6am-3.30am.)*

Open Spaces

Designed in 1891, **Carl Schurz Park** *(East End Avenue and the East River, between 84th and 90th Streets)* is named after the German immigrant who became a Civil War general, U.S. Senator, editor of the *New York Evening Post* and *Harper's Weekly* and, eventually, President Rutherford B. Hayes' Secretary of the Interior from 1869-1875.

The highlight of this grassy park is a long, wide sidewalk, named **John Finley Walk**, after the former editor of the *New York Times*, who was an avid hiker. The promenade provides great views of the East River and Queens, a path for rollerbladers and joggers and a pleasant place to relax and watch the boats on the river. Within the park,

Carl Schurz Park on the East River

Gracie Mansion (page 189), the mayor's residence, dates back to 1799. The park also features a children's playground and fenced-in playgrounds for pets – one for big dogs, the other for small.

Carl Schurz Park

Roosevelt Island's **Octagon Park** contains a promenade which provides magnificent views of the Manhattan skyline and the East River. The park also contains recreational areas with tennis courts and picnic grounds. The island is encircled by a path which makes an excellent route for walking, jogging or rollerblading.

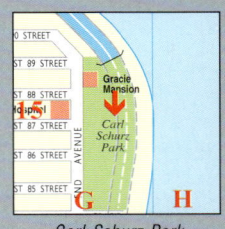

Carl Schurz Park

On the northern tip of Roosevelt Island, **Lighthouse Park** has open green spaces and views of the East River.

Inside The **Metropolitan Museum of Art** (page 178-179), **Astor Court** offers museum-goers an opportunity to relax in a tranquil Ming-style garden. It was designed by a team of Chinese artisans in 1979. In addition, the rooftop **Sculpture Garden**, which is above the 20th-century wing of the museum, features a number of outdoor sculptures and provides wonderful views of the city and Central Park.

Eating and Drinking

Madison Avenue is the pinnacle of New York art and fashion. It is *the* place for window shopping, bistro dining and people-watching. All along the avenue you will find gourmet food and specialty shops like **Caviarteria** *(29 East 60th Street, ☎ 759-7410)* and **Sherry-Lehmann** *(679 Madison Avenue, ☎ 838-7500)*, one of the best-known wine stores in New York.

Gourmet food shop on the Upper East Side

Some of Manhattan's best restaurants are tucked away in the townhouses lining the shady streets of the Upper East Side. **Aureole** *(34 East 61st Street, ☎ 319-1660)* and **Daniel** *(60 East 65th Street, ☎ 288-0033)* are just two of the many top-ranked restaurants in the area.

In the exclusive Carlyle Hotel, **Café Carlyle** *(35 East 76th Street, ☎ 744-1600)* is one of the more elegant places in town, perfect for after-dinner drinks and celebrity-watching, while being entertained by cabaret star **Bobby Short**.

Elaine's *(1703 Second Avenue, ☎ 534-8103)* has always been a favorite with theater and film celebrities, more for the social scene than the food. Another classic New York City haunt is the **Oak Room** *(Fifth Avenue at 59th Street, ☎ 759-3000)* at the Plaza Hotel.

Sharz Cafe (page 193) is a cozy Upper East Side bistro which has one of the best wines-by-the-glass selections in the city. For a moderately-priced meal in an elegant surroundings, **La Folie** (page 193) charms with its candle-lit dining room, grand piano and fireplace.

Across the street from Bloomingdale's department store, **Contrapunto** (page 194) and **Yellowfingers** (page 194) are two long-standing Italian eateries which are great places to unwind after a day of shopping and sightseeing.

East of Park Avenue, especially along Second and Third Avenues, the restaurants and shops tend to be less expensive. Some very good ones give discounts to *for less* cardholders (see pages 193-198). **Hunan Balcony Gourmet** (page 193) and **Chinatown East** (page 195) offer high quality, reasonably priced Chinese food. Nearby, **Doc Watson's** (page 195) is an amiable Irish pub which serves hearty meals at good prices.

Sharz Cafe and Wine Bar

Italian / Mediterranean

1177 East 90th Street
☎ 369-1010

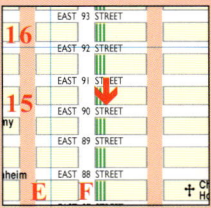

Average meal: $20-25
for less discount: 25%
AM/MC/VS/DC

This cozy Mediterranean bistro has more than 40 wines by-the-glass. Entrées include more than 16 different pastas as well as various daily specials, such as delicious rosemary lamb chops. Reservations are recommended.

HOURS

Mon-Sat: 11.30am-
3.30pm and
Mon-Thu: 5pm-10pm
Fri-Sat: 5pm-12midnight
Sun: 11am-4pm

La Folie

French

1422 Third Avenue
☎ 744-6327

Average meal: $20-25
for less discount: 25%
AM/MC/VS/DC

This elegant restaurant features a pleasant dining room with a fireplace and a grand piano. Candles and soft music enhance the atmosphere. Reasonable prices for a high quality dinner make this a great value.

HOURS

Mon-Thu: 6pm-10pm
Fri-Sat: 6pm-11pm
Sun: 12noon-4pm,
6pm-10pm

Hunan Balcony Gourmet

Chinese

1417 Second Avenue
☎ 517-2088

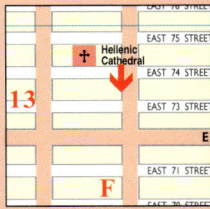

Average meal: $10-15
for less discount: 25%
AM/MC/VS/DC

Hunan Balcony serves Chinese cuisine in a modern restaurant featuring a sunny atrium overlooking the avenue. Try the Hunan flower steak or the crispy shrimp and scallops with walnuts.

HOURS

Mon-Sun:
12noon-12midnight

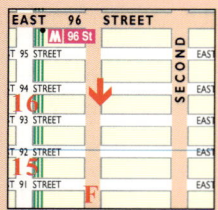

HOURS

Sun-Thu: 5pm-11pm
Fri-Sat: 5pm-12midnight

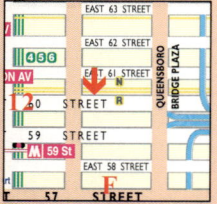

HOURS

Mon-Thu: 12noon-11pm
Fri-Sun: 12noon-
12midnight

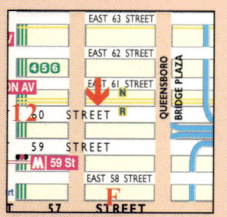

HOURS

Mon-Thu and Sun:
11.30am-12midnight
Fri-Sat: 11.30am-2am

Go Fish

Seafood

1675 Third Avenue
☎ 410-4900

Average meal: $20-25
for less discount: 25%
AM/MC/VS

On the menu at Go Fish is an incredible selection of fresh seafood. Try the mussels, any style, the Maine lobster ravioli or the coconut shrimp tempura. A glass-enclosed terrace offers views of a lovely private sculpture garden.

Contrapunto

Italian

200 East 60th Street
☎ 751-8616

Average meal: $20-25
for less discount: 25%
AM/MC/VS/DC

Located across the street from Bloomingdales, Contrapunto has been serving fine Italian cuisine for more than ten years. Favorites include the salmon with asparagus, wild mushrooms and cauliflower mousse.

Yellowfingers

Italian / American

200 East 60th Street
☎ 751-8615

Average meal: $15-20
for less discount: 25%
AM/MC/VS/DC

For 30 years, this lively trattoria has been a neighborhood favorite. Its second floor location offers you great views of the streets below. Try the rosemary chicken salad or grilled shrimp with tequila.

Chinatown East

Chinese

1650 Third Avenue
☎ 987-3500

Average meal: $10-15
for less discount: 25%
AM/MC/VS

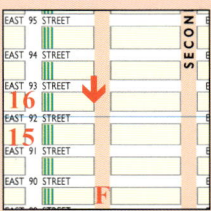

HOURS

Mon-Sun: 12noon-
12midnight

Chinatown East offers an extensive menu at very reasonable prices. The chef's specialties include sesame chicken and seafood delight. There is also a sushi bar where you can watch your food being prepared.

 # Doc Watson's

Irish / American

1490 Second Avenue
☎ 988-5300

Average meal: $10-15
for less discount: 25%
AM/MC/VS/DS

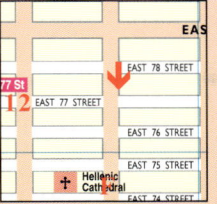

HOURS

Sun-Thu: 12noon-
12midnight
Fri-Sat: 12noon-2pm

This friendly Irish-American restaurant serves good food at reasonable prices. The atmosphere is informal and a pleasant garden is open in the summer. Try one of the burgers or the Guinness stew.

 # The Barking Dog Luncheonette

American

1678 Third Avenue
☎ 831-1800

Average meal: $10-15
for less discount: 25%
No credit cards accepted.

HOURS

Mon-Sun: 8am-11pm

The Barking Dog offers classic American food interpreted for the nineties. This comfortable spot is great for any meal, including Sunday brunch. In warm weather, sample the homemade dishes while dining outdoors.

Shopping . . .

The ultra expensive shops and galleries on Madison Avenue give testament to the wealth of their patrons. This fashionable thoroughfare is home to just about every major designer including **Calvin Klein** *(654 Madison Avenue, ☎ 292-9000)*, **Polo / Ralph Lauren** *(867 Madison Avenue, ☎ 606-2100)*, **Yves Saint Laurent** *(855 Madison Avenue, ☎ 472-5299)*

Bloomingdale's

and **Giorgio Armani** *(815 Madison Avenue, ☎ 988-9191)*.

Also on Madison Avenue, **Crate and Barrel** *(650 Madison Avenue, ☎ 308-0011)* is one of New York's most popular home decoration and furnishing stores. Though the merchandise is stylish, modern and practical, the prices are very reasonable. There are also plenty of items small enough to easily transport home.

Bloomingdale's *(1000 Third Avenue, ☎ 705-2000)* provides the quintessential Upper East Side shopping experience. Here you will find all of the major clothing brands under one roof. You will find everything from simple basics to outrageous *haute couture.*

Upper East Side boutiques

Barney's New York *(Madison Avenue at 61st Street, ☎ 945-1600)* sells top designer fashions with price tags to match. Elegant and hip, Barney's is a favorite with the fashion cognoscenti.

The Upper East Side also offers high quality, less expensive shopping alternatives (though few and far between). **Second Avenue Army Navy** (page 198) sells an assortment of clothing and accesories at very reasonable prices. It is a perfect place to pick up a pair of jeans or some T-shirts.

Take home a poster or print from **Decor Art Gallery**

. . . Shopping

(page 197) or **Metropolitan Graphic Arts** (page 198) and receive a 20% discount with your *for less* card.

Most of the museums on **Museum Mile** have shops offering unusual gifts and souvenirs. At the **Museum of the City of New York** (page 184), *for less* cardholders are entitled to a discount in the gift shop.

For a truly unique gift, make your own at **Our Name is Mud** (page 197). From mugs to hand-made pottery, you can customize just about anything in the shop.

Rather than bring home rolls of film, why not take home pictures instead? **Fromex 1 Hour Photo** (page 198) will have your color photos ready for you before you can finish shopping.

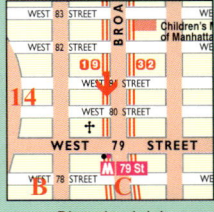

Bloomingdale's

Our Name is Mud

Crafts & Gifts

1566 Second Avenue
☎ **570-6868**

for less discount: 20%
AM/MC/VS

Handmade crafts and gifts are available in this lively shop and art studio. It sells pottery, scented candles and other creations. Visitors can observe artists at work or create their own art at the paint bar.

Decor Art Gallery

Poster Shop & Framing

1156 Second Avenue
☎ **688-7078**

for less discount: 20%
AM/MC/VS

Decor Art carries a large selection of posters and art, both with or without frames. Classic and modern art from well-known artists can be purchased. This shop can also fit a frame to any poster, photograph or artwork.

HOURS

Mon-Sat: 11.30am-8pm
Sun: 11.30am-6pm

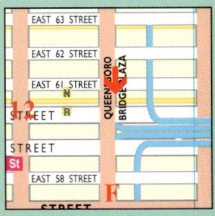

HOURS

Mon-Sat: 10am-7.30pm
Sun: 11am-6pm

Introduction . . .

The construction of Central Park was begun in 1858 by journalist and landscaper **Frederick Von Olmstead** and English architect **Calvert Vaux** on seemingly

undesirable swampland. Its creation, which took 20 years, involved moving millions of tons of soil and rocks, planting over five million trees and building ponds, lakes, a reservoir and roadways.

The terrace at Belvedere Castle

The result is an incredible wilderness in the heart of the busy metropolis. Its various areas incorporate many different types of natural landscape, which runs the gamut from open fields to thicketed forests.

Ball games, picnics and summertime outdoor concerts help make this 843-acre park a vibrant center of activity. At one famous open-air concert in 1981, more than half a million people came to the **Great Lawn** to watch Simon and Garfunkel perform.

While Americans around the country spend their summers lounging by swimming pools and walking barefoot on their lawns, the closest many New Yorkers get to the "great outdoors" is Central Park. This does not, however, stop them from putting on bathing suits, applying sunscreen and throwing their beach towels onto the sloping greens of the **Sheep Meadow** as if it were a sandy beach.

North of the Lake, **The Ramble** *(Between 72nd and 79th Streets, ☎ 772-0210)* has over 30 acres of sylvan wonderland filled with dirt paths and trickling brooks. Known as an excellent spot for bird-watching, excursions are held from Tuesday through Sunday from 11am-4pm. Binoculars and sketching materials are available free of charge.

Joseph Papp's **New York Shakespeare Festival** was founded in 1954, and its *Shakespeare in the Park* productions are a favorite summertime event. Two different plays are staged throughout the summer at the outdoor **Delacorte Theater** *(West 81st Street, ☎ 861-7277)*. Tickets are free, but obtaining them is not so easy. New Yorkers wait in shifts, staggering their lunch hours to be

Joggers in Central Park

staggered with friends until the tickets are given out sometime after 1pm (arrive early). You can also get tickets at the Public Theater (page 99) on Lafayette

INSIDER'S TIP

To find out about special events and happenings, the Department of Parks and Recreation (☎ 360-3456) has a 24-hour recorded information line which provides information on activities in this and other city parks.

. . . Introduction

Street – the same procedure applies. The tickets become more difficult to obtain towards the end of each production's run, when all the last-minute Shakespeare fans turn up in droves.

Summerstage is another free summer event that takes place at **Rumsey Playfield**. Whether the performances are reggae or opera, they always attract crowds who set up blankets and picnic anywhere within hearing distance.

Sledding in Central Park, 1898

Best known for its extremely popular walking and jogging route, the **Reservoir** (*Between 86th and 97th Streets*) has recently been renamed to honor **Jacqueline Kennedy Onassis**, who used to jog here regularly. Madonna is sometimes spotted jogging incognito with her bodyguards.

Take a stroll along the Mall – a grand tree-lined boulevard in the midst of the park. Little has changed since its days as a popular place to promenade during the late 19th century. **Horse-drawn carriages** are another popular way of seeing the park. You can check the rates and buy a ticket from a booth at **Grand Army Plaza** (*59th Street at Fifth Avenue*).

To step into another time zone altogether, visit the impromptu roller-skating rink just west of the Mall. Skaters here wear the four-wheeled rollerskates that seem so perfectly suited to the 1970s disco music that blasts from the fabricated D.J. booth in the center. Nearby, **Wollman Rink** (page 202) is one of the most popular outdoor attractions in the city and the main attraction in Central Park.

Rollerbladers at Wollman Rink

Although crime in the park is not commonplace, there have been a few very unpleasant and well-publicized incidents. Keep to the more populated areas if the park is unfamiliar to you and avoid roaming the park after dark. There are emergency phone boxes and telephones throughout the park as well as a 24-hour Park Line (☎ *570-4820*).

INSIDER'S TIP

Getting temporarily lost in the park is not uncommon (even for seasoned New Yorkers), but it is easily remedied. All of the lampposts have a sign which informs you of the nearest city street. Look at the first two digits on the post, and it will tell you which is the closest city block.

Other Attractions . . .

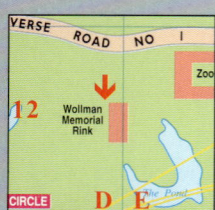
Wollman Rink

for less Skating at **Wollman Rink** is a unique New York tradition. With its wide open space and fantastic views of the midtown skyline, it is perhaps one of the most spectacular outdoor skating rinks in the world.

Outdoor tables and a terrace overlook the rink, allowing you to watch the skaters below. Inside, there is a snack bar and a sports shop. The view of the skyscrapers bordering the park is especially beautiful at night, and the rink is open late most evenings.

Ice skating at Wollman Rink

All sessions are accompanied by music, you can stay for as long as you like and lessons are available. If you don't have your own skates, you can rent them at the rink. In the winter, ice skaters fill the rink, but from April to October in-line skating becomes the main event.

The best way to reach Wollman Rink, located in the southeast corner of the park, is from the Grand Army Plaza entrance at 59th Street and 5th Avenue. *(Central Park at 63rd Street, ☎ 396-1010. Mon-Tue: 10am-3pm. Wed: 10am-9.30pm. Thu: 10am-5pm. Fri-Sat: 10am-11pm. Sun: 10am-9pm. Adult $7, child $3.50, senior $3.50, student $7, Skate rental $3.50. 50% discount on admission with voucher on page 281.)*

Located in the southern portion of the park, the wooden, Gothic-style **Dairy** was built in 1870 and now serves as the main visitors' center. Inside, a short video about the history of the park as well as other park-related information is available. This is a good place to start a visit to the park, and to find out about any special events taking place. *(65th Street Transverse,*

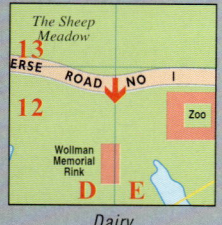
Dairy

☎ 794-6564. Winter: Tue-Sun: 11am-4pm. Fri: 1pm-4pm. Summer: Tue-Sun: 11am-5pm. Fri: 1pm-5pm.)

The **Carousel**, which was imported from its old home at Coney Island (page 226), is a now a Central Park favorite with children. *(65th Street Transverse, ☎ 879-0244. Summer: Mon-Fri: 10.30am-8pm. Sat-Sun: 10.30am-6.30pm. Winter: Sat-Sun: 10.30am-5pm. 90¢.)*

Carousel

The **Central Park Wildlife Conservation Center** has been creatively restored to maximize its small space. The 5½-acre zoo is home to more than 130 species

. . . Other Attractions . . .

and has three climate zones: the Tropics, the California coast and the Polar Circle. The Polar Circle exhibit contains a special tank that allows you to watch the polar bears on land and in the water. A gallery, located outside the main entrance to the zoo, displays wildlife art. *(Fifth Avenue and 64th Street, ☎ 439-6500. Apr-Oct: Mon-Fri: 10am-5pm. Sat-Sun: 10.30am-5:30pm. Nov-Mar: Mon-Sun: 10am-4:30pm. Adult $2.50,*

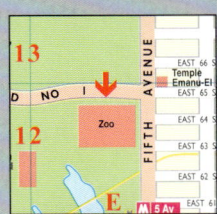

Central Park Wildlife Center

Central Park Wildlife Conservation Center

child 50¢ (under 3 free), senior $1.25, student $2.50.)

By the entrance to the Children's Zoo, the **Delacorte Musical Clock**, is also a favorite with children. Every half hour from 8am to 6pm the clock reveals animals that put on a musical performance. *(64th Street at Fifth Avenue, ☎ 861-6030.)*

Also known as the **Model Boat Pond**, the **Conservatory Water** is the site of model boat races every Saturday from March to November. On the north side of the pond is the Alice in Wonderland sculpture. Close by, a statue of Hans Christian Andersen is the site of summertime storytelling sessions. *(East 74th Street, ☎ 360-8133.)*

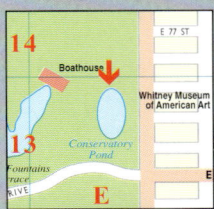

Conservatory Water

Bethesda Terrace

In the center of the park, the **Lake**, with its **Bow Bridge**, resembles a scene from a 19th-century painting thanks in part to the row boats that can be seen here on warm days. *(Between West 71st and 77th Streets.)*

Loeb Boathouse rents rowboats for $10 per hour, plus a $20 deposit. Private gondola tours are given for $30 per hour. You can also rent bicycles for $8-10 an hour. The boathouse has a restaurant and a café with outdoor seating available in warm weather. *(East 74th Street, ☎ 517-4723.)*

Bethesda Fountain and Terrace, the architectural centerpiece of the park, overlooks the Lake and offers one of the most scenic views in the park. *(72nd Street, ☎ 517-2233.)*

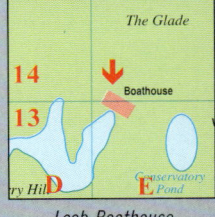

Loeb Boathouse

Beginning at 66th Street, **The Mall** is a tree-lined thoroughfare that leads up to an open area by the **Bandshell**, which has become a favorite impromptu

. . . Other Attractions

spot for in-line skaters. *(Between 66th and 72nd Streets.)*

Strawberry Fields is an international peace garden commemorating the life and death of John Lennon who lived nearby. There are 161 varieties of plant life on this three-acre preserve – a tribute to the 161 nations of the world. *(West 72nd Street.)*

Belvedere Castle, the highest point in the park, is a fairy-tale structure with great views of the heavily forested Ramble to the south and the Great Lawn to the north. **The Discovery Chamber** is an educational center where children can learn about the park through fun-filled activities. Family workshops are available on Saturdays from 1pm to 2.30pm. The castle also serves as the headquarters for the Urban Park Rangers. *(West 79th Street, ☎ 772-0210.)*

Toy boats in the Conservatory Water

The **North Meadow Recreation Center** is located north of the Reservoir. The center has basketball courts and sponsors other recreational programs, including rock climbing courses. *(West 97th Street, ☎ 348-4867.)*

Showcasing the wrought-iron gates that once stood at Cornelius Vanderbilt's mansion is the **Conservatory Garden**. Thousands of plants, trees and shrubs adorn the three formal gardens. In the summer, free tours are given on Saturdays. *(West 104th Street, ☎ 860-1382. Mon-Sun: 8am-dusk.)*

Strawberry Fields

Just above the Conservatory Garden, is the recently refurbished **Harlem Meer**. The **Charles A. Dana Discovery Center** features ongoing educational exhibitions and programs relating to Central Park. In the summer, you can rent a fishing rod from the center and cast a line in the meer. *(110th Street and Fifth Avenue, ☎ 860-1370. Tue-Sat: 11am-5pm. Sun-Mon: closed.)*

Bethesda Fountain

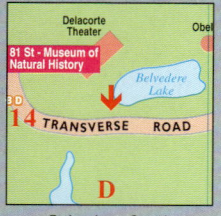

Belvedere Castle

Belvedere Castle

Conservatory Garden

New York
by Night

Introduction

More than any other city in the world, New York is known for its nightlife. "The city that never sleeps" offers endless nighttime opportunities well past midnight every night of the week. From quiet dining and classical performing arts to all-night clubbing and live music of every type, the city has something to offer everyone.

Manhattan skyline at night

Among the best things to do in New York at night are: sightseeing from the top of the **Empire State Building** (page 114), which is open until midnight, and taking a **sightseeing cruise** (page 214) around the tip of Manhattan where you can enjoy magnificent views of the Statue of Liberty and the illuminated Manhattan skyline.

Throughout New York's neighborhoods, especially along the avenues, there are dense concentrations of **restaurants and bars**, while the majority of **clubs and live music venues** can be found downtown. Almost all bars are open late, some as late as 4am on weekends.

Midtown West is home to the world-renowned **Theater District** and its **Broadway** productions. In addition to commercial Broadway shows, there are many excellent secondary productions staged throughout the city.

REFLECTIONS

'New York attracts the most talented people in the world in the arts and professions. It also attracts them in other fields. Even the bums are talented.' – Edmund Love, *Subways Are for Sleeping* (1957)

Off-Broadway, in particular, presents quality plays and musicals, often starring well-known film and television actors.

Webster Hall

Further downtown, **Greenwich Village** and **Soho** are late night hot spots for dining, bar hopping and clubbing. One of the best and biggest nightclubs is **Webster Hall** (page 210), which gives a discount to *for less* cardholders.

Free newspapers the *New York Press* and the *Village Voice*, available throughout the city, give up-to-date and detailed listings of events and venues, as do weekly magazines such as *New York* and *Time Out New York*.

The subway runs 24 hours every day and will accommodate any nightlife schedule, no matter how rigorous.

Nightlife. . .

THEATERS

The **TKTS** booth *(West 47th Street and Broadway)* in Times Square sells tickets for Broadway shows at 50% off (plus a surcharge of $2.50). They must, however, be purchased on the day of performance only and no credit cards are accepted. Another drawback is that the lines can be daunting. As an alternative to TKTS, you can use your *for less* card to purchase tickets for Broadway shows in advance, while obtaining discounts of up to 50% (see page 209).

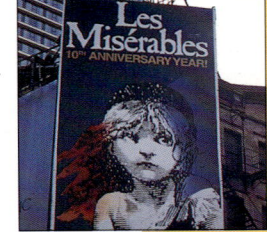
Les Misérables

DANCE

The **New York City Ballet** *(Lincoln Center, ☎ 870-5570)* performs at the New York State Theater, Lincoln Center. It is perhaps best-known for its production of *George Balanchine's The Nutcracker*, performed each holiday season. Leading dancers such as Mikhail Baryshnikov and Rudolf Nureyev have performed with the **American Ballet Theater** *(30 Lincoln Center Plaza, ☎ 362-6000)* whose productions are staged at the Metropolitan Opera House.

The **Joyce Theater** *(175 Eighth Avenue, ☎ 242-0800)* is the permanent home of Feld Ballets/NY and hosts performances in many different dance styles. Other venues for modern dance include **City Center** *(131 West 44th Street, ☎ 581-1212)*, **BAM** (page 209) and **The Merce Cunningham Studio** *(55 Bethune Street, ☎ 691-9751)*.

OPERA

The Metropolitan Opera has hosted legendary performers like Placido Domingo and Luciano Pavarotti. Performances are held from October to mid-April. *(Lincoln Center, ☎ 362-6000)*. Performing at Lincoln Center's New York State Theater, **New York City Opera** (page 209) offers a discount to *for less* cardholders. It has received critical acclaim for a varied repertoire of works from classics to world premieres. High-tech "supertitles" allow you to read English translations projected above the stage during the performance.

Evening in the Theater District

CONCERT HALLS

Carnegie Hall *(156 West 57th Street, ☎ 247-7800)* is the most historic concert hall in the city, dating back to 1891 (see page 141). **Avery Fisher Hall** is home to the prestigious **New York Philharmonic** *(10 Lincoln Center, ☎ 875-5030)*.

. . . Nightlife

FILM

For general information about movies playing around town, call **Moviephone** (☎ 777-3456). To see

Times Square at night

independent, foreign and rare films, try the **Anthology Film Archives** (*32 Second Avenue,* ☎ *505-5181)* or the **Angelica Film Center** (*18 West Houston Street,* ☎ *995-2000).* You can also enjoy a unique cinematic experience at the **Sony IMAX Theatre** (page 163) where your *for less* card entitles you to two admissions for the price of one.

COMEDY CLUBS

Stand-up New York (page 210), one of New York's top comedy clubs, offers a discount to *for less* cardholders. Other good venues for catching stand-up comedy are **Caroline's** (*1626 Broadway,* ☎ *757-4100)* and **Dangerfield's** (*1118 First Avenue,* ☎ *593-1650),* owned by comedian and actor Rodney Dangerfield.

JAZZ CLUBS / LIVE MUSIC CLUBS

Much of New York's thriving jazz scene can be found in Greenwich Village, including blues club **Mondo Cane** (page 210). Jazz enthusiasts can also enjoy venues like the **Blue Note** (*131 West 3rd Street,* ☎ *475-8592),* the **Village Vanguard** (*178 Seventh Avenue,* ☎ *255-4037)* and Tribeca's

New York nightlife

Knitting Factory (*74 Leonard Street,* ☎ *219-3055).* Popular rock clubs include the **Beacon Theater** (*2124 Broadway,* ☎ *496-7070)* and **Roseland** (*239 West 52nd Street,* ☎ *245-5761)* as well as many smaller clubs downtown, especially in the **East Village** (see page 97).

NIGHTCLUBS

Dancing at Webster Hall

New York's club scene changes rapidly, with new clubs springing up constantly. A select few have managed to remain popular for a long period. Among these, try **Limelight** (*680 Sixth Avenue,* ☎ *807-7780),* the **Palladium** (*126 East 14th Street,* ☎ *473-4141)* and **Webster Hall** (page 210) which offers reduced admission, front-of-the-line status and a complimentary champagne toast to *for less* cardholders.

Broadway Theater Discounts

226 West 47th St., 3rd Flr
☎ 398-8383, ext. 30
or (800) 223-7565, ext. 30

Save on orchestra or front
mezzanine tickets. Buy in
advance with a credit card or at
the above address ($10 service
charge applies with credit card).
AM/MC/VS

With **New York for less**, you can obtain discounts of up
to 50% off tickets for top Broadway shows. Call in
advance to see which shows are available. Book by
credit card, or purchase tickets at the ticket office.

 Brooklyn Academy of Music

30 Lafayette Ave., Brooklyn
☎ (718) 636-4100 (info),
(212) 307-4100 (tickets)
Fax: (718) 857-2021

With your for less card: 15% off
any BAM ticket. Buy tickets by
phone, fax or mail (advance
purchase possible).
MC/VS

Save 15% on tickets for any production at the oldest
performing arts center in America. If you are purchasing
your tickets by mail or fax, be sure to include alternate
dates and a phone number where you can be reached.

 New York City Opera

New York State Theater,
Lincoln Center
☎ 870-5570 (info only)

With your for less card:
$10 off all orchestra seats.
Buy tickets at box office
on day of performance.
AM/MC/VS

Enjoy an evening of opera at world-famous Lincoln
Center. New York City Opera's seasonal performances
include time-honored classics like La Bohème and
exciting new productions.

HOURS

Telephone reservations
are accepted
Mon-Fri: 10am-5pm

HOURS

Box office open:
Mon-Fri: 10am-6pm
Sat: 12noon-6pm
Sun (performance days
only): 12noon-4pm.

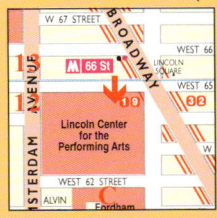

HOURS

Box office open:
Mon: 10am-7.15pm
Tue-Sat: 10am-8.15pm
Sun: 11.30am-7.15pm

Webster Hall

Nightclub

125 East 11th Street
☎ 353-1600

$15 Thu, $20 Fri-Sat
$5 off admission
with your
for less card.
AM/MC/VS/DS

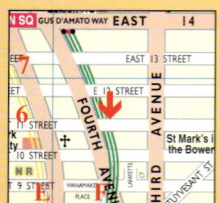

HOURS

Thu-Sat: 10pm-4am

Webster Hall is New York City's premier nightclub. It encompasses over 40,000 square feet on 4 floors and has four DJs. With your **for less** card you get a discount, priority entrance *and* a free glass of champagne.

Mondo Cane

Live Music / Blues

205 Thompson Street
☎ 254-5166

$5 entrance
2 admissions for
the price of 1 with
your for less card.
AM/MC/VS/DC

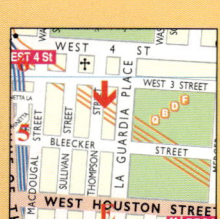

HOURS

Mon-Sun: 10am-3am

This live music club specializes in blues and jazz. It is situated right in the heart of Greenwich Village. Stop here for after-dinner drinks while watching the performance.

Stand Up New York

Comedy Club / Restaurant

236 West 78th Street
☎ 595-0850

Average meal: $15-20
2 admissions for the price of 1
and 25% discount on your
meal with voucher on page 281.
AM/MC/VS/DC/DS

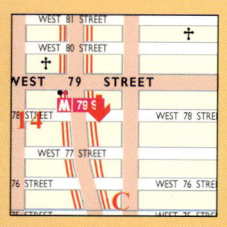

HOURS

Mon-Fri: 6:30pm-1am
Sat: 6:30pm-12midnight

This well-established comedy club is also a high quality restaurant. Top comedians from all over the world perform nightly. American cuisine is served while you watch the show. The baked ziti is highly recommended.

Tours

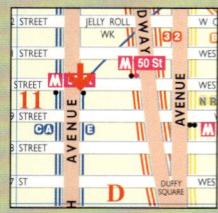

ADDRESS

Purchase tickets at the Visitors Information Center: 777 Eighth Avenue at 53rd Street.
☎ (800) 876-9868 or (212) 944-9200.

TOUR HOURS

Mon-Sun: 9am-6pm

PRICES

Full City Tour:
Adult: $35
Child: $22

Full City Tour Plus range of tours:
Prices vary, inquire at the Visitors Information Center for more details.

DISCOUNT

$5 off any Full City Tour or Full City Tour *Plus* with your *for less* card when you buy your ticket from the New York Apple Tours Visitors Information Center at 777 Eighth Avenue. Over time, it is possible that tour names, itineraries and prices will change. However, your *for less* card will ensure that you receive a discount on the tours most similar to the ones described here.

New York Apple Tours . . .

Whether you have two days or two weeks to spend in New York, taking New York Apple Tours is the best way to maximize your time while visiting all the major sightseeing attractions in the city.

All tours are conducted on **double-decker buses** imported from London. Open and closed-top buses allow you to tour New York City in any weather. As you see the sights of Manhattan, you are given a **live commentary** by an experienced on-board guide.

You can **hop on and off** as many times as you like, allowing you to customize your own sightseeing tour.

The **Full City Tour** allows you to travel on the entire route for two consecutive days. Use it to get to all the most popular sights from Lower Manhattan to Harlem, including the Empire State Building, Times Square, Rockefeller Center and Lincoln Center. The bus travels the length of Manhattan, allowing you to visit neighborhoods from Chinatown to Soho to the Upper East Side. Spend some time exploring a neighborhood in one part of the city, before re-boarding the bus to visit another.

A new addition to the Full City Tour is the Brooklyn route. Covering many of Brooklyn's best-known neighborhoods, including Brooklyn Heights and Park Slope, the tour will take you past sights

Enjoying the ride

such as the Promenade (for fantastic views of Manhattan), Grand Army Plaza and Prospect Park. For more information about the borough of Brooklyn, see pages 222-226.

New York Apple Tours has bus stops which are convenient for nearly every attraction in this book, including those which give a discount to *for less* cardholders. In the right-hand margin, you will find a list of some of the most popular attractions along the Full City Tour route, together with their corresponding page numbers in this book.

. . . New York Apple Tours

With the **Full City Tour *Plus*** range of tours, you can combine the two-day tour Full City Tour with a host of other options, all on one ticket. For example, the **Full City Tour *Plus* World Trade Center** or **Full City Tour *Plus* Empire State Building** will not only get you to your destination, but will also provide you with an entrance ticket once you get there.

Some of the more popular tours from the Full City Tour *Plus* range are listed below. Please note that these tours change from time to time so not all of the ones featured here may be available when you visit.

New York Apple Tours double-decker bus

The **Statue of Liberty Express** includes the Full City Tour *plus* the ferry ticket to the Statue of Liberty and Ellis Island (page 52-55). This a great way to avoid the inevitable lines for buying ferry tickets.

With the **Full City Tour *Plus* Cruise**, you can combine your Full City Tour with a 90-minute river cruise through New York Harbor. Cruises are seasonal, so it is best to phone ahead for times.

For the more adventurous in spirit, take the **Full City Tour *Plus* Helicopter Tour** where your excursion includes a breathtaking helicopter ride high above the skyscrapers of New York City.

For the ultimate touring experience, go with the **Super New York Package**. This includes the Full City Tour, a ferry ticket to the Statue of Liberty and Ellis Island, entrance to the Empire State Building Observatory, a McDonald's lunch or dinner and a 90-minute harbor cruise.

If you have time to travel beyond New York, take the **Full City Tour *Plus* Washington, D.C.** or **Full City Tour *Plus* Boston**. These day trips allow you to travel at your own pace. They include breakfast in New York, unreserved round-trip train transportation via Amtrak to Washington D.C. or Boston and the Full City Tour in New York.

In order to receive your *for less* discount, you must purchase your tickets from the New York Apple Tours Visitors Center, located at 777 Eighth Avenue. Tickets may *not* be purchased at any of the bus stops nor from any New York Apple Tours representatives along the route, nor may they be purchased at hotels or retail shops – only at the 777 Eighth Avenue Visitors Center can you obtain the discount.

DON'T MISS

Most of New York's top attractions lie within a short walk of a New York Apple Tours stop. Below you will find a list of some of the most popular sights and their corresponding pages in *New York for less*

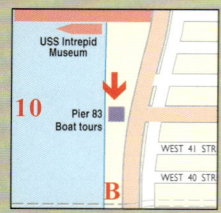

10

ADDRESS

Pier 83, Hudson River at
West 42nd Street
☎ 563-3200

HOURS

Full Island Cruise:
Hours vary depending
on the season from
9:15am-4:30pm.

Harbor Lights Cruise:
Sets sail at 5:30pm or 7pm
depending on the season.

PRICES

Full Island Cruise:
Adult $22
Child $12
Senior $19
Student $22

*Semi-Circle and Harbor
Lights Cruise (90 minutes):*
Adult $18
Child $10
Senior $14
Student $18

Music Cruises: prices vary,
call 563-3200 for
schedule and fares.

DISCOUNT

10% off the regular price
of any Circle Line cruise
with your *for less* card.

 # Circle Line Sightseeing Cruises

Circle Line Sightseeing cruises have been providing
guided tours of the New York waterways for more than
50 years.

The most
comprehensive
cruise is a three-
hour tour, which
makes a complete
circle around the
island of
Manhattan.
Known as the **Full
Island Cruise**,

Circle Line Cruise

because it circles the entire island, this tour covers 35
miles of coastline and travels past major sights and
attractions.

The Statue of Liberty, Ellis Island, World Trade Center,
Empire State Building and Yankee Stadium are just
some of the highlights visible from the boat, and are
included in the lively commentary. You will also sail
underneath the Brooklyn and George Washington
Bridges. This cruise sails daily from early March
through late December.

The 90-minute **Semi-Circle Cruise** is a great way to
see most of the major sights and is perfect if you are
short on time. During the
evening, the tour is called
the **Harbor Lights Cruise**.
This romantic cruise sets sail
at dusk – providing both
sunset and nighttime views
of Manhattan. It sails
around the tip of Manhattan
and out to the Statue of
Liberty as the sun sets.

In addition to sightseeing
tours, **live music cruises** are
also scheduled throughout
the summer (June through
September). On board these
2½-hour cruises you can
enjoy live jazz or a DJ while taking in skyline views.
Reservations are necessary on all music cruises.

*Empire State Building
at sunset*

Other custom cruises sail throughout the season
including two-hour **Family Cruises** and the **Circle Line
Captain's Club** – a series of cruises organized just for
seniors. The **Big Day Rate** promises a free cruise for
anyone celebrating their 50th Birthday.

World Yacht Dinner Cruises

There are quite a few restaurants in New York that offer great views of the city. None of them, however, can rival the ever-changing view of Manhattan offered by a cruise which circumnavigates the island.

World Yacht has combined an excellent meal with a luxury cruise, for an unparalleled entertainment, dining and sightseeing experience. The fleet of ships is comprised of five luxury dining yachts, all climate-

World Yacht

controlled for year-round cruising. From the stately glass-enclosed dining areas, every table offers spectacular views of New York's famous skyline.

Departing from midtown on the Hudson River, the yacht sails past sights such as Ellis Island, the South Street Seaport, United Nations and the

illuminated Brooklyn, Manhattan and Williamsburg Bridges before turning around to complete its three-hour tour. The highlight of the trip is when the boat sweeps right under the Statue of Liberty, allowing you a close-up view of this flood-lit monument.

A **four-course dinner** is served at a leisurely pace so that diners are free to explore the various decks or head to the dance floor where an orchestra plays.

All meals are prepared fresh on board and are known for their quality. World Yacht is a member of organizations such as The Culinary Institute of America, Commanderie des Cordons Bleus de France and the National Restaurant Association.

Dining aboard World Yacht

Some dishes from past menus include appetizers such as *porcini ravioli*, shrimp cocktail and caviar, as well as entrées like *filet mignon*, rack of lamb and the Fulton Fish Market selection of the day. There is also a wide range of desserts, cakes and pastries.

Reservations are necessary for all cruises and proper attire is required. Jeans and sneakers are not permitted and gentlemen must wear a jacket. *For less* cardholders are entitled to a discount of $14 off the price of a dinner cruise Sunday through Friday evenings with the voucher on page 283.

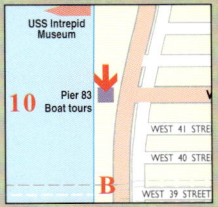

ADDRESS

World Yacht Marina
Pier 81 at West 41st Street
and the Hudson River.
☎ 630-8100

HOURS

Mon-Sun: boards at 6pm,
sails 7pm-10pm.
Call ahead to confirm
time and to reserve.

PRICES

Prices vary, call ahead for
availability and prices.

DISCOUNT

$14 off the regular price of
dinner cruises Sun-Fri with
voucher on page 283.

Seaport Liberty Cruises

Seaport Liberty Cruise by the Statue of Liberty

ADDRESS

Pier 16 at the South
Street Seaport.
☎ 630-8888

HOURS

Seaport Liberty Cruise:
Sails from 12noon-
7:30pm, hours vary
depending on the season.

Music Cruises:
Sets sail at 7pm, 9:30pm
and 10pm, depending on
the season.

PRICES

Seaport Liberty Cruises:
Adult $12
Child $6

Music Cruises:
Adult $20-$35

DISCOUNT

2 tickets for the
price of 1 with voucher
on page 283.

Seaport Liberty Cruises offer one-hour guided
sightseeing tours of Lower Manhattan and the Statue
of Liberty.

Highlights include attractions such as the Brooklyn
Bridge, Wall Street, Ellis Island and the World Trade
Center – all of which are visible from the ship. The live
commentary enriches your viewing of these attractions
and provides additional information about the
maritime history of South Street Seaport.

Seaport Liberty **one-hour cruises** sail on a regular
schedule from mid-March through late December. It is
best to call ahead to confirm the schedule.

From June to September you can also enjoy **live music
cruises** which present contemporary blues and jazz
artists against the backdrop of the Manhattan skyline.

Friday and Saturday nights, from May to October, two-
hour **DJ cruises** feature New York disc jockeys spinning
dance tunes on board.

Departing from Pier 16 at the South Street Seaport
(page 58), Seaport Liberty Cruises fits in well with a
visit to this historic district and is the official
sightseeing cruise of the South Street Seaport
Museum (page 59).

Snacks, sandwiches, beverages (including cocktails
and beer) and famous New York hot dogs are available
on board. You can also purchase T-shirts, hats and
other souvenirs.

The *for less* voucher on page 283 entitles you to
receive two tickets for the price of one on any of the
Seaport Liberty Cruises. Reservations are necessary
only for the music cruises.

Liberty Helicopter Tours

You can experience spectacular views of Manhattan on any of Liberty Helicopters sightseeing tours. Each of the two heliport locations offer pilot-narrated tours – all of which give a 20% discount to **for less** cardholders.

From the **Downtown Heliport** you can fly over New York Harbor past the Statue of Liberty, the South Street Seaport, Ellis and Governor's Islands and other Lower Manhattan sites in only 4½ minutes on the **Lady Liberty**.

From the **VIP Heliport**, the 4½-minute **A Taste of New York** takes you past the USS Intrepid, the Empire State and Chrysler Buildings, then up the Hudson River to Central Park.

Available from both locations on weekdays, **The Big Apple** begins with a close-up view of the Statue of Liberty, past the 110-story twin towers of the World Trade Center, the World Financial Center, the Empire State and Chrysler Buildings, the George Washington Bridge and Central Park.

A helicopter tour over New York Harbor

In addition, **New York, New York** (offered at both locations on weekdays) is the most comprehensive tour available, covering all five boroughs. It provides nearly twenty minutes of sightseeing from the Statue of Liberty to the Bronx. Soar through the canyons of Manhattan's skyscrapers while getting a bird's-eye view of all the attractions included in the other tours plus Yankee Stadium, the George Washington Bridge and the East and Harlem Rivers. You will also see the U.S.S. Intrepid, the Cathedral of St. John the Divine and Yankee Stadium close up.

All tours are conducted in state-of-the-art jet helicopters, featuring climate-controlled cabins and unobstructed views from every seat – perfect for picture taking. Known for having high safety standards, Liberty Helicopters has continuously received the annual safety award from the Helicopter Association International.

Purchase tickets at the heliport only. In addition to a 20% discount on tours, **for less** cardholders are *not* charged the regular heliport surcharge.

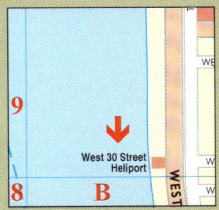

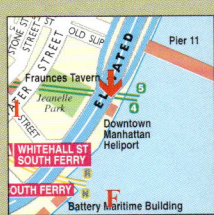

ADDRESS

The VIP Heliport: West 30th Street and 12th Avenue

Downtown Heliport: Pier 6 and the East River ☎ 487-4777 or ☎ (800) 542-9933 for either location

HOURS

The VIP Heliport: Open daily (including holidays): 9am-9pm.

Downtown Heliport: Mon-Fri: 9am-7pm.

PRICES

Prices range from $46 to $159 depending on tour. Weekend tours have different names and prices.

DISCOUNT

20% off the regular price of any helicopter tour with voucher on page 285.

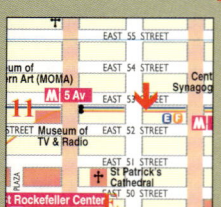

ADDRESS

457 Madison Avenue
☎ 439-1049 for tour
schedule and meeting
places. Call 935-3960 to
make reservations.

PRICES

Guided walking tour:
Adult $10
Child $5
Student $8
Senior $8
(prices may vary per tour)

DISCOUNT

Guided walking tour:
20% discount off the
regular price of any
"Discover New York"
tour with your
for less card.

Discover New York Walking Tours

Discover New York is a tour series sponsored by the **Municipal Art Society**. These architectural and historical walking tours provide you with the seasoned expertise of the society while highlighting the best of New York City's cultural and geographical diversity.

Founded in 1893, The Municipal Art Society is a private, non-profit organization whose original aim was to beautify New York with public art. It has adapted its goals to the times and today directs its efforts toward making New York a more habitable city (an enterprise welcomed by harried New Yorkers). It champions preservation in New York City by assisting

Colonnade Row on a walking tour of Greenwich Village

organizations that need guidance with planning, land use, zoning and development issues. The Municipal Art Society has been critical in the survival of many historical buildings.

The tours, which are led by architectural and urban historians, explore famous neighborhoods and districts such as Greenwich Village, the Flatiron District and Wall Street. Ethnic historians lead tours of Little Italy, Chinatown and the Lower East Side, pointing out New York City's rich multi-cultural communities.

They also explore themes that are both cultural and seasonal, such as the holiday tour "Best Dressed Landmarks of the Holidays", which takes a look at New York's most beautifully decorated buildings and plazas from Cartier and 19th-century Fifth Avenue mansions to Trump Tower.

Every Wednesday at 12:30pm the Municipal Art Society sponsors free tours of **Grand Central Terminal** (page 149).

Since tours and meeting times vary, call ahead to request a listing of the upcoming scheduled tours. Reservations are not required for weekday walking tours, but are sometimes necessary for Saturday walking tours. Your *for less* card entitles you to a 20% discount on any Discover New York walking tour.

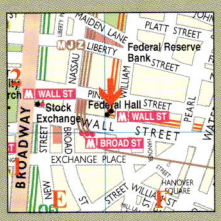 Heritage Trails New York

Lower Manhattan is one of the best places to begin sightseeing in New York City. The concentration of major sights and attractions offers a sweeping overview of the historical and modern metropolis.

As you walk along the streets of Lower Manhattan, you will notice a trail of brightly colored dots on the sidewalks. They map the "trails" of one of New York's most popular guided walking tours – Heritage Trails New York.

Following in the footsteps of Boston's Freedom Trail, New England's most popular tourist attraction, Heritage Trails is designed to interest visitors by enticing them with the historical sites and stories of one of America's oldest modern cities.

Four different trails highlight more than fifty landmarks and historical sites, covering four-and-a-half miles throughout historic Lower Manhattan.

The **Green Trail** is the most comprehensive and includes Federal Hall National Monument, the New York Stock Exchange, the Dutch City Hall Archeology Site, Castle Clinton National Monument and more. The trails are always updated and

New York Stock Exchange

new sites are added regularly. Highlights of some of the other trails include the South Street Seaport, Brooklyn Bridge and the World Trade Center.

Guided tours begin at the **Heritage Trails Visitor Center** located at Federal Hall National Memorial (page 61), just around the corner from the New York Stock Exchange. Call ahead to find out more information about times and itineraries.

With the voucher on page 277, all guided tours are $3 off for adults and $2 off for children.

ADDRESS

Heritage Trails Visitor Center: Federal Hall National Memorial 26 Wall Street
☎ (888) 487-2457
☎ (212) 269-1500, ext. 207

HOURS

Mon-Sun: 9am-5pm

PRICES

Guided walking tours:
Adult $15
Child (7-12) $7
(under 6 free)
Senior $10
Student $10

DISCOUNT

Guided walking tour:
Adult $3 off
Child $2 off
(when accompanied by an adult) with the voucher on page 277.

Other Tours

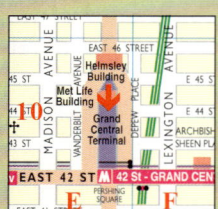

Gray Line Sightseeing Terminal

The amazing Manhattan skyline

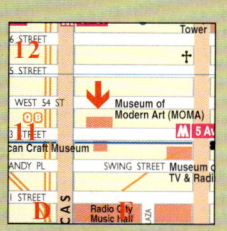

Museum of Modern Art

Grand Central Terminal

for less A great way to tour New York is by deluxe motorcoach. With **Gray Line New York**, you can take the fully-escorted **Manhattan Comprehensive Tour** and save 20% with *New York for less*. This full-day tour includes sightseeing throughout upper and lower Manhattan, admission to the Top of the World Trade Center (page 56-57) and a ticket for the Statue of Liberty / Ellis Island ferry. It also includes lunch served amidst the art-deco chandeliers, marble walls and live piano music in what may be the world's most sophisticated McDonald's. *(Gray Line Sightseeing Terminal, Port Authority Bus Terminal, 42nd Street and 8th Avenue, Street Level, ☎ 397-2600. Adult $55, child $41, senior $55, student $55. Tour departs Mon-Sun: 9am. Arrive 30 minutes prior to departure. Reservations not necessary. 20% discount with voucher on page 285.)*

Tours of attractions provide an informative overview, as well as detailed information otherwise unavailable. While visiting **Ellis Island**, audio tours (page 55) include taped reminiscences which allow you to share the experiences of immigrants who passed through the island on their way to the new world. Your *for less* card entitles you to two audio tours for the price of one.

At the **Museum of Modern Art** (page 130), audio tours help bring an enormous collection into perspective. The random-access digital format allows you to browse the collection at your own pace, viewing the works in any order. For every digital audio guide purchased, *New York for less* entitles you to one for free.

One great benefit of a tour is that it often allows you to go behind-the-scenes. At **Radio City Music Hall** (page 133) and **Lincoln Center** (page 162), go backstage and explore parts of these New York institutions that theater-goers never see. Learn about the history and some of the famous artists that have graced their stages.

The impressive renovation of **Grand Central Terminal** (page 149) is the talk of New Yorkers, but find out just how it was done by taking the free tour sponsored by the **Municipal Art Society** (page 218).

Cruise Central Park on two wheels, while enjoying a fully-escorted bicycle tour, with **Central Park Bicycle Tours** (☎ *(212) 541-8759)*. For the less athletic, a **horsedrawn hansom cab** (☎ *(212) 246-0520)* is another way to enjoy the park.

Outer Boroughs

Introduction to Brooklyn . . .

In the early 1800s, Brooklyn was made up of a number of small independent communities isolated from Manhattan. This was changed forever by the advent of Robert Fulton's Manhattan steamship service in 1807.

Speculators snatched up real estate hoping to lure Wall Street workers who could quickly and conveniently commute from Brooklyn to Manhattan's Financial District.

By the mid-19th century, the prosperous city of Brooklyn was the third largest in the country. The building of the **Brooklyn Bridge** (page 63) in 1883 linked the city to Manhattan and, in 1898, by a close vote, Brooklyn officially became part of New York City.

View of Brooklyn from Manhattan

Today, the Brooklyn Bridge is as popular as it was when it was opened over 100 years ago. Nearly a mile across, it has a pedestrian pathway that offers unrivaled views of the Manhattan skyline and Brooklyn.

Another great place to enjoy a wonderful view is the waterfront **Promenade** in **Brooklyn Heights**, where you can watch the sun set behind the Statue of Liberty. Officially declared New York's first historic district in 1965, Brooklyn Heights contains beautiful 19th-century brownstone buildings. Some of the best of these grand houses are those skirting the promenade, facing Manhattan. Plenty of restaurants can be found here as well, especially along Montague Street. At the top of Montague Street, **Borough Hall** is Brooklyn's oldest building. Built in 1851, in the Greek-Revival style, it was originally used as Brooklyn's city hall.

Brooklyn Promenade

INSIDER'S TIP

Ride the subway to Brooklyn during the day to enjoy the museums, parks and restaurants. Stroll the promenade before making your way to the foot of the Brooklyn Bridge. Walk over the bridge to Manhattan at dusk to enjoy the sweeping views of the Manhattan skyline as the sun sets.

Although Brooklyn Heights remains the borough's most visited and historic neighborhood, **Carroll Gardens**, **Park Slope** and **Cobble Hill** also contain blocks of beautifully preserved brownstones, quiet tree-lined streets and vibrant communities. Young, well-to-do Manhattanites are stretching their dollars as far as possible, moving deeper and deeper into the heart of Brooklyn, following inexpensive rents and leaving in their wake a path of gentrification and escalating real

. . . Introduction to Brooklyn

estate prices. In addition to being a desirable residential area, **Park Slope** also has historical significance as the site of General George Washington's 1776 retreat during the **Revolutionary War**.

Yet another New York City park created by Central Park planners Olmsted and Vaux, **Prospect Park** (page 224), completed in 1867, is considered to be their finest achievement.

They are also responsible for the design of **Grand Army Plaza** which was constructed in 1870 at the entrance to Prospect Park. In

Mask from Zaire at the Brooklyn Museum

1892, the **Soldiers' and Sailors' Memorial Arch** was added to commemorate those from Brooklyn who died during the Civil War. Every June, the plaza hosts the **Welcome Back to Brooklyn Festival**, which honors all its native sons and daughters.

Eastern Parkway, originating at Grand Army Plaza passes both the **Brooklyn Museum** (page 224) and the **Brooklyn Botanic Garden** (page 225). When it opened in 1897, the Brooklyn Museum was intended to be the largest museum in the world. Although it never reached this lofty ambition, it is nonetheless one of the great American cultural institutions. Close by, the **Brooklyn Children's Museum** is the oldest museum of its kind in the United States.

The **Brooklyn Academy of Music** (page 209), world-renowned for the quality of its productions, is America's oldest performing arts center in continuous operation and gives a discount to *for less* cardholders.

DON'T MISS

The New York Transit Museum (page 224) documents the history of mass transit, including New York City's subway system, with unique memorabilia and exhibits.

In southern Brooklyn, along the Atlantic coast, is **Brighton Beach**. Dominated by the largest Russian immigrant community in the U.S., and known as "Little Odessa", Brighton Beach is an ethnic treasure and a great place to enjoy specialties like vodka and smoked sausages at authentic local eateries.

A little further west, **Coney Island** was once a resort for rich New Yorkers. In the early 1900s, it was transformed into a place for

Little Odessa, Brighton Beach

the general public when the subway made access cheap and easy for everyone. Today, you can visit the beach, walk along the boardwalk and see the 1927 Cyclone rollercoaster and 1920 Wonder Wheel.

Brooklyn Attractions . . .

The **New York Transit Museum** is housed in the old Court Street subway station in Brooklyn Heights. The museum contains 19 subway and elevated cars, an operating signal tower, antique turnstiles and a gift shop.

More than 100-years worth of artifacts and memorabilia include vintage trains with wicker seats and ceiling fans. The 1904 Brooklyn Union elevated car is one of the oldest in the museum's collection. This self-propelled train has a wooden body with a steel underframe powered from either an elevated trolley line or from the subway's third rail.

1904 Brooklyn Union elevated car

An art gallery features subway memorabilia once used to brighten riders' daily commutes plus custom-designed plaques, mosaics and other decorative elements.

The gift shop sells transit-themed items like token watches, strap-hanger ties and postcards. Other gift shops are located in Manhattan at Penn Station at 34th Street and Grand Central Terminal at 42nd Street and both offer discounts to **for less** card holders.

The museum also offers special transit-related exhibitions and programs. Tours include "Nostalgia Rides" which allow you to travel on vintage trains and buses via subway tunnels and New York City streets. *(Schermerhorn Street and Boerum Place, ☎ (718) 243-8601. Tue-Fri: 10am-4pm. Sat-Sun: 12noon-5pm. Mon: closed. Adult $3, child $1.50, senior $1.50, student $3. 2 admissions for the price of 1 plus 10% discount in the gift shop with vouchers on page 283. Subway: 2,3,4,5 to Borough Hall.)*

Prospect Park, which opened in 1867, contains 526 acres of rich historical landscapes, including the 90-acre Long Meadow which is the largest open space in a U.S. urban park. At the top of Prospect Lake, Lookout Hill was notorious as a Revolutionary War burial ground. Another notable park sight is the Camperdown Elm, a large twisted tree dating from the 1870s. During the summer, the Music Grove bandstand holds open-air musical performances. Other park highlights include Lefferts Homestead *(☎ (718) 965-6505)*, the 1912 Coney Island carousel and the 1905 Italianate Boathouse which serves as the park's cafe and main information center. *(Flatbush Avenue at Grand Army Plaza, ☎ (718) 965-8951. Subway: 2,3 to Grand Army Plaza.)*

The Brooklyn Museum, founded in 1823 as the

. . . Brooklyn Attractions . . .

Brooklyn Apprentices' Library Association, is one of the oldest and largest art museums in the United States. Designed in the late 19th century by the prestigious architectural firm McKim, Mead and White, this Beaux Arts building measures 450,000 square feet.

Brooklyn Museum

The museum's permanent collection features more than 1.5 million objects, from ancient Egyptian masterpieces to contemporary art. The collection of Egyptian art is one of the best-regarded in the world. Highlights include statues, papyri, sarcophagi, mummy cases and the world-famous Brooklyn Black Head of the Ptolemaic Period.

The museum's collection of painting and sculpture includes American and European works dating from the 14th century to the present. The Brooklyn Museum was also the first museum to show African objects as art, and its display of works from central Africa is one of the most comprehensive and important in the world. Impressive art collections from the Pacific, Americas and Asia are also on display.

The Brooklyn Black Head, ca. 50 B.C.

The museum also has 28 period rooms ranging from a 17th-century Dutch-colonial farmhouse to a 19th-century Moorish Room, and from John D. Rockefeller's Manhattan mansion to a 20th-century Art Deco library. Two research libraries and an archive have extensive visual and textual materials on art, archeology and ethnology from ancient to modern times. *(200 Eastern Parkway, ☎ (718) 638-5000. Wed-Fri: 10am-5pm. Sat: 11am-6pm. Mon-Tue: closed. Suggested admission: adult $4, child free, senior $1.50, student $2. Subway: 2,3 to Eastern Parkway-Brooklyn Museum.)*

The Brooklyn Botanic Garden, next to the Brookyln Museum, has 52 acres of botanical treasures. The main attractions are the Japanese hill-and-pond garden and the new Steinhardt Conservatory Gallery, which houses one of the largest collections of bonsai trees in the U.S. There is also an outdoor café and an immense rose garden. *(1000 Washington Avenue, ☎ (718)*

DON'T MISS

Visit the Brooklyn Museum's vast ancient Egyptian collection – the most extensive outside of Cairo and London. Some of the worlds finest pieces are on display here, including the Brooklyn Black Head which dates back to 50 B.C.

. . . Brooklyn Attractions

622-4433. Tue-Fri: 8am-4.30pm. Sat-Sun: 10am-4.30pm. Mon: closed. Suggested admission $3. Subway: 2,3 to Eastern Parkway-Brooklyn Museum.)

New York Aquarium

The Brooklyn Children's Museum, founded in 1899, was the first museum specifically designed for children. The museum offers a wide variety of hands-on exhibits and interactive educational programs. *(145 Brooklyn Avenue, ☎ (718) 735-4432. Wed-Fri: 2pm-5pm. Sat-Sun: 10am-5pm. Mon-Tue: closed. Suggested admission $3. Subway: 3 to Kingston Avenue.)*

Located on Grand Army Plaza, the **Brooklyn Public Library** makes its home in an impressive 1941 Art Deco building. The library is appreciated nearly as much for its architectural splendor as its superb collection of books. On the second floor, art exhibits are presented on a rotating basis. *(Grand Army Plaza, Flatbush Avenue and Eastern Parkway, ☎ (718) 230-2100. Mon and Fri-Sat: 10am-6pm. Tue-Thu: 9am-8pm. Sun: 1pm-5pm. Subway: 2,3 to Eastern Parkway-Brooklyn Museum.)*

In the 1920s, **Coney Island** was calling itself the "World's Largest Playground". This seaside amusement park, complete with a boardwalk and piers filled with rides and games, once attracted more than one million visitors a day. Today, Coney Island is still a fun place to ride the amusements, visit the **New York Aquarium** and eat a famous Nathan's hot dog. *(Boardwalk and West 8th Street, ☎ (718) 265-3400. Subway: B,D,F,N to Stillwell Avenue-Coney Island.)*

The Brooklyn Academy of Music (page 209), also known as BAM, is one of New York's pre-eminent entertainment venues. Hosting musical and theatrical performances of every kind, it is known for its avant garde productions. It is also home to the Brooklyn Philharmonic. *(30 Lafayette Avenue, ☎ (718) 636-4100. Subway: D,Q,2,3,4,5 to Atlantic Avenue.)*

DON'T MISS

In warm weather, visit Coney Island for a uniquely New York maritime experience. Spend an afternoon enjoying the beach, strolling along the boardwalk and enjoying rides like the Cyclone rollercoaster.

Coney Island

Introduction to the Bronx

In the early 20th century, the Bronx was an affluent suburb. Its main thoroughfare, the **Grand Concourse**, was lined with expensive shops and apartment buildings. Today, mention of the Bronx conjures up images of the South Bronx, eroded by economic hardship and urban decay. This is not an accurate portrait of the entire borough, however, and there are a number of places worth visiting.

The North Bronx contains some charming residential areas, ethnic communities and a few major attractions. The Bronx Zoo, now renamed the **Bronx International Wildlife Conservation Park** (page 228), encompasses 265 acres and is the largest urban zoo in the country. Adjacent to the zoo, the **New York Botanical Garden** (page 228) contains 12 outdoor gardens, a conservatory and a series of walking trails, many of which offer glimpses of the area's natural landscape.

South Bronx

New York Yankees

For less cardholders can receive two admissions to the garden for the price of one.

Facing the garden's entrance, **Fordham University** *(Southern Boulevard,* ☎ *(718) 817-1000)*, founded in 1841, has a pleasant campus consisting of Gothic-style stone buildings and green open spaces. A short walk from the zoo and botanical gardens, the **Belmont** section boasts a **Little Italy** more authentic than its Manhattan cousin. It is a great place to have lunch or dinner after a visit to one of the North Bronx attractions.

The South Bronx has one extremely popular New York attraction – **Yankee Stadium** (page 228). The stadium has its own subway stop and can be reached safely and easily from Manhattan.

On the northeast shore of Long Island Sound, **Pelham Bay Park** is home to **Orchard Beach** and the historic **Bartow Pell Mansion** *(895 Shore Road,* ☎ *(718) 885-1461)*. Nearby, **City Island** is a tiny maritime village complete with seafood restaurants and marinas.

Fordham University

Bronx Attractions . . .

for less Founded in 1891, the **New York Botanical Garden** consists of over 250 acres of beautiful gardens and unspoiled forest, making it one of the oldest and largest gardens of its kind in the United States.

Visitors can enjoy a series of flower and rock gardens as well as walking trails. The Rose Garden contains close to 3,000 roses of various species.

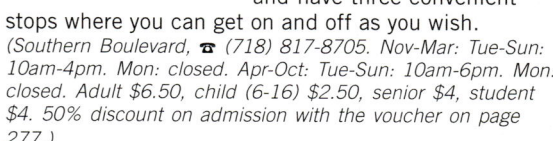

New York Botanical Garden

In 1902, the Enid A. Haupt Conservatory was constructed. It contains 11 separate areas, each featuring a distinct botanical and geological focus.

Narrated tram tours accent the wide array of natural wonders contained within the various areas of the garden and have three convenient stops where you can get on and off as you wish. *(Southern Boulevard, ☎ (718) 817-8705. Nov-Mar: Tue-Sun: 10am-4pm. Mon: closed. Apr-Oct: Tue-Sun: 10am-6pm. Mon: closed. Adult $6.50, child (6-16) $2.50, senior $4, student $4. 50% discount on admission with the voucher on page 277.)*

International Wildlife Conservation Park (formerly the Bronx Zoo) was founded in 1899 and is the largest city zoo in the United States. This immense preserve is home to over 4,000 animals. Among the exhibits are Jungle World, World of Darkness, Himalayan Highlands, World of Birds and the Children's Zoo. Wild Asia features a 25-minute narrated tour on a monorail train. For an excellent aerial overview of the park you can ride the Skyfari tramway. *(Fordham Road and the Bronx River Parkway, ☎ (718) 220-5100. Oct-Apr: Mon-Sun: 10am-4.30pm. May-Sep: Mon-Fri: 10am-5pm. Sat-Sun: 10am-5.30pm. Adult $4, child $2, senior $2, student $4. Free on Wednesdays. Subway: C,D to Fordham Road.)*

Camel ride at the International Wildlife Conservation Park

INSIDER'S TIP

Before going to the Botanical Garden, stop by Mike's Deli in Little Italy's Arthur Avenue Retail Market for a picnic lunch. *(2344 Arthur Avenue, ☎ (718) 295-5033)*

Yankee Stadium has been home to New York's beloved baseball team since 1923. Babe Ruth and Joe DiMaggio, two of baseball's greatest players, wore the

. . . Bronx Attractions

famous blue and white pin stripes of the team. The ball park received a make-over in the 1970s and now seats up to 54,000 people. The stadium was particularly full during the 1996 and 1998 seasons as the Yankees battled their way to win the World Series. *(East 161st Street at River Avenue, ☎ (718) 293-6000. Subway: 4,C,D to 161st Street.)*

The Van Cortlandt House Museum, originally the residence of wealthy New Yorker Frederick Van Cortlandt, is a preserved 1748 Georgian Colonial-style home. The interior contains American, English and Dutch period furnishings, and the dining room was used by General George Washington as a meeting place during the Revolutionary War. *(Van Cortlandt Park, ☎ (718) 543-3344. Tue-Fri: 10am-3pm. Sat-Sun: 11am-4pm. Mon: closed. Adult $2, child free, senior $1.50, student $1.50. Subway: 1,9 to 242nd Street, Van Cortlandt Park.)*

Wave Hill is a landscaped estate featuring manicured lawns, gardens and greenhouses which overlook the Hudson River. Formerly the home and estate of financier George W. Perkins, the grounds at Wave Hill are now open to the public, and the Grand Hall is used regularly for concerts. *(West 249th Street and Independence Avenue, ☎ (718) 549-3200. Tue-Sun: 10am-4:30 pm (later in summer). Mon: closed. Adult $4, child (under 6) free, senior $2, student $2. Tue and Sat year round and everyday mid-Nov through mid-Mar: admission is free. Subway: 1,9 to 231st Street.)*

Aerial view of Yankee Stadium

Woodlawn Cemetery is the resting place for many of New York's most significant former residents. This burial ground is filled with impressively crafted mausoleums and tomb stones. Author Herman Melville, jazz great Duke Ellington and department store founder Richard H. Macy are all buried here. *(East 223rd Street and Webster Avenue, ☎ (718) 920-0500. Mon-Sun: 9am-4.30pm. Subway: 4 to Woodlawn Avenue.)*

North Wind Undersea Institute, located on City Island, is a small maritime museum featuring diving memorabilia and displays on the history of whaling. Interestingly, the museum has tanks containing seals that are trained to assist the police in underwater procedures. *(610 City Island Avenue, ☎ (718) 885-0701. Mon-Fri: 10am-5pm. Sat-Sun: closed. Adults $3, child $2, senior $3, student $3. Subway: 6 to Pelham Bay Park, then BX21 bus to City Island.)*

Introduction to Queens

Just north of Brooklyn, Queens is geographically New York's largest borough, comprising more than a third of the city and stretching over a hundred miles into Long Island. Originally named after **Queen Catherine**, the wife of Charles II of Great Britain, the borough was annexed by New York City in 1898, along with Brooklyn and Staten Island. It is now home to some 2 million residents.

American Museum of the Moving Image

Although it lacks a defined city center, it is home to a multitude of distinct ethnic

Flushing Meadow-Corona Park

enclaves including the mainly Greek area of **Astoria**, which is known as the Athens of New York. In fact, more than one-third of the population claims to have been born abroad.

Two of the three main airports in the New York area are located in Queens – **John F. Kennedy** and **LaGuardia** (page 18). Both airports are easily accessible to Manhattan.

Near J.F.K. Airport, **Aqueduct Racetrack** *(110-00 Rockaway Boulevard, ☎ (718) 641-4700)* offers world-class horse racing. The former is the world's largest thoroughbred track and home of the Belmont Stakes, the third jewel in horse racing's triple crown.

The **Unisphere** globe, which stands in **Flushing Meadow-Corona Park** (page 231), marks the location of the 1939 and 1964 **World's Fairs**. The park also contains **Shea Stadium** (page 231)

Aquaduct Racetrack

and the **USTA National Tennis Center** (page 231).

Queens Museum (page 231) has a collection of memorabilia from both World's Fairs, including the Panorama, an 18,000-square-foot model of New York City. The **American Museum of the Moving Image** (page 231), housed in one of the Kaufmann-Astoria movie studios, provides a behind-the-scenes look at the art of the cinema. W.C. Fields and the Marx Brothers made films here.

DON'T MISS

Both children and adults will be fascinated by the immense collection of movie memorabilia at the American Museum of the Moving Image (page 231).

Queens Attractions . . .

for less **American Museum of the Moving Image** holds the nation's largest public collection of film and video artifacts – more than 70,000 items. Housed in what was once Paramount Pictures film studio, the museum documents the production, promotion and exhibition of motion pictures and television through a series of unique temporary and permanent exhibits. "Behind the Screen" gathers highlights from the permanent collection with an emphasis on the making and marketing of media over the last 100 years.

You can learn about filmmaking techniques through hands-on exhibits like those which allow you to work with sound effects or read a scene from a movie and see how it was filmed.

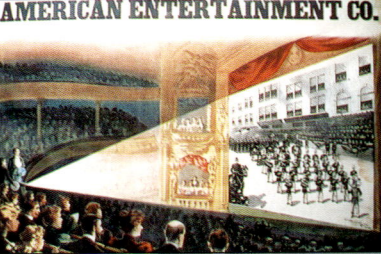

American Museum of the Moving Image

There is also a variety of movie merchandise, costumes and memorabilia including the original Yoda from the *Empire Strikes Back* and a "gold-plated" chariot from the 1959 epic film *Ben Hur*. *(35th Avenue at 36th Street, Astoria, ☎ (718) 784-0077. Tue-Fri: 12noon-5pm. Sat-Sun: 11am-6pm. Mon: closed. Adult $8.50, child $4.50, senior $5.50, student $5.50. 50% discount on admission plus 10% off in the museum shop with vouchers on page 283.)*

Flushing Meadow-Corona Park, the site of the 1939 and 1964 World's Fairs, features a number of cultural and historical attractions. **Shea Stadium** *(☎ (718) 507-8499)* is home to the New York Mets, and the **US Tennis Center** *(☎ (718) 760-6200)* hosts the annual U.S. Open tennis championship every August. Also within the park, the **Unisphere**, a huge steel globe and remnant from the 1964 World's Fair, stands 12 stories high and weighs 350 tons. Aside from its attractions, the park is also an enjoyable place to simply relax. *(Flushing. Subway: 7 to Willets Point-Shea Stadium.)*

Also located inside the park, **Queens Museum** is housed in a building originally constructed for the 1939 World's Fair. The museum has an excellent collection of contemporary art including its prized possession – the Panorama. This model of New York City, designed for the 1964 World's Fair, was built to scale and contains every building in the city at the time. It takes up close to 20,000 square feet. *(Flushing Meadow-Corona Park, ☎ (718) 592-9700. Wed-Fri: 10am-5pm. Sat-Sun: 12noon-5pm. Mon-Tue: closed. Suggested Admission: Adult $4, child (under 5) free, senior $2, student $2. Subway: 7 to Willets Point-Shea Stadium.)*

. . . Queens Attractions

The New York Hall of Science, also built for the 1964 World's Fair, is now an interactive museum for science and technology. This hands-on museum has over 160 exhibits with a wide range of topics including color, sound and light. *(111th Street and 48th Avenue, Flushing Meadow-Corona Park,*

☎ (718) 699-0005. Mon-Wed: 9.30am-2pm. Thu-Sun: 9.30am-5pm. Adult $6, child $4, senior $4, student $6. Free admission Thu-Fri: 2pm-5pm. Subway: 7 to 111th Street.)

New York Hall of Science

Bowne House, built in 1661, was originally a Quaker Friends' Meeting House and is the oldest religious site in the United States. Its owner, John Bowne, was banished here by Dutch governor Peter Stuyvesant for continuing to attend Quaker meetings after it had been outlawed. Tours of the colonial house are available, but you must call ahead to reserve. *(137-16 Northern Boulevard, between Main and Union Streets, ☎ (718) 358-9636. Subway: 7 to Main Street.)*

View of Queens and the Triborough Bridge from Manhattan

Kingsland House, within walking distance of Bowne House, now serves as the home of the **Queens Historical Society**. The society sponsors historical exhibitions and provides information about other borough attractions. Built in 1785, the farmhouse itself is a fine example of both English and Dutch architectural styles. *(Weeping Beach Park, 143-35 37th Avenue at Parson's Boulevard, ☎ (718) 939-0647. Tue and Sat-Sun: 2.30pm-4.30pm. Adult $3, child $2, senior $2, student $2. Subway: 7 to Main Street.)*

Jamaica Bay Wildlife Refuge is an ecological preserve managed by the National Parks Service. The site is home to a wide variety of plants and animals including over 300 species of birds. Park rangers give guided nature tours on the weekends. *(Cross Bay Boulevard at Broad Channel, ☎ (718) 318-4340. Mon-Sun: sunrise to sunset. Admission is free. Subway: A to Broad Channel.)*

Introduction to Staten Island

Named Staaten Eylandt in 1609 by Dutch explorer **Henry Hudson**, Staten Island became a Dutch settlement in the early 1660s. Legend has it that the island was the grand prize in a boat race sponsored by England's **Duke of York** in 1687.

The first ferry service was introduced in 1713 to link Staten Island to Manhattan. Today the free ride on the **Staten Island Ferry** (page 65) is reason enough to go there. It provides stunning views of Lower Manhattan, the Statue of Liberty and New York Harbor.

After a successful stint as an oyster village, Staten Island was officially annexed to New York City in 1898. The island remains fairly rural – filled with expansive parks, rolling hills, residential neighborhoods and beautiful harbor views.

Staten Island has a number of historical sites and attractions of interest to visitors. The **Snug Harbor Cultural Center** (page 234) has a number of beautiful 19th-century buildings and serves as a center for cultural events, museums and gardens.

The **Richmondtown Historic Restoration** (page 234), containing buildings dating from the 17th to the 19th centuries, all painstakingly restored; and the **Alice Austen House** (page 234), which overlooks New York Harbor and

Verrazano-Narrows Bridge

displays a vast collection of photographs of Staten Island and its residents taken in the late 19th and early 20th centuries.

In 1964 the imposing **Verrazano-Narrows Bridge** was built connecting the island to Brooklyn. Measuring 4,260 feet, it became the largest bridge in the United States, usurping the title from San Francisco's Golden Gate Bridge by only 60 feet. It also ranks as the world's second largest suspension bridge, falling short of England's Humber Bridge.

Recently, a campaign has been waged by Staten Island residents for secession from New York City. One sentiment is that tax dollars are being applied to inner city problems rather than their own. Another red-hot residential issue is the unwanted Fresh Kills, the largest landfill in the world, which is currently being used to dispose of New York City's garbage.

Staten Island Attractions

Founded in 1801 as a retirement home for sailors, the
Snug Harbor Cultural Center now has 28 beautiful
19th-century buildings and serves as a center for
cultural institutions and events. The Main House
contains the Newhouse Center for Contemporary Art (☎
(718) 448-2500) and the Staten Island Children's
Museum (☎ *(718) 273-2060)*. The Veterans' Memorial
Hall is now a performance space for musicians. The

Historic Richmond Town on Staten Island

28-acre Staten Island Botanical
Garden (☎ *(718) 273-8200)* features
plants, flowers and a butterfly
house. *(1000 Richmond Terrace.
Grounds to the cultural center are always
open and without admission charge.
Staten Island Ferry, change to S40 bus
or Snug Harbor trolley.)*

The **Richmondtown Historic
Restoration** encompasses 103
acres and contains over 25
buildings dating from the 17th to
the 19th centuries, meticulously restored to their
original splendor. This authentic village and museum
complex features a general store, courthouse, tavern
and houses, and is devoted to documenting three
centuries of Staten Island life, culture and history.
*(441 Clarke Avenue, ☎ (718) 351-1611. Sep-Jun: Wed-Sun:
1pm-5pm. Mon-Tue: closed. Jul-Aug: Wed-Fri: 10am-5pm.
Sat-Sun: 1pm-5pm. Mon-Tue: closed. Adult $4, child $2.50*

DON'T MISS

Tours of Richmondtown
Historic Restoration begin
every half hour,
originating at the Historic
Museum. Highlights
include the Voorlezer's
House, which is the oldest
elementary school house
in the U.S.

*(under 6 free), senior
$2.50, student
$2.50. Staten Island
Ferry, change to S74.)*

The **Alice Austen
House**, built in
1710, overlooks
New York Harbor.
The house has a
collection of

Staten Island Ferry

approximately 8,000 of Austen's photographs of
Staten Island and its residents taken from 1880 to
1930. *(2 Hylan Boulevard, ☎ (718) 816-4506. Thu-Sun:
12noon-5pm. Mon-Wed: closed. Jan-Feb: closed. Adult $2,
child free, senior $2, student $2. Staten Island Ferry, change
to S51 bus to Hylan Park.)*

Built in 1947, the **Jacques Marchais Center of Tibetan
Art** houses one of the largest collections of Tibetan art
outside of Tibet. In 1991, it was visited by the Dalai
Lama. *(338 Lighthouse Avenue, ☎ (718) 987-3500. Apr-
Nov: Wed-Fri and Sat-Sun: 1pm-5pm. Nov-Mar: Wed-Fri:
1pm-5pm. Adult $3, child $1, senior $2.50, student $2.50.
Staten Island Ferry, change to S74 bus.)*

Beyond
New York

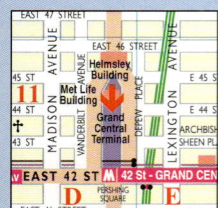

Grand Central Terminal

Traveling Beyond New York

There are a large number of exciting destinations within few hours of New York. Cities such as Boston, New Haven, Philadelphia, Atlantic City and Washington D.C. all offer a unique perspective on the history and culture of the United States. This chapter gives a brief description of some of the best places to visit, how to get there and what to do and see when you arrive. Listed below are some suggestions on the various modes of transportation for excursions from Manhattan.

TRAINS

New York has two train stations – **Grand Central Terminal** and **Pennsylvania Station** (referred to as Penn Station). **Amtrak** (☎ 582-6875), departing from Penn Station, operates long-distance trains to national destinations as well as regional cities along the eastern corridor (Boston, Philadelphia, Washington, D.C.). **Long Island Railroad** (☎ (718) 217-5477) and **New Jersey Transit** (☎ (973) 762-5100) also depart from Penn Station and serve Long Island and New Jersey respectively. **Metro-North Commuter Railroad** (☎ 532-4900) runs trains to Connecticut and New York's Westchester County (including a stop at Fordham Road which is

Atlantic City beaches

convenient for the Bronx attractions on pages 232-233) from Grand Central Terminal. **PATH** (☎ 1-800-234-7284) trains service several stops in northern New Jersey and on Manhattan's west side.

BUSES

Long-distance and commuter bus lines depart from **Port Authority Bus Terminal** (☎ 564-8484). **Greyhound** (☎ 1-800-231-2222) services the entire nation. **Adirondack Pine Hill Trailways** (☎ 1-800-225-6815) service upstate New York; **Peter Pan Bus Lines** (☎ 1-800-343-9999) and **Bonanza Bus Lines** (☎ 1-800-556-3815) service New England; and **New Jersey Transit** services New Jersey (☎ (973) 762-5100).

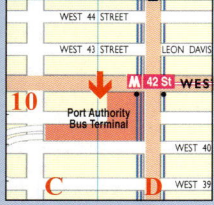

Penn Station

PLANES

New York is a major hub for national and international air travel. Prices for regional flights are often comparable to those for the train and are much faster (especially from New York to Boston or Washington, D.C.). Major national carriers include **American Airlines** (☎ 1-800-433-7300), **Continental** (☎ 1-800-231-0856), **Delta** (☎ 1-800-241-4141) and **United Airlines** (☎ 1-800-241-6522).

Port Authority

Car Rental

For visitors planning a trip out of town, renting a car is often the most convenient way to travel. From New York City, you can access every major roadway that runs along the east coast to the destinations mentioned on the following pages. Renting a car can also be more economical than regional transportation, especially when traveling with a family.

Oldsmobile 88

Avis has been setting the standard in car rentals for more than 50 years. With your *for less* card, you can receive a **20% discount off Avis' SuperValue rates**. If there is a lower rate available at the time you make your reservation, your *for less* card entitles you to a **5% discount off the special rate** (whatever that happens to be). This discount is valid at all participating Avis locations in the U.S.

In addition to a special rate on rentals, you can also receive a **free upgrade** at any participating New York City location. Reserve any Avis Intermediate through Full Size 4-door car, then present the coupon (voucher) on page 285 at participating locations in Manhattan or at New York City airports. You will then be upgraded one car group at no extra charge. The upgrade applies to weekend, weekly and daily rates (minimum of 2 days rental required) and is subject to the terms and conditions listed on the coupon.

INSIDER'S TIP

Avis has 10 locations in Manhattan. For reservations and information, call 1-800-831-8000.

Buick Skylark

Obtaining these discounts is easy. Simply dial the toll-free reservations line at 1-800-831-8000. Inform the reservations agent of the Avis Worldwide Discount (AWD) number **#K194100**. This code will access the *for less* discount mentioned above. If you would like to take advantage of the free upgrade, you must inform the reservations agent of this as well. When you pick up your car, you should turn in the upgrade voucher on page 285.

Renters must meet Avis age, driver and credit requirements. The minimum age is 25, but may vary by location.

Washington, D.C. . . .

Founded in 1791, specifically as the capital of the United States, Washington, D.C. is not part of any state, but is a unique "Federal district".

Jefferson Memorial

Famous historical attractions, monuments and memorials include the **Library of Congress** *(101 Independence Avenue SE,* ☎ *(202) 707-8000)*, **National Archives** *(7th and Pennsylvania Avenue NW,* ☎ *(202) 501-5000)*, **Vietnam Veterans Memorial** *(Constitution Avenue and Henry Bacon Drive NW,* ☎ *(202) 426-6841)*, and, of course, the home of the president – the **White House** *(1600 Pennsylvania Avenue NW,* ☎ *(202) 456-2200)*.

FOR VISITOR INFORMATION

Tourist Information
1212 New York Avenue
Suite 600
NW, Washington, D.C.
20005
☎ (202) 789-7000

The White House

You can take a free tour of the White House by picking up tickets (available on a first-come, first-served basis) at the **White House Visitor Center** *(1450 Pennsylvania Avenue NW)* which is open from 8am to 12noon Tuesday through Saturday. You can get recorded information by calling (202) 456-7041.

You can also visit the **Supreme Court** *(1st Street and Maryland Avenue NE,* ☎ *(202) 479-3211)*, the **Federal Bureau of Investigation** (FBI) *(9th and Pennsylvania Avenue NW,* ☎ *(202) 479-3211)* and the **U.S. Capitol** on Capitol Hill *(☎ (202) 225-3121)*, the home of Congress.

INSIDER'S TIP

With New York Apple Tours Full City Tour *Plus* Washington, D.C. (page 213), you can combine a double-decker tour of New York with a trip to the nation's capital.

Just three quarters of a mile from the Lincoln Memorial, in Arlington Virginia, you can find the final resting place of

Vietnam Veterans' Memorial

many important historical figures and past presidents, such as John F. Kennedy, at **Arlington National Cemetery** *(☎ (202) 426-6841)*.

. . . Washington, D.C.

Many of these attractions are free to the public and open seven days a week.

Although federal government plays a critical role in the economy and industry of Washington, there is also a wealth of cultural attractions, galleries, stores, restaurants and performing arts which attract some 20 million annual visitors to the city.

The Capitol Building

The **National Gallery of Art** *(4th and Constitution Avenue NW, ☎ (202) 737-4215)* displays a permanent collection of both American and European art, as well as a temporary exhibition of art from around the world.

The museums and galleries which comprise the **Smithsonian Institution** *(Visitor Center: 1000 Jefferson Drive SW, ☎ (202) 357-2700)* are known throughout the world for their amazing collections. In 1996, the Smithsonian celebrated its 150th anniversary. Perhaps the best-known museum, and one of the world's most-visited, the **National Air and Space Museum** *(☎ (202) 357-2700)* is a must-see on a visit to

Washington Monument and Lincoln Memorial

Washington D.C. Here you will find a wealth of information about this country's aviation history and space program, as well as incredible artifacts including the Apollo 11 lunar command module and Charles Lindbergh's plane *Spirit of St. Louis*.

Throughout the year, there are plenty of festivals and special events such as the **Cherry Blossom Festival** held in early April and **Independence Day Celebrations** each July 4th. Solemn ceremonies take place on **Veterans' Day**, November 11, and **Pearl Harbor Day**, December 7th.

GETTING THERE

From Penn Station, take Amtrak national railway (☎ 1-800-872-7245). Trains depart frequently throughout the day and the trip takes 3-4 hours.

Philadelphia . . .

In 1682, Quaker William Penn founded Philadelphia, the "City of Brotherly Love", as a haven for religious freedom in the New World.

Philadelphia's role in the Revolutionary War and the birth of the new nation was critical. Its attractions and sights provide an overview of early American history.

The Liberty Bell

FOR VISITOR INFORMATION

Philadelphia Convention & Visitors Bureau
1515 Market Street
Suite 2020,
Philadelphia, PA 19102
☎ 1-800-537-7676

Philadelphia is also a city of "firsts". The first public school opened here in 1689, while the first public library was opened in 1731 by Benjamin Franklin. He also reprinted Samuel Richardson's *Pamela*, making it the first novel printed in America. Philadelphia was also home to the new nation's first volunteer fire company, hospital and life insurance company, as well as the first stock exchange.

Philadelphia Museum of Art

Today, visitors can see many remnants of its illustrious past, including two of the nation's most recognizable and important historical monuments, the **Liberty Bell** *(Market Street, between 5th and 6th Streets, ☎ (215) 567-1000)* and **Independence Hall** *(1523 Walnut Street, ☎ (215) 597-8974)*. The Liberty Bell, perhaps best known for its famous crack, was once used to announce each victory won by the patriots during the Revolutionary War. Independence Hall was the place where the Declaration of Independence was adopted on July 4, 1776 and where the Constitution of the United States was drafted in 1787. It was also home to Congress from 1790-1800, during the ten years that Philadelphia was capital of the new nation.

Independence Hall

The city has a number of historical areas including **Society Hill** and **Olde City**. These neighborhoods, once frequented by George Washington, Thomas Jefferson and Benjamin Franklin, feature picturesque

. . . Philadelphia

cobblestone streets and Federal-style townhouses. The **Betsy Ross House** *(239 Arch Street, ☎ (215) 627-5343)* claims to be the place where the famous seamstress designed the first American flag.

Founded in 1876, the imposing **Philadelphia Museum of Art** *(26th Street and Benjamin Franklin Parkway, ☎ (215) 763-8100)* has a permanent collection of more than 2,000 years worth of art and artifacts from around the world. In addition to painting, sculpture, prints and drawings, there is also an impressive range of furniture and decorative arts, including furnished rooms from historic houses. The museum also hosts important temporary exhibitions.

The skyline of Philadelphia

Nearby, the **Rodin Museum** *(22nd Street and Benjamin Franklin Parkway, ☎ (215) 763-8100)* features a fine collection of the artist's sculptures and drawings, the largest outside of Paris. Among them, you can find *The Thinker* and *Gates of Hell*. Across the street, the **Franklin Institute Science Museum** *(20th Street and Benjamin Franklin Parkway, ☎ (215) 448-1208)* has a multitude of interactive exhibits plus one of the world's premier dinosaur exhibits.

Beginning at the Benjamin Franklin Parkway, **Fairmount Park** *(☎ (215) 685-0000)* is the largest landscaped urban park in the world.

The Schuylkill River

Its 8,900 acres encompass creeks, trails and meadows as well as 100 miles of bicycle, jogging and bridle paths. The park also features historic mansions, the nation's first zoo, a Japanese house and garden and the Victorian **Boat House Row**, where crew races are held throughout the year on the **Schuylkill River**.

Philadelphia is also known as one of the best restaurant cities in America. The nation's number one and two top-ranked restaurants - the five-star **Le Bec-Fin** *(1523 Walnut Street, ☎ (215) 567-1000)* and **The Fountain** *(Four Seasons Hotel, One Logan Square, ☎ (215) 963-1500)* can be found here. If fine dining is not what you are looking for, try one of "Philly"'s famous cheesesteaks, pretzels or water ices.

GETTING THERE

From Penn Station, take Amtrak national railway (☎ 1-800-872-7245). Trains depart frequently throughout the day and the trip takes approximately 2 hours.

Boston

Rich in American history, Boston played an instrumental role in the nation's struggle for independence. Until the mid-18th century, its status as a prestigious port town made it the largest and most important city in America.

Boston at night

Today, Boston remains one of the nation's top cultural, historical and financial cities. It combines historic charm with modern sophistication and innovation. Unlike many other major U.S. cities, most of Boston's best sites can be seen on foot.

Visitors can walk the **Freedom Trail**, marked by a red line on the ground, which covers 16 historic sites. The tour begins at the **Visitor Information Center at Boston Common** (☎ *(617) 536-4100)*. Follow the line past government buildings, churches and burial grounds, including the **Old State House**, which was built in 1712 and made history on July 18, 1776 when the **Declaration of Independence** was read there.

Boston Harbor

The city of Boston is also home to an array of museums including the **Museum of Fine Arts** (☎ *(617) 267-9300)* and the **Children's Museum** (☎ *(617) 426-6500)*. The **Boston Tea Party Museum** (☎ *(617) 338-1773)* commemorates the colonists' 1773 dumping of a ship load of British tea into the harbor to protest unfair taxes.

The **Faneuil Hall Marketplace**, formerly a place for political debate, is now a restored market filled with shops and eateries. In Beacon Hill, the **Bull and Finch pub** (*84 Beacon Street,* ☎ *(617) 227-9605)* was the motivation for the long-running hit TV show *Cheers*.

Boston Harbor

Across the Charles River lies Cambridge, home of **Harvard University** (☎ *(617) 495-1000)*. Harvard's annual regatta on the river draws university students and visitors from all around New England.

FOR VISITOR INFORMATION

Greater Boston Convention and Visitors' Bureau
P.O. Box 490
Prudential Tower
Suite 400
Boston, MA 02199
☎ 1-800-888-5515

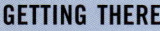

GETTING THERE

From Penn Station, Amtrak (☎ 1-800-872-7245) operates frequent service to Boston. Trip takes 4-6 hours.

INSIDER'S TIP

With New York Apple Tours Full City Tour *Plus* Boston (page 213), you can combine a double-decker tour of New York with a trip to Boston.

Atlantic City and New Jersey

Across the Hudson River from Manhattan is **Liberty State Park**. Take the weekend ferry service (☎ *1-800-533-3779*) to the park for great views of the Statue of Liberty, a picnic lunch and a visit to the **Liberty Science Center** (☎ *(201) 451-0006*). The biggest science museum in the New York area, Liberty Science

Atlantic City casino

Center is a favorite with children who enjoy the hands-on exhibits and modern displays.

Atlantic City is one of the most popular vacation destinations in the country with over 37 million annual visitors. The city is known for its 24-hour casinos, entertainment and luxurious accommodation. The boardwalk, built in 1870, has 4½ miles of attractions, amusements, shops and food vendors where you can try local specialties such as saltwater taffy and frozen custard.

Nearby, historic **Cape May** is a charming town that has a number of Victorian-style mansions, pleasant shopping areas and quality seafood restaurants. Other similar South Jersey shorefront resort towns are Ocean City, Sea Isle City, Stone Harbor and Wildwood.

Atlantic City Boardwalk

Princeton is best known as the home of New Jersey's only Ivy League institution, **Princeton University** (☎ *(609) 258-3000*). Chartered in 1746 as

Princeton University

the College of New Jersey, Princeton University is one of the oldest and finest schools in the U.S. Princeton Battlefield State Park commemorates General George Washington's victory at the Battle of Princeton in 1777.

Six Flags Great Adventure (☎ *(732) 928-1821*) is the largest theme park in the state and has the largest drive-through safari outside Africa. **Vernon Valley/Great Gorge Action Park** (☎ *(973) 827-2000*) has over 50 trails for winter skiing and a large theme park with water sports and other activities.

FOR VISITOR INFORMATION

New Jersey
Division of Tourism
CN 826
Trenton, NJ 08625
☎ 1-800-537-7397

Atlantic City Convention
& Visitors Authority
2314 Pacific Avenue
Atlantic City, NJ 08401
☎ (609) 449- 7130
☎ 1-888-228-4748

GETTING THERE

From the Port Authority
Bus Terminal,
New Jersey Transit
(☎ (973) 762-5100)
operates bus service
between New York
and many destinations
in New Jersey

New England and New Haven

Davenport College, Yale University

The colony of New Haven was established in 1638 by a group of Puritans. It evolved as an important seaport and, eventually, as an industrial center.

Yale College was founded in 1701 when the "Collegiate School", which was based in several Connecticut towns, was moved to New Haven. Today you can take guided tours of **Yale University**'s ivy-covered campus for a glimpse of the institution which counts amongst its graduates four U.S. presidents, including George Bush and President Clinton.

Yale's **Peabody Museum of Natural History** (☎ *(203) 432-5050*), built in 1866, is one of the oldest natural history museums in the U.S. **Beinecke Rare Book and Manuscript Library** (☎ *(203) 432-2977*) possesses one of the finest collections of its kind in the world (including a Gutenberg Bible), housed in an architecturally unique building that uses translucent pieces of marble in lieu of windows. **Yale University Art Gallery** (☎ *(203) 432-0600*) is the oldest

Beinecke Rare Book and Manuscript Library, Yale

university art museum in the country. Founded in 1832, it contains over 100,000 objects and works of art starting from Egyptian times, and includes paintings by Van Gogh, Monet and Picasso.

Long Wharf Theater (☎ *(203) 787-4282*) is known for its excellent theatrical productions which sometimes star famous actors like Al Pacino, Kathleen Turner and Joanne Woodward. **Yale Repertory** (☎ *(203) 432-1234*) and the **Shubert Performing Arts Center** (☎ *(800) 228-6622*) also host quality productions from the classics to new works.

New Haven Symphony Orchestra

Further along the Connecticut coastline, **Mystic Seaport** (☎ *(860) 572-5315*), recreates the area's maritime history. Highlights include restored houses, shops and tall ships.

One of the newest attractions in Connecticut is the **Foxwoods Resort Casino** (☎ *(860) 312-3000*), New England's answer to Atlantic City.

FOR VISITOR INFORMATION

The Greater New Haven Convention and Visitors Bureau
1 Long Wharf Drive
New Haven, CT 06511
☎ (203) 777-8550
☎ 1-800-332-STAY

Yale University Visitor Center
149 Elm Street
New Haven, CT 06520
☎ (203) 432-2300

GETTING THERE

From Grand Central Terminal, take Metro-North commuter rail (☎ 532-4900) or, from Penn Station, Amtrak (☎ 1-800-872-7245) runs express. Service from either station is frequent and the trip lasts less than 2 hours.

Long Island

Long Island is the largest island connected to the continental U.S. It is separated from the state of Connecticut on the north by the Long Island Sound

Long Island beaches

and surrounded by the Atlantic Ocean to the south and east.

Long Island has quaint towns, pretty villages, historic museums and numerous sights. The island is also becoming well-known for its wines, which come from more than 15 **vineyards**.

The main reason New Yorkers visit Long Island, however, is for the beach. There are more than 150 **public beaches** on the island, many of which encourage recreational activities like fishing, hiking and picnicking. The largest of the Long Island beaches (six miles long), **Jones Beach** *(☎ (516) 785-1600)*, is a 240-acre park which is also known for the outdoor concerts held in its marine theater.

The Hamptons are *the* place for Manhattanites with cash and time to spare. Magnificent beach-side mansions strewn along the coast are the summer homes of many celebrities and rich businessmen. As a tribute to excess and luxury, there is even a "beauty bus" which offers patrons beauty services *en route* to their weekend retreats.

Fire Island is a unique, 26-mile strip of land located off the coast of the south shore. Much of the island is part of a national park. **Shelter Island** is very peaceful, but can only be reached by ferry.

Westbury House, Old Westbury Gardens

Long Island Railroad makes frequent stops across the island which are convenient to Long Island's beaches and attractions.

Less than an hour from Manhattan, Nassau County has a multitude of historical, cultural and recreational opportunities. There are 114 museums and historical societies ranging in focus and settings from the **Cold Spring Harbor Whaling Museum** *(☎ (516) 367-3418)* to the **Sagamore Hill National Historic Site** *(☎ (516) 922-7866)* to the **Vanderbilt Museum**, **Mansion**, **Marine Museum**, **Planetarium and Park** *(☎ (516) 854-5555)*.

FOR VISITOR INFORMATION

Long Island Convention & Visitors Bureau 350 Vanderbilt Motor Pkwy Hauppauge, NY 11788 ☎ (516) 951-3440

GETTING THERE

From Grand Central Terminal, Long Island Railroad (☎ (718) 217-5477) services many destinations on Long Island.

New York State

To most people, New York means New York City and its immediate surrounds. Beyond the densely populated metropolitan area, however, New York State offers visitors a variety of recreational activities, cultural events and historic sites.

Niagara Falls

New York State is best seen by car (see page 237). It is an ideal way to enjoy the scenic countryside, which is most impressive in autumn when the leaves turn various shades of red and gold. The **Finger Lake Vineyards** (☎ *(800) 548-4386*) are a good destination at this time of year. In the winter, "upstate" is popular with New Yorkers who like to ski at the state's mountain areas (☎ *(800) 342-5826*).

The **Adirondacks** (☎ *(800) 487-6867*) are one of the most popular mountain ranges for skiing and summertime recreation. **Lake George** (☎ *(518) 668-5044*) is a 32-mile lake that was carved into the Adirondack Mountains by retreating Ice Age glaciers. The village of **Lake Placid** (☎ *(800) 447-5224*) and its Olympic Mountain was the site of the 1932 and 1980 Winter Olympics and is still a popular resort for winter sports.

Aerial view of the Thousand Islands

Baseball fans will probably not want to miss **Cooperstown**, home of the **National Baseball Hall of Fame** (☎ *(607) 547-7200*). For horse racing, head to Saratoga and the **Saratoga Racetrack** (☎ *(518) 584-6200*), the oldest in the country.

The state's most popular natural attraction is **Niagara Falls** (☎ *(800) 338-7890*). Tourists line-up at **Prospect Point** (☎ *(716) 278-1770*) or board the **Maid of the Mist** (☎ *(716) 284-8897*), which heads into the base of the falls, to witness the 40-million gallons of water that rush over the falls every minute.

Saratoga Racetrack

The **Thousand Islands** (☎ *(800) 847-5263*) and **Seaway Trail** (☎ *(800) 732-9298*) comprise a 454-mile-long region sprinkled with islands in both the **St. Lawrence River** and **Lake Ontario**. Some islands are so small that they can barely hold a tent, others are large enough to be occupied by small cabins. Camping, fishing, boating and **Boldt Castle** (☎ *(315) 482-9724*) make the Thousand Islands area a summertime getaway option.

FOR VISITOR INFORMATION

Division of Tourism
One Commerce Plaza,
Albany, NY 12245
☎ 1-800-225-5697

GETTING THERE

From Penn Station, Amtrak (☎ 1-800-872-7245) travels to many locations in Upstate New York. From Port Authority Bus Terminal, take Greyhound (☎ 1-800-231-2222).

Visitor Information

Calendar of Events

January

Chinese New Year celebrations. *(First full moon after January 19. Chinatown.)*

February

Black History Month, celebrating African-American culture and history nation-wide.

March

St. Patrick's Day Parade *(March 17. Fifth Avenue.)*

April

Easter Parade, celebrate wearing your Easter bonnet *(Easter Sunday. Fifth Avenue.)*

May

Martin Luther King Jr., Memorial Parade *(Second Sunday in May. Fifth Avenue.)*

June

Museum Mile Festival *(First or second Tuesday in June. Fifth Avenue, between 82nd and 105th Streets, ☎ 535-7710.)*

July

Summerstage free outdoor concerts and performances. *(Jun-Aug. Rumsey Playfield, Central Park, ☎ 360-2777.)*

August

Shakespeare-in-the-Park presents free Shakespeare plays performed in an open-air theater. *(Jun-Sep. Delacorte Theater, ☎ 861-7277.)*

Mostly Mozart classical music performances at Lincoln Center. *(Jul-Aug. Avery Fisher Hall, ☎ 875-5030.)*

September

Washington Square Music Festival *(Late Jul-Sep. Washington Square Park, ☎ 431-1088.)*

Feast of San Gennaro, Little Italy's famous street fair. *(Third week of Sep. Mulberry Street.)*

October

Columbus Day Parade *(Second Monday in October. Fifth Avenue, between 44th and 86th Streets.)*

Big Apple Circus *(Oct-Jan. Lincoln Center, ☎ 875-5400.)*

Greenwich Village Halloween Parade *(Oct 31. Sixth Avenue, between Spring and 23rd Streets.)*

New York City Marathon *(Last Sun in Oct or first Sun in Nov. ☎ 860-4455.)*

November

Macy's Thanksgiving Day Parade *(Last Thursday in November. Central Park West and Broadway to Herald Square, ☎ 494-4495.)*

December

Lighting of the Christmas Tree *(Early Dec. Rockefeller Center.)*

Christmas Spectacular *(Dec. Radio City Music Hall, ☎ 632-4000.)*

New Year's Eve celebrations throughout the city, from the dropping of the ball in Times Square to fireworks at the South Street Seaport.

Children's New York

New York has many **attractions** that will keep children entertained throughout their visit to the city. Of these, some of the best offer special discounts on children's admission with **New York for less**.

The Empire State Building and New York Skyride (page 116-117) are wonderful places to keep children entertained, and a 20% discount will keep the parents happy as well. Sony IMAX Theatre (page 163), the Children's Museum of Manhattan (page 165), Wollman Rink (page 202), Intrepid Sea-Air-Space Museum (page 134), Chelsea Piers Sports and Entertainment Complex (page 116), South Street Seaport Museum (page 59), the schooner *Pioneer* (page 59) and the American Museum of the Moving Image (page 231) are other children's favorites that offer substantial discounts to **for less** cardholders.

Carousel at Central Park

Other places of interest for children include the New York Hall of Science (page 232), New York Aquarium (page 226), the Central Park Wildlife Conservation Center (page 202) and the Bronx International Wildlife Center (page 228).

Children's museums are custom designed for the young set. The Children's Museum of Manhattan (page 165), Brooklyn Children's Museum (page 226), Children's Museum of the Arts *(72 Spring Street, ☎ 941-9198)* and the Staten Island Children's Museum *(1000 Richmond Terrace, ☎ (718) 273-2060)* are sure to please.

Throughout the year, **special events and festivals** such as the Big Apple Circus *(Oct-Jan. Lincoln Center, ☎ 875-5400)* and Barnum and Bailey Circus *(Mar-May. Madison Square Garden, ☎ 465-6741)* are among the most anticipated.

Kids will think they have gone to heaven when they visit New York's most famous **toy store**, F.A.O. Schwarz (page 155). Other kids favorites include Warner Bros. Studio Store (page 156) and Noodle Kidoodle *(112 East 86th Street, ☎ 427-6611)*. Also popular are the magical Enchanted Forest (page 90) and Tootsies (page 106) which give a 20% discount to **for less** cardholders. These shops carry an imaginative selection of children's books, games and stuffed animals.

Theme restaurants such as Planet Hollywood (page 138), Hard Rock Cafe (page 138) and Motown Cafe (page 138) have good choices of food and interesting memorabilia for children to enjoy.

INSIDER'S TIP

A beautiful day at the park is something to be enjoyed by parents and children alike. Many of New York's parks have children's playground areas. Central Park (page 200), Hudson River Park (page 67) and Carl Schurz Park (page 191) are perhaps the best.

Visitor Information . . .

CLIMATE

See "When to Go" page 16.

CUSTOMS

See "Visas and Entry Requirements" page 16.

ELECTRIC CURRENT

The U.S. uses 110V (60 hz) and most appliances from overseas will require a transformer. Check with your hotel regarding sockets for electrical devices.

EMBASSIES / CONSULATES

Australia (☎ 351-6500); Canada (☎ 596-1700); France (☎ 606-3688); Germany (☎ 610-9700); Great Britain (☎ 745-0200); Ireland (☎ 319-2555); Israel (☎ 499-5300); Italy (☎ 737-9100); Japan (☎ 371-8222); Netherlands (☎ 246-1429); South Africa (☎ 213-4880); Spain (☎ 355-4080); Sweden (☎ 583-2500); Switzerland (☎ 599-5900).

EMERGENCIES

For ambulance, fire or police, dial 911 from any telephone (free call, open 24 hours).

Hospitals (with 24 hour emergency rooms) - Bellvue Hospital (First Avenue and East 29th Street, ☎ 562-4141); Cabrini Medical Center (227 East 19th Street, ☎ 995-6120); Mount Sinai Hospital (Fifth Avenue and 101st Street, ☎ 241-6500); New York Hospital (East 70th Street at York Avenue, ☎ 746-5454); Roosevelt Hospital (428 West 59th Street, ☎ 523-4000); St. Vincent's Hospital (Seventh Avenue at 11th Street, ☎ 604-7000).

Health care and emergency treatment in New York can be very expensive. You will be required to pay for any medical treatment you receive, so it is advisable to take out a comprehensive travel and health insurance policy before arriving in New York.

ETIQUETTE

By law, smoking in New York is not allowed in public places, including the subway, buses, museums, theaters and in many restaurants' dining areas. Be sure to inquire at each restaurant if, and where, there are special areas for smoking.

Although New Yorkers are often portrayed in the movies as being rude, most simply have very busy schedules and tend to keep to themselves. However, in general people will be friendly and helpful, particularly to foreigners and will be happy to help you with directions.

INSIDER'S TIP

You will find additional visitor information that will be helpful before you go to New York, when you arrive, and when planning your itinerary on pages 16-21.

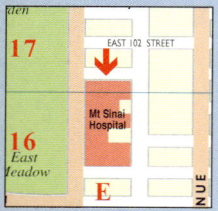

Mt. Sinai Hospital

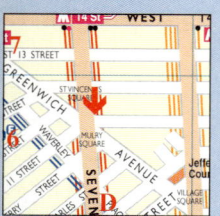

St. Vincent's Hospital

. . . Visitor Information . . .

HEALTH AND SAFETY

Doctors - In the Yellow Pages, look under "Physicians and Surgeons" to find doctors.

Drugstores / Pharmacies (open 24 hours) - Kaufman's *(557 Lexington Avenue, ☎ 755-2266)* and Duane Reade *(1279 3rd Avenue, ☎ 744-2668)*.

Safety - In contrast to its TV image, recent years have seen a dramatic fall in New York City's crime levels. However, as in any other large city, you should protect your valuables and watch out for pickpockets in crowded areas, particularly in and around Times Square. Areas to avoid after dark are Central Park, Alphabet City (the area east of Avenue B) and desolate areas along the rivers and piers.

See also Emergencies on page opposite.

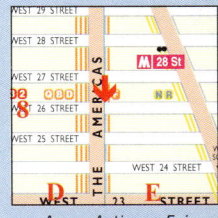
Annex Antiques Fair

LOST PROPERTY

For lost property on subways or buses, phone the MTA *(☎ (718) 625-6200)*; for taxis, phone the Taxi and Limousine Commission *(☎ 302-8294)*. For property lost more than 48 hours, call the Police Property Clerk *(☎ 374-5084)*.

LUGGAGE STORAGE

Due to security reasons, there are no longer any public lockers for storing personal belongings in the main transportation centers. You can, however, check baggage at Grand Central Station, Penn Station and Port Authority for approximately $2 per day.

MARKETS

There are a variety of interesting antique markets, fairs and greenmarkets.

Chelsea's Annex Antiques Fair and Flea Market

The **Annex Antiques Fair and Flea Market** is a huge flea market where you can find antiques, furniture, clothing and jewelry. *(Sixth Avenue at 26th Street, ☎ 243-5343. Sat-Sun: 9am-5pm.)*

Around the corner, the **Chelsea Antiques Building** contains 12 floors of antiques and collectibles. *(110 West 25th Street, ☎ 929-0909. Mon-Sun: 10am-6pm.)*

Greenwich Village Flea Market is small, but is known for having good bargains. *(P.S. 41, Greenwich Street at Charles Street. Sat: 12noon-7pm.)*

. . . Visitor Information . . .

The **Soho Antique Fair and Collectibles Market** sells inexpensive clothing plus odds and ends. *(Broadway at Grand Street, ☎ 682-2000. Mon-Sat: 9am-5pm.)*

At the popular **Union Square Greenmarket**, regional farmers converge to sell a plethora of freshly harvested goods. *(Union Square at 14th Street and Broadway, ☎ 477-3220. Mon, Wed and Fri-Sat: 8am-6pm.)*

Union Square Greenmarket

Antiques, collectibles and clothing can be found at the **P.S. 44 Flea Market**. *(Columbus Avenue, between West 76th and West 77th Street. Sun: 10am-6pm.)*

MAIL / POST

Post offices - Generally open Mon-Fri: 9am-6pm, Sat: 9am-12.30pm, the main post office at Eighth Avenue and 33rd Street is open 24 hours a day, 365 days a year.

Mail boxes - Letters and cards can be mailed at post offices or mail boxes (painted blue), found throughout the city.

U.S. Mailbox

Stamp and package / shipping cost - You can purchase stamps from post offices or from many shops. The cost of shipping packages depends on the size of the package, the destination and the speed of service. Mail weighing less than an ounce, sent within the U.S., is 32 cents. Sending a postcard overseas costs 50 cents and a letter (less than an ounce) is 60 cents.

MEDIA

Listings - A great way to find out what's happening in New York is to pick up one of its weekly magazines or papers. *New York* magazine and *Time Out New York* are two of the more comprehensive. The weekly *Village Voice* and *New York Press* are packed with things to see and do and are free. All contain full listings and information about the best in New York eating and drinking, cinemas, theaters, nightclubs and many other forms of entertainment.

New York newsstand

Newspapers - New York City has several daily newspapers. The most popular is the *New York Times*. The *Daily News*, *New York Post* and *New York Newsday* also have large readerships. In addition,

. . . Visitor Information . . .

the city has a multitude of weekly, monthly, foreign language and special interest papers.

Radio - New York has a multitude of radio stations that air every form of radio entertainment. The main ones are on the FM dial: 92.3 WXRK for rock music and shock-jock Howard Stern in the morning; 92.7 WDRE for modern and alternative rock; 93.9 for classical; 97.1 for hip-hop; 101.9 for contemporary jazz; 103.5 for country; and 104.3 for hard rock.

Television - The main national stations are 2 (CBS), 4 (NBC), 5 (Fox), 7 (ABC), 9 & 11 (independent) and 13 (PBS). Most hotels have cable TV which allows you to watch over 50 stations.

MONEY

Currency - The American currency is the dollar ($), consisting of 100 cents (¢). There are four commonly used American coins: penny (1 cent), nickel (5 cents), dime (10 cents), quarter (25 cents). Notes, which are also known as bills, come in $1, $2 (rare but in circulation), $5, $10, $20, $50 and $100 denominations.

Santa at Lord & Taylor

Money changing - You can change money at banks or at bureaux de change. Although bureaux de change stay open longer, they sometimes charge high commissions (transaction fees).

Credit cards - Major credit cards are accepted just about everywhere in New York. Check individual restaurant and shop entries for credit cards accepted. Also see page 16.

NATIONAL HOLIDAYS

Many attractions and shops are likely to be closed on the following days:

New Year's Day	*January 1*
Martin Luther King Day	*Third Monday in January*
President's Day	*Third Monday in February*
Memorial Day	*Last Monday in May*
Independence Day	*July 4*
Labor Day	*First Monday in September*
Columbus Day	*Second Monday in October*
Veteran's Day	*November 11*
Thanksgiving Day	*Fourth Thursday in November*
Christmas Day	*December 25*

. . . Visitor Information . . .

OPENING HOURS

Banks - Generally, banks are open Mon-Fri: 9.30am-3pm or 3.30pm. Some branches are open later and some are also open on Saturday mornings. Most banks have 24-hour cash machines from which you can withdraw money.

Bars / Restaurants - Restaurants and bars in New York City tend to be open quite late, often serving food past 11pm, with most bars closing around 2am. All of the restaurants in this guide have their hours stated.

Shops - In general, shops are open from Mon-Sat: 10am-7pm. In Greenwich Village and Soho, many shops stay open later, especially on weekends. The hours of each shop in this guide are listed.

Sundays - Typically, New York's streets are less crowded on Sundays, making them ideal for sightseeing. In addition, many shops, markets and attractions are open, though their hours are usually more restricted.

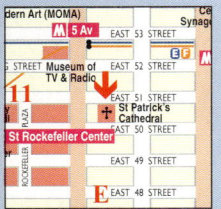

Cathedral of St. John the Divine

RESTROOMS / TOILETS

There are very few public restrooms, and none at subway stations. Museums, hotels, department stores and restaurants are your best bet when sightseeing.

RELIGIOUS SERVICES

Listed below are the addresses and phone numbers of various religious denominations and places of worship. To find a religious service close to you, contact the following:

St. Patrick's Cathedral

St. Patrick's Cathedral

Buddist *(New York Buddist Temple, 331 Riverside Drive, ☎ 678-0305)*; Episcopalian *(Cathedral of St. John the Divine, Amsterdam Avenue at 112th Street, ☎ 316-7400, or, Trinity Church, Broadway and Wall Street, ☎ 602-0800)*; Jewish *(Central Synagogue, 652 Lexington Avenue, ☎ 838-5122)*; Muslim *(Mosque of Islamic Brotherhood, 130 West 113th Street, ☎ 662-4100)*; Roman Catholic *(St. Patrick's Cathedral, Fifth Avenue at 50th Street, ☎ 753-2261)*; Unitarian *(All Souls Unitarian, 1157 Lexington Avenue, ☎ 535-5530)*.

SPECIAL TRAVELERS

Disabled - Many of New York's hotels, attractions and restaurants have facilities for the disabled. The

. . . Visitor Information . . .

Mayor's Office for People with Disabilities *(☎ 788-2830)* provides information and the free publication *Access Guide for People with Disabilities.*

Senior citizens - Seniors (generally defined as 65 or older) usually receive reduced admission at attractions. This is in addition to the discount they can obtain with *New York for less*.

Students - The International Student Identity Card is necessary for students to obtain concessions. It can be purchased from the Council on International Educational Exchange *(205 East 42nd Street, ☎ 822-2600)* or the New York Student Center *(895 Amsterdam Avenue, ☎ 666-4177)*. Proof of your student status is required to obtain the card.

Gay and lesbian - The Gay and Lesbian Switchboard *(Mon-Sun: 10am-12midnight, ☎ 777-1800)* provides information and assistance on gay activities and events happening in New York City.

SPORTS

New Yorkers take their sports very seriously, especially football, basketball and baseball. New York Yankees fans were especially pleased when their beloved "Bronx bombers" were victorious in the 1998 World Series. Tickets for all major sporting events can be ordered by calling Ticketmaster *(☎ 307-7171)*.

New York Yankees

Football - The season runs from Sep-Jan and is played at the Meadowlands in New Jersey. New York's two home teams are the Giants and the Jets.

Basketball - The Knicks play their season from Oct-Jun at Madison Square Garden.

Baseball - From Apr-Oct, you can catch a game of baseball played by the Yankees or the Mets.

Ice hockey - Hockey season runs from Oct-Apr. The Rangers and the Islanders are New York's home teams.

Working out - Many hotels have fitness facilities. At the Chelsea Piers (page 118), *for less* cardholders are entitled to a discount on one-day passes and various athletic activities.

TAXES

The U.S. does not have an export tax program or a value added tax (VAT). Instead, all shoppers are required to pay state sales tax (8½%) in addition to the marked price. Unfortunately, this tax cannot be reclaimed when a foreigner leaves the country.

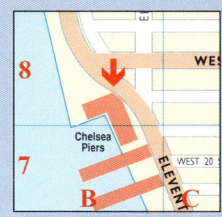
Chelsea Piers

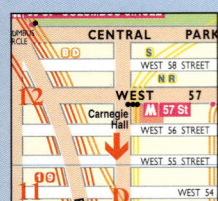

New York Convention & Visitors Bureau

INSIDER'S TIP

For more information about getting around in New York see page 19.

. . . Visitor Information . . .

TELEPHONES

When dialing within Manhattan you do not need to dial the 212 area code, but only the seven-digit telephone number. Any phone number in this book listed with an area code means that it is outside the 212 dialing area, and you must dial 1+area code+phone number (e.g. 1-718-555-1234). A call within the five boroughs of New York City (area codes 212 and 718) costs 25 cents from a public phone. For discounts on long-distance calls see page 8.

TIPPING

Tipping is customary in New York, even for the most basic services. Although tipping may seem strange or unnecessary to some overseas visitors, keep in mind that a service charge is rarely included in the bill and that employers are not required by law to pay tipped employees the minimum wage, because it is assumed that the majority of their earnings will be in tips.

Restaurants - A 15-20% tip on the total bill is standard. So that the service is not reduced by the discount, when using the *for less* card it is recommended that you tip on the total amount of the bill, before the discount is applied.

Taxis / Bartenders / Hairdressers - The standard tip is 15-20%.

Porters / Bellhops - The normal tip is $1 per bag, depending on the number of bags, the distance carried and the overall service.

TOURIST INFORMATION

New York Convention & Visitors Bureau is the main source for tourist information in the city. Multi-lingual operators are available as is a wide range of brochures and helpful information. *(810 Seventh Avenue, ☎ 1-212-397-8200. Mon-Fri: 9am-6pm. Sat-Sun: 10am-3pm.)*

Grand Central Terminal, **Penn Station** and **Port Authority Bus Terminal** also supply visitor information.

TRAVELING IN NEW YORK

Subway - The subway is the fastest and easiest way to get around New York City. Each one-way fare costs $1.50 and can be paid with a MetroCard (which are now also available with unlimited rides) or a token bought at a station. Subways run frequently, 24 hours a day, seven days a week. The last of the famous graffiti-covered subway trains was taken out of service in 1989.

A subway train in Manhattan

. . . Visitor Information

Buses - Public buses also run 24 hours a day, seven days a week. The fare is $1.50 and can be paid with a MetroCard or a token. If you need to change buses ask for a free transfer, *when you board*.

Taxis - Yellow cabs are available when the center light is on, but not when the "Off Duty" side lights are on as well. Fares are $2 for the first eighth of a mile, 30¢ for each additional fifth of a mile. There is also a 50¢ surcharge added to the fare in the evening.

Car - The cost and aggravation of city driving and parking make cars practically useless within New York City. Renting a car can, however, be very practical for out-of-town trips (see page 237).

TRAVELING OUTSIDE NEW YORK

There is a vast transportation network linking New York to other U.S. cities (see page 236).

Taxis and a horse-drawn Hansom Cab

USEFUL TELEPHONE NUMBERS

Airports - J.F.K. (☎ *(718) 244-4444)*; LaGuardia (☎ *(718) 476-5000)*; Newark (☎ *(973) 961-6000)*.

Credit cards - American Express (☎ *1-800-528-4800)*; Visa (☎ *1-800-336-8472)*; Mastercard (☎ *1-800-307-7309)*; Diners Club (☎ *1-800-234-6377)*; Discover (☎ *1-800-347-2683)*.

Emergencies - Dial ☎ 911 for police, fire and ambulance assistance. For dental emergencies, Emergency Dental Associates (☎ *972-9299)*.

Helpline - The Samaritans (☎ *673-3000)*, 24 hours.

Subway / bus information - MTA (☎ *(718) 330-1234)*.

Train information - Metro-North (☎ *532-4900)* at Grand Central Terminal; Amtrak (☎ *582-6875)*, New Jersey Transit (☎ *(973) 762-5100)* and Long Island Railroad (☎ *(718) 217-5477)* at Penn Station.

Visitor information - New York Convention & Visitors Bureau (☎ *1-800-746-6610 or* ☎ *397-8222)*.

WEIGHTS, MEASUREMENTS & CLOTHING SIZES

In the U.S., the imperial, not the metric system is used.

Clothing sizes - To convert American women's clothing sizes to British, add 2 (e.g. an American size 8 is a British 10), for shoes, subtract 2 (e.g. an American 8 is a British 6). Men's suit and shirt sizes are the same in Britain and America, but shoes are ½ size bigger in America (e.g. an American 10 is a British 9½).

Index of Hotels

HOTELS

PHOTO CREDITS

The Publishers would like to thank the following people and organizations for permission to reproduce their photographs over which they retain copyright. Any omission from this list is unintentional and every effort will be made to include these in the next edition of this publication.

Debra Sweeney (principal photography); Bob Strong (cover photo); The Museum of the City of New York: Edward Moran. The Unveiling of the Statue of Liberty Enlightening the World. Oil on canvas. 39½ x 49½", The J. Clarence Davies Collection. John Bachmann. Central Park-Summer, Looking South, New York, 1865. Colored lithograph, 11 3/4 x 17 5/8", The J. Clarence Davies Collection. DeWit View, 1672. Line engraving on copper, Gift of Mrs. William Sloane. Looking West on Wall Street, 1922, The Byron Collection. Sledding, Central Park, 1898, The Byron Collection. Immigrants on Battery Park, 1901, The Byron Collection. Broadway North from 34th Street, c.1910, The Byron Collection. Lewis Hine, Empire State Building Construction, c. 1930. Permanent Deposit of the Empire State Building. Berenice Abbott, Pike and Henry Streets, 1936. Purchase Mrs. Elon Hooker Acquisition Fund. T.H. McAllister Co., Flatiron Building, 1909. Lantern Slide. Greeley Square, 1898, The Byron Collection. West 59th Street and 5th Avenue, 1905, The Byron Collection. Brooklyn Bridge, 1912, Photographer unknown. Subway Construction Workers in Tunnel. New York Skyline. c. 1932, The Wurts Collection. Gilbert Stuart, Portrait of George Washington, 1796, Gift of John Hill Morgan. Dance on the Battery in the Presence of Peter Stuyvesant, A. Durand, 1838. City Hall Park from the NW Corner of Broadway and Chambers St. Purchase of Manhattan from the Indians, 1626, Peter Minuit and Poor Lo, The Clarence J. Davies Collection. Pulling down the statue of George III at the Bowling Green, City of New York, July 1776. 19th Century steel engraving. New York Convention & Visitors Bureau; Bridget O'Neil; Joseph O'Neil; Virgin Atlantic Airways; Soho Grand Hotel; Southgate Towers; Rihga Royal; Best Western Woodward; Doubletree Guest Suites; Hotel Gorham; Mansfield; Michelangelo; Millennium Broadway; Gayle Gleason, New York Renaissance; Novotel New York; Morgans; Paramount; Tom Vack; St. Moritz; Salisbury; Shoreham Hotel; The Warwick; Crowne Plaza; Edison Hotel; New York Palace; Omni Berkshire Palace; Dumont Plaza; Lou Hammond & Associates, Inc.; Doral Court; Doral Inn; Doral Park Avenue; Eastgate Tower; Hotel Intercontinental; Jolly Madison Towers; Loews New York; Morgans; Todd Eberle; New York Helmsley; Shelburne Murray Hotel; The Tudor; Waldorf-Astoria; Radisson Empire; Franklin; Hotel Wales; Regency; Barbizon; Hotel Delmonico; National Park Service Photos; Brain Feeney; Charley Van Pelt; South Street Seaport Museum; Frank Lusk; Fraunces Tavern Museum; The Museum for African Art; Lower East Side Tenement Museum; Steve Brosnahan; 5 & 10 No Exaggeration; Stan Ries; Deborah Jaffe; Battmann; Skyline Multimedia Entertainment, Inc.; Fred George; Roberto Johnson; John Ortner; Frank DeSisto; Eva Heyd; Dan Cornish; Chun Y. Lai; Todd Eberle; American Museum of Natural History; Scott Frances/Esto; Lincoln Center; Sony IMAX Theatres; Morris-Jumel Mansion, Inc.; Eastern National; The Metropolitan Museum of Art; David Heald; The Frick Collection, New York; Whitney Museum of American Art; National Academy of Design; The Jewish Museum; Peter Aaron/Esto; John Parnell; BAM archive; New York City Opera; Gerardo Samoza; Webster Hall; New York Cruise Lines, Inc.; Julian Olivas; Heritage Trails New York; New York Transit Museum; Kristin Holcomb; Patricia Lauman Bazelon; Peter Howard Photographer Inc.; New York Botanical Garden; Scott Bowron; Sarah Wells; Bart Barlow; Avis Car Rental Company; Photos courtesy of Washington, D.C. Convention & Visitors Association; Courtesy of Philadelphia Convention and Visitors Bureau; R. Andrew Lepley; Jim McWilliams; John D. Widmaier Jr.; Kevin Reilly; Courtesy of Greater Boston Convention and Visitors Bureau; Courtesy of Atlantic City Convention and Visitors Authority; Robert P. Matthews; Courtesy of Greater New Haven Convention & Visitors Bureau; Stuart Smith; Yale University; Michael Marsland; Courtesy of Long Island Convention & Visitors Bureau; Photos by Robert Lipper, Island-Metro Publications; NYS Department of Economic Development; Darren McGee; Tony Stone Images.

Index of Discounters . . .

ATTRACTIONS AND MUSEUMS

KEY TO ABBREVIATIONS

LM=Lower Manhattan
SO=Soho, Chinatown & the Lower East Side
GV=Greenwich Village
CH=Chelsea, Gramercy & the Flatiron District
ME=Midtown East

MW=Midtown West
UW=Upper West Side & Harlem
UE=Upper East Side
CP=Central Park
OB=Outer Boroughs
★= Hotel rating (see page 34)

. . . Index of Discounters . . .

Shops

Accessories & Hats	Hattitude	94	SO
Army Navy & Clothing	Chelsea Army and Navy	126	CH
Army Navy & Clothing	Galaxy Army & Navy	126	CH
Army Navy & Clothing	MASH Army and Navy	143	MW
Army Navy & Clothing	Second Avenue Army Navy	198	UE
Army Navy & Clothing	Village Army Navy	108	GV
Art & Clothing	MarcoArt	94	SO
Art Gallery & Poster Shop	Decor Art Gallery	125	CH
Art Gallery & Poster Shop	Triton Gallery	144	MW
Athletic Wear & Clothing	Starting Line	124	CH
Athletic Wear & Clothing	Chelsea Piers Store	116	CH
Cameras & Electronics	Cambridge Camera Shop	124	GV
Cards, Gifts & Posters	Avenue A Cards	124	CH
Chess Shop	Village Chess Shop	107	GV
Children	Tootsie's	106	GV
Children & Gifts	Enchanted Forest	90	SO
Children, Toys & Novelties	Tah-Poozie	107	GV
Clothing	Alpana Bawa	93	SO
Clothing	Authentic New York	143	MW
Clothing (Men's)	Eclipse	72	LM
Clothing (Men's)	L'Uomo	109	GV
Clothing (Vintage)	1909 Company	93	SO
Clothing (Vintage)	Garage Sale	109	GV
Clothing (Vintage)	Post War Club	107	GV
Clothing (Vintage)	What Comes Around Goes Around	91	SO
Clothing (Women's)	A Uno	91	SO
Clothing & Art	MarcoArt	94	SO
Clothing & Army Navy	Chelsea Army and Navy	126	CH
Clothing & Army Navy	Galaxy Army & Navy	126	CH
Clothing & Army Navy	MASH Army and Navy	143	MW
Clothing & Army Navy	Second Avenue Army Navy	198	UE
Clothing & Army Navy	Village Army Navy	108	GV
Clothing & Athletic Wear	Starting Line	126	CH
Clothing & Athletic Wear	Chelsea Piers Store	116	CH
Clothing & Gifts	New York 911	94	SO
Clothing & Skateshop	Swish	110	GV
Clothing (Vintage) & Western	Whiskey Dust	106	GV
Collectibles & Vintage	Garage Sale	109	GV
Collectibles & Vintage	Howdy-Do	110	GV
Crafts & Gifts	Back from Guatemala	112	GV
Crafts & Gifts	Eastern Arts	91	SO
Crafts & Gifts	Eastern Arts	108	GV
Crafts & Gifts	Our Name is Mud	174	UW
Crafts & Gifts	Our Name is Mud	197	UE
Crafts & Gifts	Truva	106	GV
Crafts & Gifts	Vision of Tibet	107	GV
Crafts, Gifts & Gallery	After the Rain	92	SO
Electronics & Cameras	Cambridge Camera Shop	125	GV
Electronics & Souvenirs	Santino Photos	144	MW
Film Developing	Fromex 1 Hour Photo	144	MW
Film Developing	Fromex 1 Hour Photo	156	ME

... Index of Discounters ...

Shops

Film Developing	Fromex 1 Hour Photo	174	UW
Film Developing	Fromex 1 Hour Photo	198	UE
Framing & Poster Shop	Decor Art Gallery	197	UE
Framing & Poster Shop	Metro Art	174	UW
Framing & Poster Shop	Metropolitan Graphic Arts	198	UE
Gallery, Crafts & Gifts	After the Rain	92	SO
Gifts	Carapan	126	CH
Gifts	Hudson Street Papers	108	GV
Gifts	Recherché	125	CH
Gifts, Cards & Posters	Avenue A Cards	124	CH
Gifts & Children	Enchanted Forest	90	SO
Gifts & Clothing	New York 911	94	SO
Gifts & Crafts	Back from Guatemala	110	GV
Gifts & Crafts	Eastern Arts	108	GV
Gifts & Crafts	Eastern Arts	91	SO
Gifts & Crafts	Our Name is Mud	197	UE
Gifts & Crafts	Our Name is Mud	174	UW
Gifts & Crafts	Truva	106	GV
Gifts & Crafts	Vision of Tibet	107	GV
Gifts, Crafts & Gallery	After the Rain	92	SO
Hats & Accessories	Hattitude	94	SO
Jewelry	Ray's Jewelers	72	LM
Jewelry (Original)	Alex Streeter	90	SO
Jewelry (Original)	Margo Manhattan	92	SO
Museum Store	Fraunces Tavern Museum	60	LM
Museum Store	L.E.S. Tenement Museum	79	SO
Museum Store	Museum for African Art	78	SO
Museum Store	Museum of the City of New York	184	UE
Museum Store	Museum of the Moving Image	231	OB
Museum Store	New York Transit Museum	224	OB
Museum Store	Pierpont Morgan Library	148	ME
Museum Store	South Street Seaport Museum	59	LM
Museum Store	The Museum of Modern Art	130	MW
Museum Store	The Museum of TV & Radio	132	MW
Music	Norman's Sound & Vision	109	GV
Natural History	Evolution	93	SO
Novelties, Toys & Children	Tah-Poozie	107	GV
Optical Boutique	Selima Optique	92	SO
Poster Shop & Art Gallery	Decor Art Gallery	125	CH
Poster Shop & Art Gallery	Triton Gallery	144	MW
Poster Shop & Framing	Decor Art Gallery	197	UE
Poster Shop & Framing	Metro Art	174	UW
Poster Shop & Framing	Metropolitan Graphic Arts	198	UE
Posters, Gifts & Cards	Avenue A Cards	124	CH
Skateshop & Clothing	Swish	110	GV
Souvenirs & Electronics	Santino Photos	144	MW
Sports Collectibles	Future Sports	156	ME
Sporting Goods & Athletic Wear	Chelsea Piers Store	116	CH
Toys, Novelties & Children	Tah-Poozie	107	GV
Vintage & Collectibles	Howdy-Do	110	GV
Western & Clothing (Vintage)	Whiskey Dust	106	GV

. . . Index of Discounters . . .

Restaurants

American	The Barking Dog Luncheonette	195	UE
American	Boomer's Sports Club	171	UW
American	Firehouse	172	UW
American	John Street Bar and Grill	70	LM
American	Mercantile Grill	69	LM
American	Mike's American Bar & Grill	141	MW
American	Miss Elle's	172	UW
American	Nice Guy Eddie's	104	GV
American / Brewery	Heartland Brewery	122	CH
American / Coffee & Tea Shop	Basset	85	SO
American / Continental	P. J. Charlton's	87	SO
American / International	Barocco Kitchen	122	CH
American / International	Barocco to Go	102	GV
American / Irish	Doc Watson's	195	UE
American / Italian	Ottomanelli's	154	ME
American / Italian	Yellowfingers	194	UE
American / Steakhouse	Broadway Joe's Steakhouse	140	MW
Argentinian / Continental	Caffe Novecento	86	SO
Asian / Vegetarian	Tiengarden	88	SO
Brazilian / Continental	Caffe Novecento	86	SO
Brewery / American	Heartland Brewery	122	CH
Brewery / International	Commonwealth Brewing Co.	139	MW
Burmese	Mingala West	171	UW
Cabaret / Continental	5 & 10 No Exaggeration	87	SO
Café	Café Mozart	121	CH
California / Mediterranean	Cafe Inferno	123	CH
Chinese	Chinatown East	195	UE
Chinese	Hunan Balcony	172	UW
Chinese	Hunan Balcony Gourmet	193	UE
Chinese	Mao Mao	86	SO
Chinese	Panda	154	ME
Coffee & Tea Shop / American	Basset	85	SO
Continental	MK Restaurant	141	MW
Continental / American	P. J. Charlton's	87	SO
Continental / Brazilian	Caffe Novecento	86	SO
Continental / Cabaret	5 & 10 No Exaggeration	87	SO
Creole / French	La Belle Epoque	103	GV
Delicatessen / Kosher	Mendy's East	123	CH
Delicatessen / Kosher	Mendy's West	170	UW
French	La Folie	193	UW
French / Creole	La Belle Epoque	103	GV
German / Swiss	Roettele A.G.	104	GV
Indian	Akbar	153	ME
Indian	Haveli	104	GV
Indian	Mitali West	102	GV
International	Nadine's	102	GV
International	The Beekman	69	LM
International / American	Barocco Kitchen	122	CH
International / American	Barocco to Go	102	GV
International / Brewery	Commonwealth Brewing Co.	139	MW
Irish / American	Doc Watson's	195	UE
Italian	Barocco	86	SO

. . . Index of Discounters

Restaurants

Italian	Cafe Bondi	123	CH
Italian	Contrapunto	194	UE
Italian	Il Bocconcino	103	GV
Italian	Il Brunello	140	MW
Italian	L'Oro di Napoli	103	GV
Italian	Maristella	140	MW
Italian	Portfolio	122	CH
Italian	Rocky's	88	SO
Italian	Sambuca's Cafe	88	SO
Italian	Zi Teresa	141	MW
Italian / American	Ottomanelli's	154	ME
Italian / American	Yellowfingers	194	UE
Italian / Mediterranean	Sharz Cafe and Wine Bar	193	UE
Kosher / Delicatessen	Mendy's East	123	CH
Kosher / Delicatessen	Mendy's West	170	UW
Mediterranean	Cafe Soleil	154	ME
Mediterranean / California	Cafe Inferno	123	CH
Mediterranean / Italian	Sharz Cafe and Wine Bar	199	UE
Peruvian	El Pollo	87	SO
Pizzeria	Pranzo Pizzeria	70	LM
Seafood	Go Fish	194	UE
Steakhouse / American	Broadway Joe's Steakhouse	140	MW
Swiss / German	Roettele A.G.	104	GV
Thai	Bennie's Thai Cafe	70	LM
Vegetarian / Asian	Tiengarden	88	SO
Viennese	Cafe Mozart	171	UW
Wine Bar	Sharz Cafe and Wine Bar	193	UE

NIGHTLIFE

Broadway Theater Discounts	209	Broadway shows
Brooklyn Academy of Music	209	Performing arts
Mondo Cane	210	Live music
New York City Opera	209	Opera
Stand Up New York	210	Comedy
Webster Hall	210	Nightclub

TOURS

Circle Line Sightseeing Cruises	214	Boat tours
Discover New York Walking Tours	218	Walking tours
Gray Line New York	220	Coach tours
Heritage Trails New York	219	Walking tours
Liberty Helicopter Tours	217	Helicopter tours
New York Apple Tours	212-213	Double-decker bus tours
Seaport Liberty Cruises	216	Boat tours
World Yacht Dinner Cruises	215	Boat tours

Ellis Island Immigration Museum (page 54)

No. of paid audio tours: 1 or 2   (please circle)

Voucher valid for up to 4 people:
maximum 2 free audio tours

South Street Seaport Museum (page 59)

No. of paid admissions: 1 or 2   (please circle)

Voucher valid for up to 4 people:
maximum 2 free admissions

South Street Seaport Museum Shop (page 59)

Save 10% on goods purchased in the
South Street Seaport Museum Shop

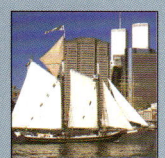

Schooner Pioneer (page 59)

No. of adults	1	2	3	4	Circle as appropriate: voucher valid for up to 4 people
No. of children	1	2	3	4	
No. of seniors	1	2	3	4	
No. of students	1	2	3	4	

Fraunces Tavern Museum (page 60)

No. of adults	1	2	3	4	Circle as appropriate: voucher valid for up to 4 people
No. of children	1	2	3	4	
No. of seniors	1	2	3	4	
No. of students	1	2	3	4	

Fraunces Tavern Museum Shop (page 60)

Save 10% on goods purchased in the
Fraunces Tavern Museum Shop

This voucher entitles the holder of a valid **for less** card to the following discount at the **Ellis Island Immigration Museum** (page 54):

2-for-1 Audio tours: one free audio tour with each audio tour of equal or greater value purchased (maximum 2 free audio tours)

Cannot be combined with any other promotional offer.

This voucher entitles the holder of a valid **for less** card to the following discount at the **South Street Seaport Museum** (page 59):

2-for-1 Admission: one free admission with each admission of equal or greater value purchased (maximum 2 free admissions)

Cannot be combined with any other promotional offer.

This voucher entitles the holder of a valid **for less** card to the following discount at the **South Street Seaport Museum Shop** (page 59):

10% discount in the museum shop

Cannot be combined with any other promotional offer.

This voucher entitles the holder of a valid **for less** card to the following discounts on the **Schooner Pioneer** (page 59):

Adult	20% discount	Senior	20% discount
Child	20% discount	Student	20% discount

Cannot be combined with any other promotional offer.

This voucher entitles the holder of a valid **for less** card to the following discounts at **Fraunces Tavern Museum** (page 60):

Adult	50% discount	Senior	50% discount
Child	50% discount	Student	50% discount

Cannot be combined with any other promotional offer.

This voucher entitles the holder of a valid **for less** card to the following discount at the **Fraunces Tavern Museum Shop** (page 60):

10% discount in the museum shop

Cannot be combined with any other promotional offer.

Guggenheim Museum Soho (page 78)

No. of paid admissions: 1 or 2   (please circle)

Voucher valid for up to 4 people:
maximum 2 free admissions
[code: NYL]

Museum for African Art (page 78)

No. of paid tours: 1 or 2   (please circle)

Voucher valid for up to 4 people:
maximum 2 free tours

Museum for African Art Shop (page 78)

Save 10% on goods purchased in the
Museum for African Art Shop

Lower East Side Tenement Museum (page 79)

No. of adults	1	2	3	4	Circle as
No. of children	1	2	3	4	appropriate:
No. of seniors	1	2	3	4	voucher valid
No. of students	1	2	3	4	for up to 4 people

L.E.S. Tenement Museum Shop (page 79)

Save 10% on goods purchased in the
Lower East Side Tenement Museum Shop

Eldridge Street Synagogue (page 80)

No. of adults	1	2	3	4	Circle as
No. of children	1	2	3	4	appropriate:
No. of seniors	1	2	3	4	voucher valid
No. of students	1	2	3	4	for up to 4 people

This voucher entitles the holder of a valid **for less** card to the following discount at the **Guggenheim Museum Soho** (page 78):

2-for-1 Admission: one free admission with each admission of equal or greater value purchased (maximum 2 free admissions)

Cannot be combined with any other promotional offer.

This voucher entitles the holder of a valid **for less** card to the following discount at the **Museum for African Art** (page 78):

2-for-1 Admission: one free admission with each admission of equal or greater value purchased (maximum 2 free admissions)

Cannot be combined with any other promotional offer.

This voucher entitles the holder of a valid **for less** card to the following discount at the **Museum for African Art Shop** (page 78):

10% discount in the museum shop

Cannot be combined with any other promotional offer.

This voucher entitles the holder of a valid **for less** card to the following discount at the **Lower East Side Tenement Museum** (page 79):

| Adult | 50% discount | Senior | 50% discount |
| Child | 50% discount | Student | 50% discount |

Cannot be combined with any other promotional offer.

This voucher entitles the holder of a valid **for less** card to the following discount at the **Lower East Side Tenement Museum Shop** (page 79):

10% discount in the museum shop

Cannot be combined with any other promotional offer.

This voucher entitles the holder of a valid **for less** card to the following discount at the **Eldridge Street Synagogue** (page 80):

| Adult | 50% discount | Senior | 50% discount |
| Child | 50% discount | Student | 50% discount |

Cannot be combined with any other promotional offer.

New Museum of Contemporary Art (page 80)

No. of adults	1 2 3 4	Circle as
No. of children	1 2 3 4	appropriate: voucher valid
No. of seniors	1 2 3 4	for up to
No. of students	1 2 3 4	4 people

Merchants House Museum (page 98)

No. of adults	1 2 3 4	Circle as
No. of children	1 2 3 4	appropriate: voucher valid
No. of seniors	1 2 3 4	for up to
No. of students	1 2 3 4	4 people

Chelsea Piers (page 116)

No. of adults	1 2 3 4	Circle as
No. of children	1 2 3 4	appropriate: voucher valid
No. of seniors	1 2 3 4	for up to
No. of students	1 2 3 4	4 people

Chelsea Piers (page 116)

No. of adults	1 2 3 4	Circle as
No. of children	1 2 3 4	appropriate: voucher valid
No. of seniors	1 2 3 4	for up to
No. of students	1 2 3 4	4 people

Chelsea Piers Store (page 116)

Save 20% on goods purchased at the
Chelsea Piers Store

The Museum of Modern Art (page 130)

No. of adults	1 2 3 4	Circle as
No. of children	1 2 3 4	appropriate: voucher valid
No. of seniors	1 2 3 4	for up to
No. of students	1 2 3 4	4 people

This voucher entitles the holder of a valid **for less** card to the following discounts at the **New Museum of Contemporary Art** (page 80):

Adult	50% discount	Senior	50% discount
Child	50% discount	Student	50% discount

Cannot be combined with any other promotional offer.

This voucher entitles the holder of a valid **for less** card to the following discounts at the **Merchant's House Museum** (page 98):

Adult	50% discount	Senior	50% discount
Child	50% discount	Student	50% discount

Cannot be combined with any other promotional offer.

This voucher entitles the holder of a valid **for less** card to the following discounts on general admission to the **Chelsea Piers Sports and Entertainment Complex** (page 116):

Adult	20% discount	Senior	20% discount
Child	20% discount	Student	20% discount

This offer applies Mon-Fri from opening time to 5pm only.

This voucher entitles the holder of a valid **for less** card to the following discounts on general admission to the **Chelsea Piers Sports and Entertainment Complex** (page 116):

Adult	20% discount	Senior	20% discount
Child	20% discount	Student	20% discount

This offer applies Mon-Fri from opening time to 5pm only.

This voucher entitles the holder of a valid **for less** card to the following discounts at **the Chelsea Piers Store** (page 116):

Save 20% on goods purchased
in the Chelsea Piers Store

Cannot be combined with any other promotional offer.

This voucher entitles the holder of a valid **for less** card to the following discounts at **The Museum of Modern Art** (page 130):

Adult	$1 off	Senior	$1 off
Child	$1 off	Student	$1 off

Cannot be combined with any other promotional offer.

MoMA Audio Guides (page 130)

No. of paid audio guides: 1 or 2 (please circle)

Voucher valid for up to 4 people:
maximum 2 free audio guides

MoMA Stores (page 130)

Save 10% on goods purchased in the
MoMA Stores

Museum of TV & Radio Shop (page 132)

Save 20% on goods purchased in the
Museum of TV & Radio Shop

Radio City Music Hall Grand Tour (page 133)

No. of paid tours: 1 or 2 (please circle)

Voucher valid for up to 4 people:
maximum 2 free tours

Intrepid Sea-Air-Space Museum (page 134)

No. of adults	1	2	3	4	Circle as appropriate: voucher valid for up to 4 people
No. of children	1	2	3	4	
No. of seniors	1	2	3	4	
No. of students	1	2	3	4	

American Craft Museum (page 134)

No. of adults	1	2	3	4	Circle as appropriate: voucher valid for up to 4 people
No. of children	1	2	3	4	
No. of seniors	1	2	3	4	
No. of students	1	2	3	4	

This voucher entitles the holder of a valid *for less* card to the following discount at **The Museum of Modern Art** (page 130):

2-for-1 Audio guides: one free audio guide with each audio guide of equal or greater value purchased (max. 2 free guides)

Cannot be combined with any other promotional offer.

This voucher entitles the holder of a valid *for less* card to the following discount in the **MoMA Stores** (page 130):

10% discount in the MoMA Stores

Cannot be combined with any other promotional offer.

This voucher entitles the holder of a valid *for less* card to the following discount at **The Museum of TV & Radio shop** (page 132):

20% discount in The Museum of TV & Radio Shop

Cannot be combined with any other promotional offer.

This voucher entitles the holder of a valid *for less* card to the following discount at **Radio City Music Hall** (page 133):

2-for-1 Grand Tours: one free Grand Tour with each Grand Tour of equal or greater value purchased (maximum 2 free tours)

Cannot be combined with any other promotional offer.

This voucher entitles the holder of a valid *for less* card to the following discounts at the **Intrepid Sea-Air-Space Museum** (page 134):

Adult	20% discount	Senior	20% discount
Child	20% discount	Student	20% discount

Cannot be combined with any other promotional offer.

This voucher entitles the holder of a valid *for less* card to the following discounts at the **American Craft Museum** (page 134):

Adult	50% discount	Senior	50% discount
Child	50% discount	Student	50% discount

Cannot be combined with any other promotional offer.

ICP Midtown (page 135)

No. of adults	1	2	3	4	Circle as
No. of children	1	2	3	4	appropriate:
No. of seniors	1	2	3	4	voucher valid
No. of students	1	2	3	4	for up to 4 people

Pierpont Morgan Library Shop (page 148)

Save 10% on goods purchased in the
Pierpont Morgan Library Shop

New York Botanical Garden (page 228)

No. of adults	1	2	3	4	Circle as
No. of children	1	2	3	4	appropriate:
No. of seniors	1	2	3	4	voucher valid
No. of students	1	2	3	4	for up to 4 people

Heritage Trails New York (pages 66 & 219)

No. of adults	1	2	3	4	Circle as
No. of children	1	2	3	4	appropriate:
No. of seniors	1	2	3	4	voucher valid
No. of students	1	2	3	4	for up to 4 people

Lincoln Center Classic Tour (page 162)

No. of adults	1	2	3	4	Circle as
No. of children	1	2	3	4	appropriate:
No. of seniors	1	2	3	4	voucher valid
No. of students	1	2	3	4	for up to 4 people

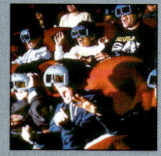

Sony IMAX Theatre (page 163)

No. of paid admissions: 1 or 2 (please circle)

Voucher valid for up to 4 people:
maximum 2 free admissions

This voucher entitles the holder of a valid *for less* card to the following discounts at the International Center of Photography Midtown (page 135):

Adult	50% discount	Senior	50% discount
Child	50% discount	Student	50% discount

Cannot be combined with any other promotional offer.

This voucher entitles the holder of a valid *for less* card to the following discount at the **Pierpont Morgan Library Shop** (page 148):

10% discount in the Pierpont Morgan Library Shop

Cannot be combined with any other promotional offer.

This voucher entitles the holder of a valid *for less* card to the following discounts at the **New York Botanical Garden** (page 228):

Adult	50% discount	Senior	50% discount
Child	50% discount	Student	50% discount

Cannot be combined with any other promotional offer.

This voucher entitles the holder of a *for less* card to the following discounts on **Heritage Trails New York** walking tours (pages 66 & 219):

Adult	$3 off	Senior	$3 off
Child	$2 off	Student	$3 off

Cannot be combined with any other promotional offer.

This voucher entitles the holder of a valid *for less* card to the following discounts on **Lincoln Center Classic Tour** (page 162):

Adult	50% discount	Senior	50% discount
Child	50% discount	Student	50% discount

Cannot be combined with any other promotional offer.

This voucher entitles the holder of a valid *for less* card to the following discount at the **Sony IMAX Theatre** (page 163):

2-for-1 Admission: one free admission with each admission of equal or greater value purchased (maximum 2 free admissions)

Cannot be combined with any other promotional offer.

Morris Jumel Mansion (page 164)

No. of adults	1	2	3	4	Circle as
No. of children	1	2	3	4	appropriate:
No. of seniors	1	2	3	4	voucher valid
No. of students	1	2	3	4	for up to
					4 people

Children's Museum of Manhattan (page 165)

No. of adults	1	2	3	4	Circle as
No. of children	1	2	3	4	appropriate:
No. of seniors	1	2	3	4	voucher valid
No. of students	1	2	3	4	for up to
					4 people

Guggenheim Museum (page 180)

No. of adults	1	2	3	4	Circle as
No. of children	1	2	3	4	appropriate:
No. of seniors	1	2	3	4	voucher valid
No. of students	1	2	3	4	for up to
	[code: NYL]				4 people

The Frick Collection (page 182)

No. of adults	1	2	3	4	Circle as
No. of children	1	2	3	4	appropriate:
No. of seniors	1	2	3	4	voucher valid
No. of students	1	2	3	4	for up to
					4 people

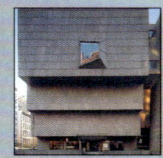

Whitney Museum of American Art (page 183)

No. of adults	1	2	3	4	Circle as
No. of children	1	2	3	4	appropriate:
No. of seniors	1	2	3	4	voucher valid
No. of students	1	2	3	4	for up to
					4 people

Museum of the City of New York (page 184)

Save 10% on goods purchased in the
Museum of the City of New York Shop

This voucher entitles the holder of a valid *for less* card to the following discounts at the **Morris Jumel Mansion** (page 164):

Adult	50% discount	Senior	50% discount
Child	50% discount	Student	50% discount

Cannot be combined with any other promotional offer.

This voucher entitles the holder of a valid *for less* card to the following discounts at the **Children's Museum of Manhattan** (page 165):

Adult	50% discount	Senior	50% discount
Child	50% discount	Student	50% discount

Cannot be combined with any other promotional offer.

This voucher entitles the holder of a valid *for less* card to the following discounts at the **Solomon R. Guggenheim Museum** (page 180):

Adult	$2 off	Senior	$2 off
Child	$2 off	Student	$2 off

Cannot be combined with any other promotional offer.

This voucher entitles the holder of a valid *for less* card to the following discounts at the **Frick Collection** (page 182):

Adult	50% discount	Senior	50% discount
Child	50% discount	Student	50% discount

Cannot be combined with any other promotional offer.

This voucher entitles the holder of a valid *for less* card to the following discounts at the **Whitney Museum of American Art** (page 183):

Adult	50% discount	Senior	50% discount
Child	50% discount	Student	50% discount

Cannot be combined with any other promotional offer.

This voucher entitles the holder of a valid *for less* card to the following discount at the **Museum of the City of New York Shop** (page 184):

10% discount in the museum shop

Cannot be combined with any other promotional offer.

National Academy Museum (page 185)

No. of adults	1	2	3	4		Circle as
No. of children	1	2	3	4		appropriate: voucher valid
No. of seniors	1	2	3	4		for up to
No. of students	1	2	3	4		4 people

ICP Uptown (page 186)

No. of adults	1	2	3	4		Circle as
No. of children	1	2	3	4		appropriate: voucher valid
No. of seniors	1	2	3	4		for up to
No. of students	1	2	3	4		4 people

The Jewish Museum (page187)

No. of paid admissions: 1 or 2 (please circle)

Voucher valid for up to 4 people:
maximum 2 free admissions

Wollman Rink (page 202)

No. of adults	1	2	3	4		Circle as
No. of children	1	2	3	4		appropriate: voucher valid
No. of seniors	1	2	3	4		for up to
No. of students	1	2	3	4		4 people

Stand Up New York (page 210)

No. of adults	1	2	3	4		Circle as
No. of children	1	2	3	4		appropriate: voucher valid
No. of seniors	1	2	3	4		for up to
No. of students	1	2	3	4		4 people

Stand Up New York (page 210)

No. of adults	1	2	3	4		Circle as
No. of children	1	2	3	4		appropriate: voucher valid
No. of seniors	1	2	3	4		for up to
No. of students	1	2	3	4		4 people

This voucher entitles the holder of a valid **for less** card to the following discounts at the **National Academy Museum** (page 185):

Adult	50% discount	Senior	50% discount
Child	50% discount	Student	50% discount

Cannot be combined with any other promotional offer.

This voucher entitles the holder of a valid **for less** card to the following discounts at the **International Center of Photography** (page 186):

Adult	50% discount	Senior	50% discount
Child	50% discount	Student	50% discount

Cannot be combined with any other promotional offer.

This voucher entitles the holder of a valid **for less** card to the following discount at **The Jewish Museum** (page 187):

2-for-1 Admission: one free admission with each admission of equal or greater value purchased (maximum 2 free admissions)

Cannot be combined with any other promotional offer.

This voucher entitles the holder of a valid **for less** card to the following discounts at **Wollman Rink** (page 202):

Adult	50% discount	Senior	50% discount
Child	50% discount	Student	50% discount

Cannot be combined with any other promotional offer.

This voucher entitles the holder of a valid **for less** card to the following discount at **Stand Up New York** (page 210):

2-for-1 Admission: one free admission with each admission of equal or greater value purchased (maximum 2 free admissions)

PLUS a 25% discount on your meal

Cannot be combined with any other promotional offer.

This voucher entitles the holder of a valid **for less** card to the following discount at **Stand Up New York** (page 210):

2-for-1 Admission: one free admission with each admission of equal or greater value purchased (maximum 2 free admissions)

PLUS a 25% discount on your meal

Cannot be combined with any other promotional offer.

New York Transit Museum (page 224)

No. of paid admissions: 1 or 2 (please circle)

Voucher valid for up to 4 people:
maximum 2 free admissions

New York Transit Museum (page 224)

Save 10% on goods purchased in the
New York Transit Museum Shop

Museum of the Moving Image (page 231)

No. of adults	1	2	3	4	Circle as
No. of children	1	2	3	4	appropriate: voucher valid
No. of seniors	1	2	3	4	for up to
No. of students	1	2	3	4	4 people

Museum of the Moving Image (page 231)

Save 10% on goods purchased in the
Museum of the Moving Image Shop

World Yacht Dinner Cruises (page 215)

No. of adults	1	2	3	4	Circle as
No. of children	1	2	3	4	appropriate: voucher valid
No. of seniors	1	2	3	4	for up to
No. of students	1	2	3	4	4 people

Seaport Liberty Cruises (page 216)

No. of paid admissions: 1 or 2 (please circle)

Voucher valid for up to 4 people:
maximum 2 free admissions

This voucher entitles the holder of a valid *for less* card to the following discount at the **New York Transit Museum** (page 224):

2-for-1 Admission: one free admission with each admission of equal or greater value purchased (maximum 2 free admissions)

Cannot be combined with any other promotional offer.

This voucher entitles the holder of a valid *for less* card to the following discount at the **New York Transit Museum** (page 224):

10% discount in the museum shop

Cannot be combined with any other promotional offer.

This voucher entitles the holder of a valid *for less* card to the following discounts at the **American Museum of the Moving Image** (page 231):

Adult	50% discount	Senior	50% discount
Child	50% discount	Student	50% discount

Cannot be combined with any other promotional offer.

This voucher entitles the holder of a valid *for less* card to the following discount at the **Museum of the Moving Image** (page 231):

10% discount in the museum shop

Cannot be combined with any other promotional offer.

This voucher entitles the holder of a valid *for less* card to the following discount on **World Yacht Dinner Cruises** (page 215):

$14 off the regular price of a
World Yacht Dinner Cruise (Sun-Fri)

Cannot be combined with any other promotional offer.

This voucher entitles the holder of a valid *for less* card to the following discount on **Seaport Liberty Cruises** (page 216):

2-for-1 Tickets: one free ticket with each ticket of equal or greater value purchased (maximum 2 free tickets)

Cannot be combined with any other promotional offer.

Liberty Helicopter Tours (page 217)

No. of adults	1	2	3	4	Circle as
No. of children	1	2	3	4	appropriate:
No. of seniors	1	2	3	4	voucher valid
No. of students	1	2	3	4	for up to 4 people

Gray Line Manhattan Comprehensive (page 220)

No. of adults	1	2	3	4	Circle as
No. of children	1	2	3	4	appropriate:
No. of seniors	1	2	3	4	voucher valid
No. of students	1	2	3	4	for up to 4 people

Gray Line New York Airport Service
Arrival Transfer (pages 18-19)

No. of adults	1	2	3	4	Circle as
No. of children	1	2	3	4	appropriate:
No. of seniors	1	2	3	4	voucher valid
No. of students	1	2	3	4	for up to 4 people

[ ] JFK   [ ] LGA   [ ] EWR

Gray Line New York Airport Service
Departure Transfer (pages 18-19)

No. of adults	1	2	3	4	Circle as
No. of children	1	2	3	4	appropriate:
No. of seniors	1	2	3	4	voucher valid
No. of students	1	2	3	4	for up to 4 people

[ ] JFK   [ ] LGA   [ ] EWR

Avis Car Rental (page 237)

Reserve an Intermediate (group C) through Full Size 4-door (group E) car at weekend, weekly or daily rates (2 days minimum rental required) and get a car from the next higher car group at no extra cost. **Advance reservation with request for upgrade is required.** For information and reservations, call your travel consultant or Avis at
1-800-831-8000. Subject to complete terms and conditions on back.

Coupon #UUFA273

This voucher entitles the holder of a *for less* card to the following discounts on **Liberty Helicopter Tours** (page 217):

20% off the regular price of any Liberty Helicopter Tour

Cannot be combined with any other promotional offer.

This voucher entitles the holder of a valid *for less* card to the following discounts on the **Gray Line Manhattan Comprehensive Tour** (page 220):

Adult	20% discount	Senior	20% discount
Child	20% discount	Student	20% discount

Cannot be combined with any other promotional offer. Voucher expires March 31st, 2001. After this date, the discount will be valid only at the discretion of Gray Line NY (212) 397-2600.

This voucher entitles the holder of a valid *for less* card to the following discounts on **Gray Line Airport Shuttle Arrival Transfer** (page 18-19): 20% discount on a one-way transfer from J.F.K., LaGuardia or Newark Airport to any Manhattan hotel between 23rd and 63rd Street. Passengers should proceed to the Ground Transportation Desk in their arriving terminal and present this voucher to the agent who will arrange the transfer.

Valid for up to 4 people. Cannot be combined with any other promotional offer. Voucher expires March 31st, 2001. After this date, the discount will be valid only at the discretion of Gray Line New York, (212) 315-3006.

This voucher entitles the holder of a valid *for less* card to the following discounts on **Gray Line Airport Shuttle Departure Transfer** (page 18-19): 20% discount on a one-way transfer from any Manhattan hotel between 23rd and 63rd Street to J.F.K., LaGuardia or Newark Airport. Reservations required one day before departure (☎ *(212) 315-3006)*. Voucher redeemable *only* at the following locations: Gray Line Sightseeing Terminal *(Port Authority Bus Terminal, 42nd St. & 8th Ave.)* or Times Square Visitors Center *(Broadway between 46th and 47th St.)*. Valid for up to 4 people. Cannot be combined with any other promotional offer. Voucher expires March 31st, 2001. After this date, the discount will be valid only at the discretion of Gray Line New York, (212) 315-3006.

AVIS Terms and conditions: Coupon valid for a one-time, one car group upgrade on an intermediate (Group C) through full-size (Group E) car. Maximum upgrade to Premium (Group G). Offer valid on weekend, weekly and daily rates only. Minimum 2-days rental required. Coupon must be surrendered at time of rental: one per rental. Coupon valid at participating Avis corporate and license locations in Manhattan and New York City airports only. **Advance reservation with request for upgrade is required.** The upgraded car is subject to availability at time of rental. Renter must meet Avis age, driver and credit requirements. Minimum age is 25, but may vary by location.

Rental Sales Agent Instructions:
Assign customer a car one group higher than car group reserved. Upgrade to no higher than Group G. Charge for car group reserved. In AWD, enter **K194100**. Complete this information:
RA:_____
Rental location:_____   Attach to coupon tape.